The Gospel according to the Beatles

Steve Turner

Westminster John Knox Press
LOUISVILLE • LONDON

Unless otherwise indicated, Scripture quotations are from The King James Version. Scripture quotations marked NIV are from *The Holy Bible, New International Version.* Copyright © 1973, 1978, 1984 International Bible Society. Used by permission of Zondervan Bible Publishers.

Excerpts from "The End," copyright 1969 (Renewed) Sony/ATV Tunes LLC. All rights administered by Sony/ATV Music Publishing, 8 Music Square West, Nashville, TN 37203. All rights reserved. Used by permission.

Excerpts from "Love Me Do" (Lennon/McCartney), © MPL Communications Ltd. All rights reserved. Used by permission.

Excerpts from "Tell Me What You See," copyright 1965 (Renewed) Sony/ATV Songs LLC. All rights administered by Sony/ATV Music Publishing, 8 Music Square West, Nashville, TN 37203. All rights reserved. Used by permission.

Excerpts from "Within You without You," copyright 1967 (Renewed) Sony/ATV Tunes LLC. All rights administered by Sony/ATV Music Publishing, 8 Music Square West, Nashville, TN 37203. All rights reserved. Used by permission.

Book design by Sharon Adams
Cover design by designpointinc.com
Cover illustration: The doorway of St Pancras Old Church, London, on July 28, 1968.
© *Don McCullin/CONTACT Press Images*

First edition
Published by Westminster John Knox Press
Louisville, Kentucky

This book is printed on acid-free paper that meets the American National Standards Institute Z39.48 standard. ♾

PRINTED IN THE UNITED STATES OF AMERICA

06 07 08 09 10 11 12 13 14 15 — 10 9 8 7 6 5 4 3 2 1

Library of Congress Cataloging-in-Publication Data is on file at the Library of Congress, Washington, D.C.

ISBN-13: 978-0-664-22983-2
ISBN-10: 0-664-22983-2

*This is dedicated to two people who
played important roles in my writing career:*

Sean O'Mahoney, who published my first-ever story in The Beatles Monthly
and gave me my first job as a writer on Beat Instrumental

Andrew Bailey, London bureau chief for Rolling Stone *during the early
1970s, who gave me the best advice I'd been given about writing.*

Contents

Preface

I'd had the idea for this book since the mid-1990s, but it became a reality after a call from David Dobson of Westminster John Knox Press, who asked me if I'd consider writing a book called *The Gospel according to Rock'n'Roll* to join the venerable series begun by Robert Short's *The Gospel According to Peanuts*. Having been a big fan of Short's book at the beginning of my writing career, I felt privileged to be asked to contribute and put forward my Beatles idea, because I felt that *The Gospel according to the Beatles* would embrace a lot of what I could say in a similar book devoted to rock 'n' roll. Fortunately David was a big Beatles fan, and it didn't take long for him to say yes.

There are apparently over a thousand books about the Beatles, so you need a good reason to add to such a huge collection. I believe that *The Gospel according to the Beatles* adds something to our knowledge of the group. It follows the same well-trodden path that you have to follow if you're going to recount one of the best-known myths of modern times, but because of its focus it looks into areas that are often only briefly touched on or sometimes completely ignored.

For example, John's involvement with his local church in Woolton was an important part of his life for at least ten years and supplied him with his introduction to the great themes of theology, the writing of words to music, and a rudimentary knowledge of singing. Yet most books gloss over that involvement and pay more attention to the games he played in the street or the drawings he did for Aunt Mimi. Similarly, Paul, George, and Ringo all had varying degrees of involvement with church that affected the development of their thought.

It was a difficult book to describe to prospective interviewees. I would generally say something like "It's a book about the philosophical/spiritual journey of the Beatles," which made it sound like a university thesis or a four-page pamphlet for a fundamentalist sect. Even Beatles experts seemed a bit nonplussed. They generally assumed that I would be concentrating on the Maharishi period. One of them thought a while and then said, "Oh, you mean like 'Let It Be'?" as if I were going to write one hundred thousand words about one hymnlike song. My friend Ray said, "You're not going to write a book that says they're all Christians at heart, are you?"

One of my earliest interviews was with Tony Carricker, an old art school friend of John's who has spent his working life laying bricks and carrying bags of cement. He loves the rock 'n' roll that first turned him and John on in the late 1950s—many of the earliest rock records that John played at home came from his collection. He thought I was barking up the wrong tree. He told me that he didn't think that John had any sense of spirituality at all. "Nothing he's ever done or said or written convinces me that he ever had any spirituality, not in the way I would understand spirituality."

I will have succeeded with *The Gospel according to the Beatles* if I can convince people like them that the search for a meaningful spirituality was an important part of the Beatles' motivation. I would like the person who thought that "Let It Be" was the only spiritual song the Beatles ever recorded to see that songs as varied as "The Word," "Nowhere Man," "Strawberry Fields Forever," and "Penny Lane" have as much to do with their quest for self-realization.

I believe that humans are fundamentally religious. The root of the word "religion" is the Latin *ligare*, meaning "to bind." Re-*ligare* is therefore "to bind back." To be religious in this sense is to want to be bound back—to be bound back to our original innocence, sense of wonder, and source of meaning. It is not surprising to me that the Beatles sought out wonder, meaning, and innocence in their lives and music and that a huge international audience looked to the Beatles to find much the same thing. To my friend Ray, and others like him, I would say that the gospel of the Beatles is not found in their conformity to an orthodox creed, especially the creeds of the Christian churches, but in their hunger for transcendence. To Tony Carricker I would point out that even during his overtly atheistic periods John was still trying to find his way back to paradise.

I thoroughly enjoyed writing this book. Working on a project about the Beatles—as I had done in the past with *A Hard Day's Write* and on the text of Linda McCartney's photographic book *Sixties: Portrait of an Era*—affords the pleasurable opportunity of living with their music, images, and stories every day of the week for months on end. I consider such times to be a great privilege. It makes me thankful that in 1963 I started my first Beatles scrapbook and never stopped collecting, although my clippings now go into sturdy archive boxes rather than books.

My research started with books, newspapers, journals, magazines, CDs, and tape recordings and then progressed to interviews with people who'd known the Beatles at various stages in their career. I was fortunate to be able to supplement these interviews carried out specifically for the book with others that I'd done for past projects with people like George Martin, Ravi Shankar, Cynthia Lennon, Timothy Leary, and Derek Taylor.

I would like to thank those who were particularly generous with their help. Maureen Cleave, author of the article that started the "more popular than Jesus" controversy, answered numerous e-mail messages and checked the relevant chapter for accuracy. David Ashton readily dredged his mind for all his memories of John in Woolton. J. Willoughby, whose father was a radio partner with Tommy Charles for many years, sent me all his clippings on the "Jesus" incident and put me in touch with Doug Layton.

Graham Paisley, the verger at St. Peter's parish church in Woolton, shared material from the church archives. Ken Horton sent me copies of letters written to him by Stuart Sutcliffe. Pauline Sutcliffe photocopied pages from her brother's art college notebooks. Raul Nunez, longtime friend to *Datebook* editor Art Unger, set me on the trail that eventually allowed me access to Unger's papers at the University of Missouri. Tony Barrell shared memories of literary Liverpool at the turn of the 1960s and also sent me rare copies of the university magazine *Sphinx* that he had edited as an undergraduate.

I am grateful to Pattie Boyd, who I had first met in 1974 when she moved into Eric Clapton's life, for being so encouraging about the subject of the book and for sharing her memories of George. I am also grateful to Cyndy Bury, who was shocked to have been tracked down but nevertheless invited me to fly out and meet her at her Mediterranean home. She is one of only three people still living who was present when John and George first sampled LSD, and her version of events has helped to clear up some persistent myths about the occasion.

When I visited Liverpool I was given wonderful, personalized guided tours by Jackie Spencer and then David Bedford of Liverpool Tours. Spencer Leigh, as ever, was generous with phone numbers and a mine of information about the city and its music. Paul Wane of Tracks and Pete Nash of the London Beatles Fan Club were great at putting me in touch with rare Beatles material and making useful suggestions of people to contact and paths to follow.

Finally, thanks to the various libraries, research centers, and other organizations that supplied me with material, contacts, or information: Apple Corps (Neil Aspinall), Associated Press New York (Susan James), BBC Written Archives Centre (James Codd), the *Birmingham News* (Bob Carlton), the

British Library, Church House, Companies House, Howard Gotlieb Archival Research Center of Boston University (for Hugh Schonfield archives), Liverpool Public Library, Liverpool University Library, Elliott Mintz, MPL (Lilian Marshall), National Newspaper Library, Summit Ministries (David Noebel), University of Missouri Western Historical Manuscript Collection (Arthur Unger archives), and *Waycross Journal Herald* (Jack Williams III).

London, March 2006

Chapter One

Tell Me What You See

If this scene is (around) in 2012 . . . the masses will be where I am today and I should be as groovy as Jesus by then.
—*John Lennon, 1968*

There are a lot of people who like us and they are influenced by us. So, you know, in a small way I may be able to influence them in another direction.
—*George Harrison, 1966*

There'd never been anything like the Beatles, who were about music but also about something more far-reaching.
—*Paul McCartney, 2004*

Some people pray to the Beatles. I know. I don't think that's wrong. If you pray you usually get something.
—*Ringo Starr, 1969*

Gospel—*euaggelion* in New Testament Greek—literally means "good message" or "good tidings." Sometimes it's interpreted as "good news." Did the Beatles really have a "gospel"? I think they did. It wasn't their intention. It wasn't the reason that they first got together and made music. But over the years they were certainly received as bearers of good news, and, in retrospect, they themselves came to see their historical significance not only in terms of having changed the course of popular music but of having been heralds of a cultural revolution. As John said in 1968, "I've changed a lot of people's heads."

There can be no doubt that, particularly from 1966 onward, they were looked to for guidance, and their songs were analyzed in much the same way as theologians analyze the Bible or literary critics analyze Shakespeare. "The temporarily ironic 'meanwhile' of 'Penny Lane' is all that holds the context of the song 'together' except for the rock provincial humanness scattered throughout," wrote Richard Meltzer in *Crawdaddy* (May 1967). "The unlikeliness of the simultaneity asserted by this 'meanwhile,' particularly in its repetition not even as a relation at the close of the song provides the song's most absurdly secure and out-of-context verbal pole."

Listeners became curious about the subtext of these apparently casually written pop songs. When Paul said that the girl selling poppies from a tray felt as if she was "in a play," was he suggesting that life is a game, that our existence is scripted by a spiritual superpower, or merely that we all have roles? Were the "friends" that helped Ringo "get by" his fellow humans or some newly developed pharmaceuticals? Was "You've Got to Hide Your Love Away" a secret message to Brian Epstein about his clandestine homosexual relationships? Old certainties were crumbling, and some thought the Beatles were supplying pointers toward a new way of life.

It wasn't just impressionable fans but fellow artists and cultural commentators who were given to thinking of the Beatles as savior figures capable of transforming lives. The highly regarded rock critic Greil Marcus wrote: "The Beatles affected not only the feel and quality of life—they deepened it, sharpened it, brightened it." In 1967 the film historian Gene Youngblood argued that, "The allure, the excitement, the glory of Beatle music is the suspicion that the Beatles might just succeed where magicians of the past have failed." Two years later rock critic Dave Marsh, writing in the pages of the rock monthly *Creem*, concluded that everything before the Beatles now seemed indistinct and unimportant to him. "'I Want to Hold Your Hand' may not seem significant, but to people my age that is a line of demarcation between history and life as we know it." The poet Allen Ginsberg concluded in 1984: "The Beatles changed American consciousness."

By the time they released *Sgt. Pepper's Lonely Hearts Club Band* with its gatefold sleeve, psychedelic inner bag, free cardboard cutouts, and clue-ridden front cover artwork, the Beatles were aware that their work was being received as more than light entertainment. "Turn the sleeve over," notes Matthew Schneider in an essay in *Anthropoetics*, "and you encounter the second quasi-religious dimension of Sgt. Pepper; for the first time on a pop album, all the words to the songs are transcribed. The lyrics thus acquire the stable, fixed status of sacred text, which can now be pored over and studied with the kind of Talmudic intensity that the Beatles knew their fans possessed."

It would be wrong to assume that this gospel came only through the lyrics of the songs, important though they were. It also came through the sound of the music, the spaces between the words, and their entire way of life. The interviews they gave in the group's later years became an important way of updating fans on the changes in their thinking. "They didn't just represent an attitude that was helpful to their fans," wrote Nick Bromell in *Tomorrow Never Knows*. "They *enacted* it, they structured it, they *were* it."

The Beatles had not started out with any thought of imparting messages to a generation. In the early days their lyric writing and grasp of social issues were the least developed of their capabilities. If you had told them in 1963 that within four years their spoken and written words would be pored over by intelligent young people in search of direction, they would have laughed you out of the room. They got into music for the kicks and the sex, not to be spreaders of good news.

This is hardly surprising. There were no precedents for Western pop singers as prophets, priests, or teachers. Elvis had sent out cultural shock waves in the fifties, but he didn't write his own songs and had no understanding of the social dimensions of his performance. No one thought that Elvis's views on sex, death, religion, and politics would be as inspiring as his legwork on stage. Chuck Berry told some great tales in his music, but, again, no one imagined that he knew the secrets of the universe. The only opinions sought from rock stars were their visions of an ideal date or their favorite movie star.

Initially the Beatles were treated in the same way. Even though they were better educated than Elvis and Chuck Berry, interviewers only wanted to know about their favorite food or what records they were listening to and almost never asked them about the sources of inspiration behind their music. Probably the songs in those early days didn't demand an explanation. In their subject matter they were not vastly different from what had gone before, although they tended to display more politeness and less raunch than people like Jerry Lee Lewis and Little Richard. (Five of their first eleven singles contained the word "please.") They were songs of teenage love, longing, and loneliness. "Love Me Do," their first single, consisted of one hundred words, twenty-two of which were "love."

However, it soon became obvious that the Beatles had things going for them that made them different from the previous wave of pop and rock outfits. First, their music had a richness and variety that enabled it to withstand the critical analysis of experts schooled in classical composition. Even though they'd received no formal training and couldn't sight read, they had an instinctive understanding of how to match mood to sound and how to introduce those surprising yet not completely outrageous chord changes that make magic of music. They didn't know that "A Hard Day's Night" contained "oscillations between a latent tonic of C and the flat seventh triad of a B flat before the answering phrase balanced the modality with descending chromatics," as musicologist Wilfrid Mellers wrote, but they'd done it anyway.

Second, their better education meant that they could see themselves as being in the same lineage as painters, poets, and playwrights. They might be entertainers, but they weren't *mere* entertainers. In fact, they had more in common with a sculptor or a dancer than a ventriloquist or a comedian. They had aspirations beyond pop. They considered writing a musical about Liverpool for the West End stage. John published a book of humorous poems, stories, and drawings. Paul equated the process of writing a song to Picasso's method of painting as captured in Henri-Georges Clouzot's 1956 documentary *Le Mystère Picasso*.

Finally, the Beatles were clearly having a cultural impact that defied obvious explanation. Girls had screamed at Frank Sinatra, Johnny Ray, and Elvis, but the excitement generated by this group seemed out of proportion to what was actually happening on stage or on record. In other words, the reaction was as much a symptom of an emerging rupture in society as it was evidence of a high level of appreciation for a particular style of music. And it wasn't in Europe and North America alone. Wherever the Beatles went they received the same response. In the places they never visited, the records worked in the same way. Russian teenagers, for example, were every bit as won over as their American or Japanese counterparts.

All this meant that the Beatles were good fodder for musicologists, sociologists, psychologists, and cultural historians. These people began to take the Beatles seriously before the Beatles took themselves seriously. When *Rolling Stone* publisher Jann Wenner asked John at what point he had noticed the first "spiritual reaction" to the records, John mentioned the music critic of the *Times* (of London), William Mann, who in December 1963 wrote an unsigned column that started: "The outstanding English composers of 1963 must seem to have been John Lennon and Paul McCartney, the talented young musicians from Liverpool whose songs have been sweeping the country since last Christmas" and went on to praise their instrumental versatility, exhilarating vocal duetting, and ability to translate "African blues or American Western idioms . . . into tough, sensitive Merseyside."

What was groundbreaking about Mann's column was that he treated the Beatles as seriously as he usually did Bach, Beethoven, or Schubert. Ignoring the "hysterical screaming of young girls," he examined the performances of the songs in their own right and described them in the same musicological terms—"flat-submediant key-switches," "melismas with altered vowels," "chains of pandiatonic clusters"—that he would use when discussing classical repertoire. In John's view it was this piece that "made us credible with intellectuals."

Yet this was only musical credibility. Mann made no reference to the words of the songs, except to comment on the way the Beatles altered vowels when singing. Lyrical credibility would come with the release of *Rubber Soul* in December 1965. John acknowledged to Wenner that "The Word" (recorded on November 10) was the first song he'd written with the intention of imparting knowledge. In essence, it was the first gospel song of the Beatles ("This could be a Salvation Army song," said Paul at the time). "We just took that position," John explained with reference to the *Rubber Soul* period. "We started putting out messages. Like, 'The word is love,' and things like that."

Songs like "Nowhere Man" and "In My Life" revealed a soul searching that hadn't been evident before. A reevaluation was taking place. Although "Help!" had been intended as a serious song, it had been swallowed up in the atmosphere of jollity and mayhem that surrounded the movie it was written for, and so no one thought of John as someone suffering from depression and anxiety. *Rubber Soul* was a distinctive move away from the heavily physical music they'd perfected in the basement clubs and toward a more cerebral sound better suited for record listening.

The first serious interview about their songwriting was given in December 1965 to the novelist Francis Wyndham for the short-lived magazine *London Life*. He had earlier met with both John and Paul but found that together they just fooled around and got lost in a labyrinth of puns. "The jokes were good," Wyndham admitted, "but no better than Beatle jokes on the cinema or television screens." To retrieve the situation he arranged to meet Paul alone at Brian Epstein's office and spent two hours in conversation. "He was ready to talk about his music, and did so with the minimum of suspicion or self-consciousness."

In the interview Paul spoke of how the group was changing. "What's the point of living in a rut? We could stay in one now for ever, repeating our early hits, and if we did come up with something exciting we'd have to scrap it." His points of reference were broadening. Instead of only talking about pop musical competitors such as Bob Dylan, the Who, and the Rolling Stones (each of whom he referred to), he mentioned the painter Francis Bacon, the playwright Eugene O'Neill, the poets Robert Graves and Dylan Thomas, and the composer Handel. "A famous painter has got to paint but he's still knocking himself out doing it. We've reached that stage. We both want to do a million more things."

Although there were no precedents in Western pop music for musicians as spiritual leaders, there were in other cultures. The most pertinent was the tradition of the shaman in areas such as Africa, South America, and Siberia. The shaman was trained to get into an ecstatic state during a ritual, usually driven by music and drugs, and be taken into the spirit world to deal with the spirits on behalf of the tribe. When the ecstasy was over and he had returned to normal consciousness, he would share with the tribe, in the form of stories, the experiences of his journey down to the lower world and up to the higher world.

The shaman played a mixture of roles. He could see into the future, guide the dead, tell the history of the tribe, diagnose and heal illnesses, settle disputes, and offer consolation. Besides being able to deal with the spirits during trances or under the influence of music and drugs, he would enjoy a rich dream life. During these dreams he would be visited by long-dead shamans who would pass on advice.

The Beatles didn't consciously base themselves on shamans (as Jim Morrison would later do with the Doors), but during the period 1966–1970 this is the role they played. It was as though the culture was involved in a giant ritual in which the Beatles got themselves stirred up with drugs and music and then reported back what they had seen and experienced. They were descending to the lower world on behalf of their public ("Let me take you down"), then ascending to the higher world ("Climb in the back with your head in the clouds") before returning to the middle world with their stories and visions ("I can show you").

The songs from the lower world were about their trials and tribulations—pain, depression, loneliness, despair, rejection, addiction—which they had endured as they acquired wisdom. These could range from Paul's "I'm Down" to John's "Yer Blues" and "Don't Let Me Down." The songs from the higher world were about visionary ecstasy: either their experiences of other dimensions ("Across the Universe," "Lucy in the Sky with Diamonds") or the everyday world renewed ("Penny Lane," "Good Day Sunshine," "Mother Nature's Son"). Their story songs were messages distilled from their visits to the higher and lower worlds ("Come Together," "Revolution," "Hey Jude," "All You Need Is Love," "Within You without You"). Appropriately, they served their apprenticeship below the surface of the earth in the cellar clubs of Liverpool and Hamburg, did their final impromptu concert on the rooftop of the Apple headquarters in London, and built their reputation in between at ground level in the concert halls and stadia of the world.

John, in particular, made great shaman material. What better summary of his character could there be than Rogan Taylor's description, in his book *The Death and Resurrection Show: From Shaman to Superstar*, of the ideal candidate for training as a shaman in Siberia? "He is the 'lazy boy,' precocious and unhappy with the ordinary world," he wrote. "He is unaccountably moody or queerly sick, often lonely and separated from his real parents. An orphan-outsider, who thinks he must be special. Above all, or rather beneath all, he is the dreamer, the visionary, who lets his imagination run away with itself. He is the man who must go to another world in order to live in *this* one."

In common with successful shamans, John enjoyed sleeping, dreaming, and other voluntary forms of loss of consciousness, later referring to the whole Beatle phenomenon as a "dream." He often wrote songs that sounded dreamlike in their delivery ("Julia," "Strawberry Fields Forever," "Tomorrow Never Knows"), described a dreamlike world ("Lucy in the Sky with Diamonds," "Glass Onion," "Cry Baby Cry"), or were about sleeping ("I'm So Tired," "Good Night," "I'm Only Sleeping"). "A Day in the Life," written with Paul, starts in the lower world of death and war and then ascends, via a "smoke" on a bus, to the dream state. The ascent is illustrated by an orchestra frenetically building up to a musical crescendo.

The shamanistic model seems more appropriate than the priestly model of the Judeo-Christian tradition because the priest passes on the word of God without having to battle with demons and consult with good spirits. The priest doesn't have to experience an altered state of consciousness to know the love and truth of God. The shaman, however, speaks of what he has been through on behalf of the tribe. He suffers for his people.

The Beatles, it seemed, went through things on behalf of their followers and then sent back their findings. They traveled the world, smoked pot, took acid, snorted cocaine, lived to excess, became addicted, consulted psychics, spent millions, meditated, and then wrote their reports up in the form of songs. The poet William Blake (1757–1827) believed that the "road of excess" led to the "palace of wisdom," and the Beatles consciously traveled along that road in the expectation of becoming enlightened. "We're in a position to try things, to show people," said George in 1968. "We can jump around and try new things which others can't or won't. Like drugs. People doing ordinary jobs just couldn't give the time we did to looking into all that."

Starting with *Revolver*, their albums were eagerly anticipated not just for their musical value but for their information. Where were the Beatles at? What were they into? Their lyrics were teased apart to see if new meanings would reveal themselves. The intricate details of the album covers were examined for clues to supplement the songs. Bunyan Davie Napier, esteemed Old Testament theologian and dean of the chapel at Stanford University, preached sermons on "Yellow Submarine" and "Eleanor Rigby," telling *Time* in September 1967 that "no entity hits as many sensitive people as these guys do."

Yet, unlike the Bible or the Qur'an, the words of the Beatles arrived embedded in music, and you couldn't arrive at the truth of a Beatles song by stripping the lyric from its backing track and hoping that it would speak to you as it lay supine on the page. What a Beatles song meant could only be experienced by immersion in the sound—the words conversing with the music—and even then it couldn't always be articulated. There was a sense in which the Beatles did "take you down," and the only way to understand the songs was to inhabit the space they created. The truth had to be felt.

Nick Bromell sums this up well in his book *Tomorrow Never Knows*:

> The Beatles came from Liverpool. They did not descend from the heavens with a roll of thunder or in a chariot of fire. But they did create an experience that cannot be adequately described if we are afraid to think of the miraculous or the divine. Words like 'divine' are just metaphors in any case. They point towards something that can be experienced but not named. They simply indicate that, alongside explanations of the Beatles phenomenon that emphasise the proclivities of capitalism and the ramifications of technology, we have to add one that acknowledges the human thirst for transcendence. Human connection without transcendence (if there has ever been such a thing) does not satisfy.

If the Beatles had a gospel, it presupposes that they believed that something was wrong with the world. You don't go around dispensing "good news" if you think everything's fine. The Christian gospel was meant to be good news to people who were enslaved to wrong desires and heading for hell. It offered them peace (with God), freedom (from guilt), and forgiveness (for sin). It also gave them the possibility of partaking in the building of the kingdom of heaven, now and on into eternity.

The central concern of the Beatles is harder to pin down because they didn't believe in a cataclysmic event such as the fall or in a definitive redemptive act such as the atonement. Also the group consisted of four people whose views sometimes diverged and who lasted as a recording entity for almost eight years, during which time their opinions changed. However, a good case can be made for saying that their unfolding philosophy always pivoted on freedom of one type or another. The human problem, in their eyes, was one of limitations and constraint. We couldn't reach our full potential if we were inhibited. "One thing I can tell you," John sang in "Come Together," "is you got to be free."

As they matured, the issues that preoccupied them changed from ones of freedom from authority and tradition to freedom from material craving, rampant ego, reduced consciousness, war, prejudice, poverty, and lies. The first questions could be answered by youthful rebellion, but the later questions increasingly took them into the area of self-realization. You could rattle human authority by growing your hair long, but you couldn't conquer your inner demons in the same way. To "change your head," as John referred to it in "Revolution," required something much more radical.

The realization that a transformed society could only come about through transformed people prompted them to explore consciousness-altering drugs and then to reconsider religion. In June 1967 Paul told *The People* newspaper, "We all know what we would like to see in the world today—peace. We want to be able to get on with each other. I believe the drug [LSD] could heal the world." A year later Ringo was saying, "If everyone in the world started meditating, then the world would be a much happier place, and there would be less wars and things. I seriously think this could happen in a few years' time."

Whether or not we think it fitting that a pop group should be looked to for guidance on such matters, that's what happened. When John said that the Beatles had become "more popular than Jesus" he was no doubt drawing attention to the fact that for a certain generation, in a certain part of the world, the Beatles were occupying the position that had traditionally been the preserve of religious leaders. Millions of young people smoked pot, dropped acid, investigated Eastern religions, and marched for peace in Vietnam as a result of things the Beatles did or said. Al Aronowitz, who chronicled the Beatles for the *Saturday Evening Post*, said: "The Beatles had become role models for the youth of the entire Western world. Whatever the Beatles did was right! Correct! Acceptable!"

In my concluding chapter I've taken the liberty of using my own life as an example of one that was influenced by the Beatles. I've done this because it's easy to discuss the "effect" of the Beatles on the "sixties" but difficult to substantiate this with reliable data. How is it possible to tell how many people grew their hair long as a direct result of seeing the Beatles or took up yoga because of something George said? The only way I can understand it and communicate it to others is to look at how one person was touched in a small town seventy miles north of London. My only advantage over any other Beatles fan of the era is that my work has given me more time than most people have to ponder the phenomenon and has enabled me to meet many of the people involved, including John, Paul, and their producer George Martin.

The sixties were a time of great spiritual turmoil. Long-standing sources of stability—Enlightenment rationalism and traditional religion—were being questioned. Rationalism, the idea that everything could be worked out by the human mind and that progress was inevitable, had no place for the inexplicable. The result was an over-mechanized, over-organized society characterized by conformity, where the imagination was devalued. In its revolt against this, the sixties generation, like the Romantics of the nineteenth century, celebrated the irrational, chance, dreams, hallucinations, and the primitive. "I don't believe that it ends with our Western logical thought," said Paul in 1967. "It can't do because that's so messed up anyway, most of it, that you have got to allow for the possibility of there being a lot more than we know about."

Traditional religion—Christianity in the West—wasn't widely considered as a solution to this problem, mainly because it seemed to have made compromises with rationalism. The soullessness and lack of mystery that the young hated about modernity was replicated in the church. The alliance between industry, politics, and the military seemed to be blessed rather than challenged by the clergy. This was partly why those disenchanted by materialism tended to be attracted to the religions of the East that showed more respect for nature and were less interested in war and the pursuit of wealth. "The religions they have in India I believe in much more than anything I ever learned from Christianity," said George in 1966 when visiting Bombay for the first time. "Their religion is not like something which Christianity seems to be, which is you turn it on Sunday morning and go to church because you're supposed to go rather than because you want to go. It's every second and every minute of their lives. It's *them*—how they act, how they conduct themselves, how they think."

A few weeks earlier, while on his last tour of America as a Beatle, he had said, "To me it seems that Western philosophy is very prejudiced because they look upon mysticism as a magical 'something else,' you know? But after everything the greatest Western philosophers have said, to me it all boils down to the fact that they still haven't hit upon what the Eastern people have."

It was into such a crisis of faith that the Beatles spoke. R. C. Zaehner, the author of *Mysticism Sacred and Profane*, said, "Loss of faith in a given religion does not by any means imply the eradication of the religious instinct. It merely means that the instinct, temporarily repressed, will seek an object elsewhere." The religious instincts of millions of young people in the sixties, which found no satisfaction in either godless rationalism or traditional Christianity, found something to hold on to in the Beatles. The Beatles may not have supplied creeds and doctrines, but they offered a model. As Bromell has said, "Their music certainly did create a framework, invisible to the eyes, in which something like enlightenment was an imagined possibility."

They suggested a way forward that combined some of the best aspects of rationalism with some of the best aspects of the old faith. They may have feared the slow disappearance of the human touch as technology improved, but they took advantage of everything it offered from the Moog synthesizer to multi-track recording. John had an in-car phone and Paul a video recorder in 1966. They were always eager to purchase new inventions as soon as they appeared on the market.

A positive feeling about the future emanated from their work. Although their 1967 song "Getting Better" was about personal progress rather than the development of the world, it encapsulated the type of optimism associated with the Beatles from the time they burst onto the recording scene in 1962. Summarizing the achievements of the group over thirty years after their breakup, George said, "I think we gave hope to the Beatle fans. We gave them a positive feeling that there was a sunny day ahead and that there was a good time to be had and that you are your own person and that the government doesn't own you. There were those kinds of messages in a lot of our songs."

They were skeptical and even dismissive of the church, yet many of their core beliefs—love, peace, hope, truth, freedom, honesty, transcendence—were, in their case, secularized versions of Christian teachings. "All You Need Is Love," written by John, owed a lot to the biblical view of love and St. Paul's words on charity in 1 Corinthians 13. George's "Within You without You," a challenge not to get so caught up in the material world that we ignore the spiritual, actually quotes from the words of Jesus. When Paul wrote "Lady Madonna" he had the image of the Virgin Mary in mind but then extended it to embrace all working-class women with children.

"We're all Jesus and we're all God," said John in 1968. "He's inside all of us and that's what it's all about. As soon as you start realizing that potential in everyone, well, then you can change it [humanity] and the person themselves [sic] can change it. That's the whole bit. Jesus wasn't God come down on earth any more than anybody else was. He was just a better example of a good guy."

Aspects of the relationship between the Beatles and their audience were similar to those between shaman and ritual participant or between guru and disciple. They were the enlightened ones who passed on their insights in three-minute sermons. When they were touring, they were regularly approached by the diseased and disabled who wanted to be touched by them in the belief that their power as performers would translate into healing power. After the breakup John admitted, "The Beatles *were* a kind of religion," and said that the festivals at Woodstock and on the Isle of Wight were more than just rock concerts. "They were the youth getting together and forming a new church, as it were."

Some will think that the claim that the Beatles had any kind of gospel to spread is preposterous. They will argue that they were four ordinary lads with not much concrete advice to offer who happened to become famous in an age that was looking for gods. They will point to the trivial and ambiguous nature of many of their songs, argue that their comments were often inconsistent and ill-informed, and point out that they were as gullible as any of their followers when it came to being hoodwinked by spiritual hucksters.

In what follows I won't be endorsing everything they said. I will simply be arguing that they had things to say and that these things were taken seriously at the time by a large proportion of young people, many of whom are still affected by those views. There are powerful people in the arts, media, and entertainment today for whom the Beatles provided the initial inspiration, not necessarily by making them want to play guitars or drums, but by giving the confidence to develop a vision and stay true to it.

It's obvious that they had an effect on fashion, but perhaps less obvious are the effects they have had on the consciousness behind such movements as those for human rights, animal rights, justice, world peace, legalization of soft drugs, and freedom of expression. Even if they didn't specifically campaign for all these causes, they helped establish the frame of mind that put them on the agenda. When John was asked in the mid-sixties whether he would be writing any songs against the war, he answered that all Beatles' songs were against war.

I'll look at what was said, how it was said, and how it changed over time. Where possible I'll attempt to discover how what was said was received at the time and whether there was a measurable cultural impact. The pilgrimage of the Beatles from the rather stuffy Christianity of their childhoods to the fascination with forms of occultism toward the end of their career was in many ways a microcosm of what would eventually happen to the spiritual underpinnings of Western culture.

For this reason I will look closely at their upbringings in Liverpool to try to detect where the dissatisfaction with the Christian gospel began and then to their early days as a group, when they became more defiantly agnostic, to see how much that was affected by their exposure to the philosophy of existentialism. In the first half of their recording career they were not consciously dealing in messages and yet their implicit concern for truth, love, hope, freedom, ecstasy, and existential experience laid the foundations for what was to come.

Hallucinogenic drugs without doubt produced the crucial turning point. The Beatles' use of them marked the point not only when they became more concerned with art than entertainment but when they became more introspective, aware of the spiritual, and concerned with spreading their views about peace, togetherness, and harmony. Without drugs it's unlikely that they would have been as receptive to the teachings of Hinduism or would have devoted so much time to learning techniques of meditation.

Information about Eastern religion was made more widely known in the West than ever before through the influence of the Beatles. It's difficult to imagine that the New Age movement would have had so great an appeal without their groundwork. Interest in Transcendental Meditation, for example, received a tremendous boost from their corporate endorsement, and the proliferation of shaved-headed men and long-haired women singing the Hare Krishna mantra on the main streets of every major city was a direct result of the financial and moral backing their organization received from the Beatles.

By the time of their final recordings they were less sure of what they believed in as a group. Each Beatle was into something different and wanted to divest himself of the burden of leadership. One of the first things John did after the breakup of the group was to try to demystify the Beatles, but this was in itself an acknowledgment of how powerful they had become. "The dream is over," he told *Rolling Stone* publisher Jann Wenner. "Nothing happened except that we all dressed up."

John was wrong to say that nothing had happened during the sixties. It was true that many of the same political, social, and economic problems remained, but there had been a massive change in the way people saw themselves, their goals, and their relationship with authority. The world of 1970 was almost unrecognizable from that of 1959, whereas there were similarities between the world of 1959 and 1949.

One of the most decisive aspects of this change was the weakening of the power that the Christian story had over the popular imagination. For centuries people in the West had looked to this story to discover where they came from, how much they were valued, why they were here, how they should live, and what lay beyond death. Local churches provided a sense of community, rites of passage, regular rituals, teaching, pastoral guidance, and an opportunity to worship.

During the sixties the Christian story no longer gripped. For various reasons ranging from the spread of scientific thinking to the influence of television, people began to desert the church. Decisions about personal and public behavior began to be made without reference to Bible teaching or church doctrine. In 1940, the year John was born, 36 percent of British children attended Sunday school. In 1960 it was 24 percent. In 2000 it was 4 percent.

The popularity of the Beatles coincided with this sudden loss of Christian influence. They were beneficiaries of new attitudes toward money and leisure. The emphasis moved from thrift, duty, and service to consumerism, self-expression, and fun, and the Beatles were magnificent providers of fun. At the same time, though, the human instinct for fellowship, ritual, and worship hadn't disappeared. It merely sought a new focus, and the Beatles found themselves as the object of an unusual level of devotion. People expected from them the sort of guidance that had once come from the pulpits.

"The Beatles had been mistaken for medicine-men or witch-doctors," said Rogan Taylor of the times when disabled fans lined up outside the Beatles' dressing rooms hoping to be touched by the "now semi-divine Liverpool lads" and perhaps cured. "Soon they [the Beatles] began to dress and talk like medicine-men. But was it simply a case of mistaken identity? Why should entertainers be expected to perform cures? Do we all attend their shows in order to 'feel better'? Are we humming the songs so that we might, like the singers, get *transformed* from the ordinary world into the *extraordinary* world? If we do, we are in a church. We are attending a religious rite."

The position they came to occupy was most perfectly encapsulated by the incident in 1966 when John was accused of claiming that the popularity of the Beatles now exceeded that of Jesus Christ. It seemed outrageous at the time that a pop singer would elevate his art to the level of religious leadership. The disgust that many Americans felt was not to do with an argument over numbers but was because someone involved in entertainment would dare compare himself to the central figure in an international, historical religion.

This was a year before the start of the great outdoor rock festivals when some idealists thought they had at last found a way of building heaven on earth. It was before the love-ins and be-ins took place in San Francisco. It was even before people started speaking of "rock culture" or suggesting that rock 'n' roll could "change the world." It was at a time when few people even treated rock seriously as a form of music, let alone a form of religion.

It's with this incident that I start the story of *The Gospel according to the Beatles* because it embraced all the conflicting energies of the period: the Christian abhorrence of rock music and rock music's rejection of Christianity, the visions of drugs and the lure of the East, the decline of the church, and the rise of commercialized popular culture for teenagers. It also happened exactly halfway through their career. It was four years after their first recordings with EMI in 1962 and four years before their official disbandment in 1970. During the first half they had been entertainers who played the fool during interviews. During the second half they became artists who took on the mantle of sages and offered "words of wisdom" to benighted people. Right in the middle came the moment of change.

Chapter Two

You Can't Do That

I'm not saying we're better, or greater, or comparing us with Jesus Christ as a person, or God as a thing, or whatever it is. I just said what I said and it was wrong, or was taken wrong. And now it's all this.
—*John Lennon, 1966*

Of course, John never meant to say that the Beatles were literally bigger than Christ. He was only referring to the lack of attendance in church. He was actually taking a sympathetic point of view.
—*Paul McCartney, 2004*

There weren't more people coming to see us than going to church.
—*Ringo Starr, 2000*

Our music is our religion. We're giving a lot of happiness to a lot of people. I'm sure that we're giving a lot more happiness to people than some of those priests.
—*George Harrison, 1966*

*T*he Beatles, at the height of Beatlemania, were agnostic and didn't hide this belief. Religion, Paul said in 1963, was something he didn't think about: "It doesn't fit in with my life." While touring Britain in October 1964 he admitted to *Playboy*, "None of us believe in God." John clarified the group's position: "We're not quite sure what we are, but I know that we're more agnostic than atheistic."

Yet just a few months later this assurance in God's nonbeing would be rocked by their first encounter with LSD. All their material dreams had been achieved so dramatically, at such an early age, that they were starting to ask themselves what was left to look forward to. Since their teen years they'd been motivated by the possibility of wealth, fame, sex, and acclaim, but now that they had these things a fresh purpose was required. Drugs seemed to offer new possibilities.

"The four of us have had the most hectic lives," said Ringo. "We have got almost anything money can buy. But when you can do that, the things you buy mean nothing after a time. You look for something else, for a new experience."

They began to question their assumptions and talk openly about belief in God. They cut down on drinking whiskey as they took up smoking pot, and read Aldous Huxley rather than Ian Fleming. George was saying that the only worthwhile pursuit was the search for the answers to the questions, who am I? why am I here? and where am I going? "We made our money and fame, but for me that wasn't it," he said. "It was good fun for a while, but it certainly wasn't the answer to what life is about."

Paradoxically, as they began to search for a meaning beyond the material, they themselves became a source of meaning to millions of fans around the world. As one father explained to *Time* in 1967, "The Beatles are explorers, trusty advance scouts. I like them to report to my kids." This was made all the more exciting because the art was enigmatic and the lyrics ambiguous. They seemed to know more than we did, but what it was that they knew was hard to determine. We emulated their dress and behavior. We combed their interviews for insights. We played their music in the hopes that it would soak into our psyches and somehow make us more like them.

John would later refer to the mid-sixties as the Beatles' "self-conscious" period, and during it he made his most contentious comment about religion: "The Beatles are more popular than Jesus." It was an artlessly delivered observation that would have unforeseen consequences, both for the Beatles as a touring group and for John as an individual. Although the controversy centered on his opinion of the crowd-pulling power of Christianity in the mid-twentieth century, he was also saying something about the religious function of rock music. For the music he played to be anything like a challenge to Christianity, wouldn't it have to satisfy some of the same yearning that traditional religion satisfied?

The life and teachings of Jesus had always intrigued John. When he and Paul were still teenagers, they started work on a play, heavily influenced by the absurdism of Harold Pinter's plays *The Birthday Party* and *The Dumb Waiter*, with a central character named Pilchard who lived in suburbia and believed he was a "Christ figure." In November 1965 Paul mentioned it to *New Musical Express*, saying that it was "about Jesus Christ coming back to earth as an ordinary person." John regularly poked fun at church dignitaries, parodied hymns, and drew blasphemous cartoons of Christ on the cross in a way that only the once-faithful can. It was as though he was trying to prove to himself that he was free from the influence of the Church of England.

When he became recognized as a leader, he began to empathize with the person Christians referred to as "the Lord." He wondered whether Christ, like the Beatles, had had divinity thrust on him by over-zealous followers. Had Jesus been someone with a gift for storytelling, insight into the human condition, and the ability to foretell the future, who had been turned into a god figure against his will? John admired his central teachings of love, justice, and seeking the kingdom of heaven but felt that Jesus had been co-opted by people with a different agenda. He speculated that Jesus' claim to be the son of God might have been a way of telling us that we're all divine but that most of us don't recognize it. When asked to nominate his heroes for the cover of *Sgt. Pepper* John included Jesus, but it was eventually decided not to use this image. "It was just too controversial," says designer Peter Blake. "I'm not even sure that he was actually made into a cut-out."

In interviews John regularly alluded to biblical events and paraphrased memory verses. When asked by *Mersey Beat* about the origin of the name "Beatles" in 1961 he wrote: "It came in a vision—a man appeared on a flaming pie and said unto them, 'From this day on you are Beatles with an A.' Thank you, Mister Man, they said, thanking him." This alluded in part to Saint Peter's vision as recorded in Acts 10: " And [he] saw heaven opened, and a certain vessel descending unto him, as it had been a great sheet knit at the four corners, and let down to the earth"; in part to the story told in Genesis 17 about the origin of Abraham's name: "And when Abram was ninety years old and nine, the LORD appeared to Abram, and said unto him . . . Neither shall thy name any more be called Abram, but thy name shall be Abraham; for a father of many nations have I made thee"; and (possibly) in part to the story in Isaiah 6: "Then flew one of the seraphims unto me, having a live coal in his hand, which he had taken with the tongs from off the altar: And he laid it upon my mouth, and said, Lo, this hath touched thy lips; and thine iniquity is taken away, and thy sin purged." In 1973 John referred to his "flaming pie" story as "imitation Bible stuff."

In 1980, when asked why the Beatles would never reform, his reply alluded to at least three Gospel stories. "Do we have to divide the fish and the loaves for the multitudes again?" he said. " Do we have to get crucified *again*? Do we have to do the walking on water again because a whole pile of dummies didn't see it the first time or didn't believe it when they saw it? That's what they're asking. 'Get off the cross. I didn't understand it the first time. Can you do it again?' No *way*. You can't do things twice."

Occasionally this empathy was so consuming that, as he later admitted, when he was under the influence of drugs, "I thought, 'Oh, I must be Christ.'" His boyhood friend Pete Shotton told of a meeting John called in May 1968 to tell Paul, George, and Ringo that he was Jesus Christ reincarnated. He wanted an authorized statement to that effect put out. Apple's press officer Derek Taylor, who was also present, listened attentively but wisely ignored the plea, knowing that the drugs would soon wear off and this new Jesus would go back to being John.

By the end of the sixties John was, like Che Guevara, a bearded Christ figure for the counterculture. His line "They're gonna crucify me" in "The Ballad of John and Yoko" evidenced the degree of identification. After all, Christ had initially been greeted by cheers when he entered Jerusalem but was later hounded by the authorities just as John was hounded by the drug squad.

When he was interviewed at home by Maureen Cleave of London's *Evening Standard* in January 1966 he'd been giving fresh thought to religion after some disturbing experiences with LSD. Cleave, who'd first interviewed the Beatles in 1963, was a trusted friend who shared his interest in books. He valued her opinions and had made changes to the lyrics of "A Hard Day's Night" and "Help!" based on her advice. Too old to be a fanatical Beatles follower (she was six years older than John), but sharp enough to be able to see the phenomenon in its cultural and historical context, she pioneered serious adult coverage of the group. She never allowed the heat of the moment to distort her judgment.

Her accent and education set her apart from the usual females the Beatles came across in their work. Born in Mussoorie, North Eastern India, she was the daughter of Major J. C. T. Cleave of the Seventh Rajput Regiment and his Irish wife, Isabella, and had been brought to Ireland at the age of four. Two years later, in September 1940, she set sail for Bombay with her mother, but three days out at sea their ship, *City of Simla*, was torpedoed by a German U-boat. After being rescued and taken to Belfast, they remained in Ireland. She read history at St. Anne's College, Oxford, and in 1959 joined the *Evening Standard* as a feature writer.

The interview with John was to be the first in a series of interviews with each Beatle and manager Brian Epstein. They would be run on successive Fridays for five weeks. There was no merchandise to promote—*Rubber Soul* had been out for three months, and the songs for *Revolver* were still being written—but Cleave was keen to document recent changes in their lives and to see the new homes of John, George, and Ringo in the "stockbroker belt" south of London. The word was that they were growing up; that they'd cut back on clubbing and were interested in theater, film, literature, art, and avant-garde music.

It was Cleave's first visit to John's twenty-thousand-pound mock-Tudor mansion in St. John's Hill, Weybridge. He gave her a tour of the property, and she noted his expanding collection of objects and toys: a suit of armor, model racing cars, a fruit machine, a gorilla suit, tape recorders, five television sets, a huge Bible (recently bought in Chester), and an altar crucifix. He proudly showed her his outdoor pool and his fleet of cars—a Ferrari, a Mini Cooper, and a Rolls Royce.

Their conversation touched on his current enthusiasms (history, poetry, religion, and Celtic mythology) with barely a mention of Beatles music. He talked about watching television and sleeping. He wondered out loud about what sort of school to send his son Julian and announced that his current painting, drawing, and writing showed that he hadn't yet found his true métier. "There's something else I'm going to do," he said. "Something I must do. Only I don't know what it is."

As published, his mention of Jesus appeared not be connected to anything discussed. There's a chance it was prompted by an album of Indian music he'd played that had led him to say that the British in India had been foolish to think they could enlighten the natives. This could have led to a comparison of Christianity and Hinduism. Maureen Cleave can no longer recall the details. "It was just John sounding off," she says. "We were used to him doing that." Forty years ago she had said: "Mr. Lennon is very interested in [religion] and has been reading several books. As I remember the interview, we discussed how the power of Christianity had declined in the modern world, and his remarks were intended to illustrate this."

Among the several books he'd been reading were *Zen Flesh, Zen Bones* compiled by Paul Reps; *Siddhartha*, by Herman Hesse; and *The Doors of Perception*, by Aldous Huxley. He may also have been reading works by theologian Paul Tillich and the atheistic philosopher Friedrich Nietzsche (he went searching for Nietzsche books four weeks after the interview was published). The book that had the most significant impact, though, was *The Passover Plot: New Light on the History of Jesus*, by Hugh Schonfield, published in London just three months before. This was only revealed after the controversy had blown up, when he told the *Washington Post* that he had been "saying in my illiterate way of speaking what I gleaned from Schonfield's book."

Hugh Schonfield, sixty-five at the time, referred to himself as "an independent Jewish historian of the Nazarene faith," arguing that Jesus was the Messiah but not as Christians understood him to be. He wasn't divine and hadn't risen from the dead. The person that Christians revered as the son of God was a religious Jew who intentionally set out to fulfill the messianic prophecies. His plan had been to feign death on the cross and then revive in the tomb so that his disciples would believe he was the Messiah, but it backfired when a Roman soldier pierced him in the side and he bled to death.

Schonfield concluded that, rather than the promised savior of Hebrew scripture, Jesus was "a son of his country, a man with the blood of kings in his veins, exercising authority, because he believed it to be his messianic destiny, in circumstances of great danger and difficulty, addressing himself to a populace looking for inspiring leadership and national liberation."

John knew from experience how impressionable the masses could be and how easy it would be to deceive them, and this conspiracy theory appealed to him. Matthew Schneider of Chapman University, writing in the anthropological journal *Anthropoetics*, says, "As the *Evening Standard* interview suggests, reading the book seems to have impelled Lennon to consider his own fame and the phenomenon of Beatlemania in their broader cultural and historic contexts, and to conclude that the psychic, political, and cultural forces that went into the making of Christianity had been revived by Beatlemania."

Schonfield didn't think that his thesis of a plot need diminish Christ's significance. "Rather should we be strengthened and encouraged," he wrote, "because he is bone of our bone and flesh of our flesh and not God incarnate. The mind that was in the Messiah can therefore also be in us, stimulating us to accomplish what those of more careful and balanced disposition declare to be impossible." In other words, everyone could be a Christ.

The essence of Schonfield's theory, as passed on to Maureen Cleave by John, came out as: "Christianity will go. It will vanish and shrink. I needn't argue about that; I'm right and I will be proved right. We're more popular than Jesus now; I don't know which will go first—rock 'n' roll or Christianity. Jesus was all right but his disciples were thick and ordinary. It's them twisting it that ruins it for me."

The sentences appear to be sound bites from a more wide-ranging conversation. The three topics—the decline of Christianity, the popularity of the Beatles, and the ignorance of the disciples—are not logically linked, unless John was thinking that the "twisting" of Christ's message ultimately had led to the weakening of the faith, which had in turn allowed the Beatles to take advantage of a spiritually ravenous generation.

Schonfield's contribution was his thesis that Christianity is based on a misunderstanding of Jesus. John didn't expressly back this view, saying only that Christians had lost sight of the core of the gospel teaching. His view of the disciples as "thick and ordinary" almost certainly came from Schonfield, who referred to them as "loyal in their own way, but of limited intelligence, simple Galileans for the most part, who would not be at all at home in the sophisticated atmosphere of Jerusalem."

Maureen Cleave's interview was published in the *Evening Standard* on March 4, 1966, as a two-thousand-word single-page feature. The only pull-out quote was: "They keep telling me I'm all right for money but then I think I may have spent it all by the time I'm 40 so I keep going." The headline was: "How does a Beatle live? John Lennon lives like this." Above the headline, in smaller print, was the sentence, "On a hill in Surrey . . . a young man, famous, loaded, and waiting for something."

The *Evening Standard* never considered capitalizing on the Jesus quote. It wasn't seen as anything out of the ordinary. In her narrative Cleave didn't even prepare the reader for a shock. She simply set the comment in the context of his current passions: "Experience has sown few seeds of doubt in him; not that his mind is closed, but it's closed round whatever he believes at the time." It was an astute observation, and not one found in the typical Beatles story of the time.

The received wisdom is that the comment was ignored in Britain and unpublished in America until five months later. Neither is true. It didn't cause a big fuss in Britain, but it didn't disappear without a trace. John Grigg picked up on it in his *Guardian* column of Monday, March 7. In a satirical tone he suggested that if the public were polled, Jesus might have a higher rating than the Beatles but that "younger age groups might go for the Beatles." Yet, he argued, spending almost two thousand years "in the charts" was in itself "a fair achievement." Two days later the *Evening Standard*'s Letter of the Day was from a "loyal reader" who found the interview "nauseating," not just because of "John Lennon's impudent assertion" about Jesus but because John said that when his estranged father had recently reappeared on his doorstep in Weybridge he'd asked him to leave. "No gentleman," wrote the correspondent, "would discuss his private family affairs for publication in a national newspaper." The comments were widely enough known for the satirical magazine *Private Eye* to feature a cartoon by Gerald Scarfe of John dressed in a heavenly gown, with a cross-shaped guitar and a halo made out of a record.

The failure of the British to go apoplectic was proof of tolerance rather than ignorance. They also held the belief that an attack on John would merely bestow dignity on the statement. The opinions of pop stars on anything other than pop music were not taken terribly seriously in the Britain of 1966. Completely unaware of what John had said, as the interview hadn't yet been published, George also had a little dig at Christianity when Cleave spoke to him. "Why is there all this stuff about blasphemy?" he said. "If Christianity's as good as they say it is, it should stand up to a bit of discussion."

The series was one of the frankest that had ever been written about the group. It revealed them as intelligent, thoughtful, questioning adults who were already shedding their image as lovable mop-tops. On publication, Brian Epstein wrote to Maureen Cleave to tell her that he was "very satisfied" with the outcome, adding that "they must rank among the best that's [*sic*] been done." On March 21, 1966, there was a brief report on John's interview in *Newsweek*. "Turning to a discussion of religion," it noted, "the many-faceted musician predicted that 'Christianity will go' and declared that it is already playing second fiddle to the Beatles: 'we're more popular than Jesus now.'"

A month later it was picked up by Charles McCabe in the *San Francisco Chronicle*. He wrote, "I don't think the young fellow is mad, or anything. He is a victim of a belief, which often erodes intelligence. It is a belief often common to those who reap the strange rewards the theatrical life can yield. He thinks he's God. Naturally, he's a bit jealous of those notices his Son has been getting through these centuries. Since he's a nice kid, I hope he gets over his delusion before it begins to hurt him. But there it is; the lightweights who don't want to play Hamlet want to play God. I take it as a given doctrine that all actors are emotional cripples. The greatest actors are very crippled indeed. . . . It's a black childhood that leads a man to the bright lights." McCabe's observation proved remarkably prescient. Over the next six years John would imagine himself as Christ, admit the pain of his childhood, and record a song called "Crippled Inside."

In May the complete interview was published in *Detroit* magazine and on July 3 the *New York Times Magazine* ran "Old Beatles—A Study in Paradox," in which Maureen Cleave reworked her four *Evening Standard* interviews with the Beatles into a single feature that included John's reference to Jesus. *Atlas*, an American digest of the world press, selected the offending quote for its July issue. However, despite the wide metropolitan readerships of these publications, there was no protest. The ungoaded American public was as calm about John's wild comparison as the British public had been.

This wasn't unexpected because the Beatles had already told journalists that they were not Christians. Popular syndicated columnist Phyllis Battelle reported from the set of *Help!* that the Beatles were "Anti-adult. Anti-religion. Anti-convention. Anti-many things." Pointing to the statue of the fictional goddess Kaili used in the film, Ringo told her, "See that idol? If you'd been brought up to believe in that you'd believe in it instead of God, wouldn't you? People say they have visions and that's how they get to believe. Well, if I had a vision, maybe I'd believe too. But, until I do . . ." He had recently told *Playboy* that the group was "anti-Pope and anti-Christian." It was left to Paul to smooth the situation by adding, "But, believe it or not, we're not anti-Christ."

They were aware at the time that comments about religion regarded as refreshingly honest in Europe could offend in America. "In America they're fanatical about God," Paul explained. "I know somebody over there who said that he was an atheist. The papers nearly refused to print it because it was such shocking news that somebody could actually be an atheist. Yeah, and admit it."

Fundamentalist Christians were already uneasy about the Beatles' influence. The view that rock 'n' roll encouraged "base animal passions," first developed in the wake of Elvis's success, was still strong. The difference was that Elvis also recorded hymns and considered himself a Christian, whereas the Beatles admitted to being unbelievers and embodied distaste for convention, tradition, and respectability. The fact that they also drank, smoke, danced, wore their hair long, and went on un-chaperoned holidays with their girlfriends didn't endear them to the faithful. When the group landed in San Francisco on August 19, 1964, they were met by Christian protesters bearing placards, one of which read, "BEATLE WORSHIP IS IDOLATRY. THE BIBLE SAYS, 'CHILDREN KEEP YOURSELVES FROM IDOLS.'"

The most high-profile Christian critic of the Beatles was a thirty-year-old youth pastor, David A. Noebel, the author of *Communism, Hypnotism and the Beatles* (1965) and *Rhythm, Riots and Revolution* (1966). Since 1962 he had worked for Billy James Hargis, a notorious right-wing preacher who had once been a speechwriter for Senator Joseph McCarthy. His thesis was that rock 'n' roll sapped the moral fiber of the young, unwittingly achieving the goals of the revolutionary left. "The Beatles in particular have a special significance to the disrupters of society for their promotion of drugs, avant-garde sex and atheism," he wrote. "The revolution, though sometimes veiled, is fundamentally against Christianity and Christianity's moral concepts. Karl Marx sought to dethrone God before he set out to destroy capitalism."

Noebel, whose preferred music was southern gospel or classical, toured churches and youth organizations urging young people to stop buying Beatles records. His books, which were carefully sourced, drew connections between rock 'n' roll, Soviet subversion, delinquency, promiscuity, drug addiction, and psychological damage. He was concerned both with the effects of the rhythms on the consciousness and the viewpoint of the lyrics. As the Beatles' career progressed, they gave him more and more reason to denounce them. What was implicit in 1964 had become explicit by 1966.

Brian Epstein later blamed the whole controversy on *Datebook*, the American teen magazine that carried John's comments in August 1966. He argued that the story was inappropriate for such a young market. The fact is that, perhaps unknown to him, his organization helped place the story. The day after John's interview came out in the *Evening Standard*, Tony Barrow, senior press and publicity officer for Epstein's company NEMS Enterprises, contacted Art Unger, *Datebook*'s editor and publisher. "I think you might be more than interested in a series of 'in-depth' pieces which Maureen Cleave is doing on each Beatle for the *Evening Standard*," he wrote. "I'm enclosing a clipping showing her piece on John Lennon. I think the style and content is very much in line with the sort of thing that *Datebook* likes to use."

Datebook was run from a one-bedroom apartment on Washington Place in Greenwich Village, New York. It had started as a quarterly, selling 250,000 copies an issue in 1965, but in July 1966 had become a monthly. Although it listed nine people on its masthead, it was essentially a one-man operation with help from friends and teenage fans who sent in field reports. Unger, then forty-one, was a graduate of the University of Missouri School of Journalism who'd worked on a variety of trade magazines before buying the *Datebook* title and spicing it up for a new generation that was in love with the Beatles.

It was an intelligent and well-written publication that covered social issues alongside music, fashion, and dating. In the Winter 1965 issue, for example, there were several stories on the Beatles, an investigation into the then-little known drug LSD, an introduction to "folk rock," a feature on Mary Quant's latest London fashion designs, and a section in which readers interviewed groups such as Herman's Hermits, the Beach Boys, the Rolling Stones, and the Righteous Brothers. The aim was to give kids what they wanted but also to make them question the values they'd inherited.

"We were much more than an entertainment magazine," says Carmel Berman Reingold, one of *Datebook*'s main feature writers. "We tried to get kids involved in social issues. When the KKK started firebombing we did a story on a girl who was trapped on a burning bus. We also did a story on some kids who were fighting for integration at a lunch counter in Woolworth's. It was a well-received magazine, recommended by libraries and schools, but during the Civil Rights period we did get pulled off a lot of stands in the South because of our views on integration."

Unger first learned about the Beatles from an article in *Variety*. Anticipating that their U.K. success could be repeated in the United States, he published a one-shot magazine called *All about the Beatles* that sold 900,000 copies. The Beatles liked the issue and as a result gave him privileged access on American tours where they got to know each other well.

On Barrow's advice, Unger wrote to Maureen Cleave asking if she could write a five-thousand-word story for *Datebook* based on her *Evening Standard* interviews, offering her a fee of $150, the same amount that the United Press Syndicate in New York was quoting for the Lennon story. Cleave found the offer derisory. "I'm afraid the whole thing is out of the question," she replied. "The fee you offer is laughable. I do not mean to be rude but you cannot have expected any journalist of any standing to write so much for so little."

So on March 28 Unger bought the syndication rights and on April 4 wrote to Barrow to thank him for the tip-off, asking as an aside if any amendments would be required. "I thought I would ask you if you or the boys felt there was any distortion in the material since there is still time to cut or correct. . . ." Barrow didn't ask for any changes when he replied on the fourteenth, merely commenting, "I am glad to hear that you managed to secure the magazine rights for the Maureen Cleave series."

Unger planned to condense the material himself into a single piece but, on reflection, decided to run all four interviews virtually uncut. With the magazine now published monthly he needed as much good Beatles material as he could get. The Ringo interview ("I'm Not Thick, Just Uneducated") and the one with George ("I Never Asked to Be Famous") were in the August 1966 issue with the cover line, "Wildest Beatles Interviews Ever." The interviews with John and Paul were held back for the controversy-driven "Shout-Out Issue" of September 1966.

Contrary to what is frequently cited in books, the interview wasn't edited to make it more appropriate for a teenage audience. Only two opening paragraphs were cut, neither of which affected the thrust of the piece. What made the difference was the use of the sentence, "I don't know which will go first—rock 'n' roll or Christianity," both as a headline and a pull-out quote on the cover. Unger's commercial sense told him it was an arresting sentence. However, it was Paul's quote about America—"It's a lousy country where anyone black is a dirty nigger!"—that he thought would get the most attention.

What hasn't been known until now is that Unger deliberately sought to stir trouble in the South, where he thought the two Beatles quotes would prompt the strongest reaction. He mailed advance copies to the most reactionary disc jockeys he knew of in the Bible Belt, "figuring if one story didn't catch their eyes, the other would," as he noted in an unpublished memoir. The tactic worked. Two of the men targeted, Doug Layton and Tommy Charles in Birmingham, Alabama, who ran a popular daily morning show on WAQY (which they also owned), jumped on it like dogs on a juicy bone. "The Bible Belt jockeys reacted immediately," Unger noted. "They disregarded Paul's explosive statements and concentrated on John's allegedly blasphemous remarks."

The Layton and Charles Show played Top 40 records, kept the airwaves humming with good-humored banter, and took phone calls from listeners. Charles, thirty-nine, was a firecracker always set to explode over a local story of injustice that would get the switchboard lighting up, and Layton, thirty-six, was his calmer, more reflective sidekick. "It was Tommy's shtick to take something and just go with it," says J. Willoughby, a Birmingham radio presenter who knew him well in later life. "He was a talented guy and he would stir things up."

The advance magazines had been mailed out during the last week of July, over a week before they were due on the newsstands. Layton opened his copy and couldn't believe what he was reading. It sounded like the ultimate statement of arrogance from an atheistic pop star and one that would be sure to provoke outrage if widely known in the South. The strength of feeling it could arouse was just what his show thrived on.

"We were on air and I happened to ask, 'Did you hear what John Lennon has said?'" recalls Layton. "Tommy said, 'No. What?' I said, 'He said that the Beatles were more popular than Jesus.' Tommy said, 'Oh! That does it for me. I'm not going to play the Beatles anymore.' It was just a spur-of-the-moment kind of thing. Nothing had been planned."

Frank Giardina, WAQY's program director, was completely taken by surprise at the decision. "I was driving into the station and heard them do it on the air," he says. "As they were the owners I didn't have any input. If it had been a promotion or a gimmick I would have been in on the planning stages, but they just fed off the audience and the audience fed off them."

They took a snap poll of their listeners and found that a massive majority— 99 percent, according to Charles—supported their decision. Feeling that they'd tapped into a popular disgruntlement, they planned to burn a mountain of Beatles records, pictures, magazines, and souvenirs in public on August 19, the day that the Beatles were booked to play in Memphis. "I think that when the other guys around the country read the interview they'll probably feel as we do," said Charles at the time. "They'll realize the influence the Beatles have and realize that these statements are not only ridiculous but way out of place."

Astonishingly, in light of what would happen, neither Charles nor Layton was particularly religious, and both were huge Beatles fans ("I thought they were the greatest thing to have come along in a hundred years," says Layton). They hardly typical of the audience they were appealing to. What irked them, they said, was John's arrogance. They also knew that this issue would push buttons in Birmingham, a city where churchgoing was almost a patriotic duty. "I suppose we went to church but not with any regularity," says Layton. "Everybody goes to church, I guess. I don't know what Tommy was thinking at the time. I didn't get the impression that he was offended on religious grounds. It was just something to talk about on our program and pretty soon it was dragging us. After it became such a big thing we had to play a role."

The Jesus controversy is most often looked back on as an example of the power of fundamentalism in the South, but it's more an example of the power of the media to feed on itself and inflame passions. By the time John's quote reached the ears of the citizens of Alabama it was a radio report of a magazine story taken from a newspaper interview. When it reached the ears of the world it was in the form of newspaper reports of record bans based on public response to radio reports of the magazine story taken from a newspaper interview.

Perhaps the most important person in the whole chain of events was twenty-six-year-old Al Benn, then the Birmingham bureau manager for the United Press International (UPI) news agency. If he hadn't happened to have been driving in Birmingham that morning and heard Layton's denouncement and his threat to burn Beatles records, the whole episode would have remained a local issue of no lasting importance. Instead it became one of the biggest scoops of his career and one that would see the story reported around the world in every medium. It wouldn't be too far-fetched to say that if Al Benn had had his car radio turned off that day, the Beatles might have continued performing for a bit longer and even that John Lennon could still be alive today.

"I heard them say to remember to send in all your Beatle albums because we're gonna burn them on a bonfire," he says. "My ears pricked up. I'd got to know Layton and Charles real well so I called them right away, and they were very helpful. I just knew that it was a good story and that it would be picked up by the Atlanta and New York news desks."

Beatle Hit Below the Bible Belt

The Beatles is dead, insists Birmingham, Ala., radio station manager Tommy Charles.

Charles, of WAQY, has organized a 'Ban the Beatles' campaign because of an article he read in a teenagers' magazine called 'Datebook.'

The story quotes John Lennon, the literary Beatle, as saying that the British foursome is more popular than Jesus.

"Christianity will go," the article quoted Lennon as saying in an interview with Maureen Cleave of the London Evening Standard. "It will vanish and shrink.

"I needn't argue about that; I'm right and I will be proved right.

"We're more popular than Jesus now.

"I don't know which will go first—rock 'n' roll or Christianity.

"Jesus was all right, but his disciples were thick and ordinary. It's them twisting it that ruins it for me."

Charles, a popular disciple of rock 'n' roll who up to now has featured the Beatles on his own disc jockey show, became incensed when he read the gospel according to Lennon.

And, apparently operating under the assumption that a group that sings together ought to be condemned together, he resolved to squelch Beatle sales in Birmingham.

To highlight his crusade, Charles is planning a book burning. Starting today, WAQY is broadcasting spot announcements every hour telling the audience to bring their Beatle records, pictures, magazines and souvenirs to pickup spots.

"We'll have a giant Beatle bonfire," Charles said gleefully, "the night they are closest to Birminhgham on their next American tour, probably when they are in Memphis."

Benn's story turned a listener-grabbing spat on local radio into a national event. The UPI story was picked up around the country and alerted the American heartlands to John's comment and every other radio station to WAQY's response. Journalists and DJs began canvassing public opinion, and the dissension spread. On August 2, he filed another story about the "Ban the Beatles drive," quoting Charles as saying, "Almost unbelievably the teen-agers, as soon as they're sure of [the quotes] become really angry, some to the point of tears. All sorts of record and book stores have called saying they are taking their Beatles records and books off the market."

Soon the wire stories were reporting that the campaign had "spread rapidly from its Southern base across the nation." The stations cited were predominantly in the South (Texas, Alabama, South Carolina), but there were a clutch in the Northeast: "The first thing I knew was that on the Wednesday I got a call from a radio station in Maine saying, 'Hey! We're going along with you,'" remembers Layton. "I said, 'I beg your pardon.' They said, 'We're not going to be playing the Beatles either. Good work.' Then we began to get calls from all over the country. The next thing we knew it was out of hand."

As the magazine was not yet even on the stands, *Datebook* was swamped with inquiries about the full story. Many Beatles fans were sure that the quote had been made up. The press officer from Capitol Records was concerned that the ban would impact record sales. *Newsweek* wanted to see the issue. Dan Donovan of WNEX in Macon, Georgia, wanted a quote. Fred Forest of WMOC, in Chattanooga, Tennessee, wanted to know if what John had been reported as saying was accurate. Asked what the reaction had been like in Chattanooga, Forest answered, "The Beatles better watch out when they hit the Southern States." Unger's message taker noted, "Forest is apparently not a Bible thumper. He was quoting from general public reaction." Unger called Epstein and told him about the planned Birmingham bonfire. Apparently Epstein giggled and said, "You know—they've got to buy the records before they can burn them."

The Associated Press (AP) story for Thursday, August 4, was headlined "Dozens of stations ban against Beatle records" and reported that in addition to the bans there were several "bonfires for the burning of Beatles records and pictures" planned. The offending comment was republished with Tommy Charles's statement: "We just felt it was so absurd and sacrilegious that something ought to be done to show them they cannot get away with this sort of thing."

The truth is that there were probably never more than forty stations that announced bans, and many of these weren't in the habit of playing Beatles records anyway. Some of them jumped on the cause as a means of getting publicity for themselves. A search through the reports of the major American newspapers and news agencies shows many of the same stations mentioned over and over again. It was a story that some people wanted to make happen. The successful, haughty, irreverent, apparently unstoppable Beatles had finally been slapped down. Decent Christian values had taken revenge on libertarian agnosticism.

Despite his lighthearted quips, Epstein was starting to panic. The Beatles were scheduled to start their American tour in Chicago on August 12, and there were fears of cancellations and lost revenue. Although few wanted to admit it, there was also the possibility that someone would take revenge. The assassination of President Kennedy was a fresh memory. On August 1, a former U.S. Marine, Charles Lee Whitman, had killed thirteen people with a gun fired from a bell tower at the University of Texas in Austin. Epstein thought it would be prudent to fly to New York to calm the situation.

By Friday, August 5, the day that *Datebook* hit the stands, the story reached the front page of the *New York Times*, and Epstein announced a press conference. Behind the scenes Epstein and Tony Barrow were trying to ensure that neither the Beatles nor Maureen Cleave said anything to deepen the crisis. It hadn't helped that a comment George had made before recent events had just been published in the British weekly music paper *Disc*. "We've got to go and get beaten up in America," he was quoted as saying, with reference to his diminishing appetite for touring.

The official line, agreed on by Barrow and Epstein, was that John was "deeply interested" in religion and had been quoted out of context. Epstein's assistant, Wendy Hanson, wrote to John to explain the position he was to take. "You had a serious and long talk about religion (in which you are very interested) and the quote came out of the fact that you were astonished and surprised that Christianity in the last 50 years in this country has gone off in its appeal. When you said the Beatles were more popular than Jesus you were not trying to upset anyone, but merely suggesting that your appeal is more immediate."

Epstein's official statement printed on Nemperor Artists Limited notepaper and dated August 5, 1966, followed this template.

The quote which John Lennon made to a London columnist more than three months ago has been quoted and represented entirely out of context. Lennon is deeply interested in religion and was, at the time, having serious talks with Maureen Cleave, who is both a friend of the Beatles and a representative for the London *Evening Standard*, concerning religion.

He did not mean to boast about the Beatles' fame. He meant to point out that The Beatles' effect appeared to be a more immediate one upon, certainly, the younger generation. The article, which was in depth and highly complimentary to Lennon as a person, was understood to be exclusive to the *Evening Standard*. It was not anticipated that it would be displayed out of context and in such a manner as it did in an American teen-age magazine.

In the circumstances, John is deeply concerned, and regrets that people with certain religious beliefs should have been offended in any way.

In claiming that the story had been used "out of context," Epstein was implicitly accusing *Datebook* of bad journalism. At the press conference Unger pointed out that none of John's words had been altered. "But nobody listened," he later said, "least of all, Epstein." *Datebook*'s lawyer suggested he sue Epstein, but Unger preferred to phone him. "What I meant," Epstein told him when they finally connected, "was that a story which appeared in a British newspaper for adults was distorted by its very appearance in an American teen magazine."

Within a week a four-month-old quote from a London newspaper was threatening ticket sales, record promotion, and the safety of the Beatles. The craze for destroying albums was spreading, senators in at least three states had attempted to get concerts banned, and there were even reports of anti-Beatles action having spread to Hong Kong, South Africa, Spain, and Mexico. "It's an example of the chaos theory," says J. Willoughby. "One little action unleashes a chain of events."

Typical of the response in the South was that of WAYX in Waycross, Georgia. On August 5 it announced that it would no longer be playing Beatles records. By the next day 564 listeners had called to express approval of the ban, 36 to express disapproval. The youth of the town were praised for "taking a stand for Christianity." Program director Howard Williamson arranged for a bonfire on the night of August 8 in the front yard of the station on Carswell Avenue. Every Beatles record in WAYX's library was burned along with copies handed in by listeners.

One of those present was fifteen-year-old Larry Purdom, now sports editor for the *Waycross Journal-Herald*. He looks back on it as a time when he was "carried along by the hype" and recalls that he immediately regretted having thrown his precious copy of the Beatles' first album into the flames. "All we knew at the time was what the adults had told us," he says. "What we heard was that John Lennon has said that the Beatles were more popular than JESUS!! As all us young folks in the Bible Belt could have told you, that just wasn't a nice thing to say. There were probably two hundred teenagers at the burning, and one of the DJs made a speech. I can't recall any of it, but it was along the lines of how bad it was that this band dared to criticize JESUS!! Of course, what Lennon actually said was much milder, but truth sometimes gets obliterated by hype. Then, after he'd finished speaking, we all approached the bonfire, and I can tell you, without any hesitation, that the second that album left my hands I regretted the hell out of it! That was a good album, and I've missed it ever since."

The burnings and bans confirmed the Beatles' suspicion that Americans were prone to religious extremism. They were surprised that few seemed prepared to examine John's statement and ask whether it was true or even partly true. What was being questioned was not so much his opinion as his right to express it. Typical of the reaction was that of a spokesperson for WTUF in Mobile, Alabama, who said that the comment was "not only deplorable but an outright sacrilegious affront to Almighty God." The Rev. Thurman H. Babbs, a black pastor of the New Heaven Baptist Church in Cleveland, Ohio, threatened to expel any member of his congregation who attended the Beatles concert in Cleveland on August 14 (although it should be pointed out that Babbs's now widely reported denunciation was first printed in the *Cleveland Plain Dealer* because he worked for the paper as a printer).

Some expressed a more liberal attitude. Norm Seeley, music director of KRUX in Phoenix, Arizona, thought that John was right in his analysis. "We have placed more emphasis on material and physical things than on religion. Religion in itself is good and wholesome, but it's our fault that it's on its way out." The Rev. Richard Pritchard of Westminster Presbyterian Church in Madison, Wisconsin, also supported John. He suggested that those who criticized him should "take a look at their own standards and values. There is much validity in what Lennon said. To many people today, the golf course is also more popular than Jesus Christ."

If John had been talking internationally, he was clearly wrong. There were far more followers of Jesus around the world than there were Beatles fans. If he was referring to intensity of devotion, he was also wrong because few people would have died for the sake of the Beatles, whereas thousands died each year around the world as a result of being persecuted for their Christian faith. But he said he was thinking specifically of Anglicanism and English teenagers. "Originally I was pointing out the fact with reference to England— that we meant more to kids at that time than Jesus did."

In this respect, he had a valid point. The average English teenager in 1966 was more interested in, and excited by, the Beatles than in Jesus Christ or the Church of England. Church attendance had declined, whereas record sales were increasing. Members of this generation could have quoted more Beatles lyrics than they could *Hymns Ancient and Modern* and would know more about John the Beatle than John the Baptist, more about Paul of Allerton than Paul of Tarsus. And the exodus would continue. Anglican Church attendance would go on to fall 50 percent between 1979 and 1999, eventually dipping below one million for the first time since records were collected.

On August 11 the Beatles flew from London to Chicago via Boston. The night before, Brian Epstein had told Art Unger that he was withdrawing his press credentials for the tour lest anyone should think the "Jesus" controversy was a publicity stunt. "It was a bad idea for you to run those interviews in the first place," Epstein told him. "But if you agree to cancel your participation in the tour there are many things I could do for you. We could make a great publishing team." Unger gracefully bowed out, but Epstein would never fulfill his part in the bargain.

A press conference was arranged in Tony Barrow's suite on the twenty-seventh floor of the Astor Towers Hotel in Chicago where the four Beatles faced a room so packed with journalists that the group was virtually pinned against one of the walls. John was briefed in private by Tony Barrow and Brian Epstein before he faced the microphones and told that to defuse the crisis he needed to make an unequivocal apology. He was torn. On the one hand he didn't want to let Paul, George, and Ringo down. On the other hand he didn't want to retract a statement that he believed to be true. "Brian told John that we might have to call the whole tour off," says Barrow. "He said that the next twenty-four hours were crucial. John actually started sobbing. I'd never seen him cry before. He tried to hide it from us, but he didn't succeed. It was so uncharacteristic of the guy."

"John was terrified," his wife, Cynthia, says. "What he'd said had affected the whole group. I didn't go on the tour, but I know that he was very frightened. In addition, he'd had warnings from clairvoyants. One had written to him saying that he was going to be shot. Another said that their plane was going to crash. Everything was so against them going on this tour, and they really didn't want to go, but they had to because they were contractually obligated. So, John had to get down on one knee and say sorry."

In front of the press he apologized in a faltering and ambiguous way. "I used the word 'Beatles' as a remote thing—not as what I think of as Beatles but as those other Beatles, like other people see us. I just said that 'they' are having more influence on kids and things than anything else, including Jesus. But I said it in that way, which is the wrong way." Was he sorry that he'd said it? "I am. Yes, you know, even though I never meant what people think I meant by it I'm still sorry that I opened my mouth." Had he meant to say that the Beatles were more popular than Christ? "When I was talking about it, it was very close and intimate with this person that I know who happens to be a reporter. And I was using expressions on things that I'd just read and derived about Christianity. Only I was saying it in the simplest form that I know, which is the natural way that I talk."

The next day, before the concert at the International Ampitheatre, the Beatles faced a second conference. The Jesus story was still at the top of the agenda. "Are you sorry about your statement concerning Christ?" one journalist asked John. "I wasn't saying whatever they're saying I was saying," said John. "I'm sorry I said it, really. I never meant it to be a lousy antireligious thing. From what I've read, or observed, Christianity just seems to be shrinking, to be losing contact." One correspondent told him that Tommy Charles from WAQY wanted an apology. Could he give it? "He can have it. I apologize to him. If he's upset and he really means it, you know, then I'm sorry. I'm sorry I said it for the mess it's made, but I never meant it as an antireligion thing, or anything. You know, I can't say any more than that. There's nothing else to say really. No more words. I apologize to him."

No one asked whether he would welcome the death of Christianity. Questioned as to whether he really thought the religion was shrinking, he said, "It just seems to me to be shrinking. I'm not knocking it or saying it's bad. I'm just saying it seems to be shrinking and losing contact." It was left to Paul to rescue the situation. "And we deplore the fact that it is," he said. "That's the point of it all."

The fifteen-concert tour went ahead, although not without problems. Many of the dates didn't sell out; firecrackers and debris were thrown at them in Memphis, where the Ku Klux Klan threatened to disrupt the show. "The Beatles made a statement that they were getting better than Jesus," announced one of their hooded leaders in a television interview. "The Ku Klux Klan, being a religious order, is going to come out the night they appear at the Coliseum to stop this performance. The Klan is going to come out because it's the only organization that will put a stop to these accusations." Robert Shelton, Grand Dragon of the Mississippi White Knights of the Ku Klux Klan, urged his followers to destroy any Beatle records that they might own and to burn their Beatles memorabilia.

The Birmingham bonfire, the announcement of which had started it all, never took place. The city authorities denied permission to burn records in public, and the alternative plan of crushing them with industrial machinery had to be aborted when the chipper teeth of a tree grinder set up in the parking lot of the Roebuck Plaza Shopping Center couldn't cope with the thick vinyl of the LPs. WAQY ended up with a basement full of undamaged, unburned albums, probably the most extensive library of Beatles' material held by an American radio station.

The enemies of the Beatles didn't halt the tour, but they put a damper on it. Paul said that this was when the laughing had to stop. "I still remember this young blond boy, no more than twelve years old, banging on the window (of the Beatles' car), raging, like we were devils. When you come up against that you think 'Who needs this?' We had religious fanatics burning our records, the KKK were making death threats. There was a whole climate of hate and fear, and we were bang in the middle of it. Of course, you look back and feel glad that those people were against you, because we were certainly against them."

The closing show, at Candlestick Park in San Francisco, was the Beatles' final concert. When George boarded the plane to fly back down to Los Angeles after the show, he turned to Tony Barrow and said, "That's it. I'm not a Beatle any more." The most sensitive and spiritually inclined member of the group, he had been particularly affected by the animosity. The experience confirmed his growing conviction that the Christian religion was more concerned with morality and power than with spirituality and humility.

A few days before in an unpublished interview George told Art Unger: "All this bit about religion seems so idiotic to me because although I'm not a Christian—I openly admit that, I'm not a Catholic, I'm not a Protestant—but the thing is, I'm very religious. I can see that the way religion is in the East is much easier."

Unger asked him if he was an agnostic.

No, no. I do believe. I believe very much and that's the laugh because a lot of these people who are preaching [against us] don't believe. I'm convinced that they can't believe. . . . You know, I believe not in God as a person who's up there doing it, but in infinity and the whole bit. . . . Man can't put a label on anything that's going on because it's so much bigger. . . . Man's mind doesn't have the capacity to work out what's going on. The thing is, to feel a part of all that.

I believe in life after death. I mean, I believe in reincarnation. I believe in a lot of things. That's why it's just so ridiculous. They [the record burners] are talking about trivialities. It's all trivial what they're talking about. And I'm sure that when these vicars die, they'll suddenly realize that they didn't really know what it was about after all.

After returning to England, George and his new wife, Pattie, traveled to India, where they mingled with musicians and spiritual teachers. After less than four years of fame and fortune, he now sought anonymity and simplicity. On October 21 he was interviewed in Bombay by BBC correspondent Donald Milner. "I'm here because, apart from learning Indian music, I'm learning things like yoga and lots of different things which will help me to work myself out," he said.

John, too, knew that the Beatles had to stop touring. "There are many things I'd like to do but there isn't time," he'd told Art Unger. "Before I know it I'll either be in the loony bin or I'll be dead. Right now, all I can tell you is that the Beatles is over." He took Unger's copy of the notorious September 1966 issue of *Datebook* and signed his photo "John C. Lennon." "The C is for Christ," he told him.

For John the intensity of the American protest was further proof that Christ's message had become twisted in the hands of his followers. Jesus, the "Prince of Peace" who commanded his disciples to love their enemies, was now represented by people who responded to criticism with anger, insults, and threats. Piles of letters found their way to Weybridge, where John told Cynthia to separate them into two piles—for and against. "Some of the mail was absolutely hateful," says Cynthia. "They had to be dumped. Nobody would want to read them." Some Christians took time to send him books that they thought might help him in his search. He read a good proportion of them. "I found out things," he said. "I've found out, for example, that the Church of England isn't very religious. There's too much politics. You can't be both. You can't be powerful and pure."

He confided to Unger that the mail that had been forwarded to him had been split fifty-fifty over the issue. "The ones that were for [me] had good, reasonable arguments," he said. "The ones that were against were the fanatic little blast-heads who couldn't even say what they meant." Unger told him that he'd just been sent a petition signed by 150 readers saying that they would never again buy *Datebook*, and John became quite vehement in denouncing them. "Well, that's good," he said. "You want to get rid of readers like that. You don't want readers who can't read the truth. Let them go on and read all the other [magazines] that just print crap for them to read. They're the ones who want to read crap all the time. They don't want to know what's going on. You're lucky to get rid of them. So are we. I hope that they don't buy *Datebook* and they don't buy our records. Let them move on. We obviously can't get through to them."

Like the other radio stations involved in the moral panic of 1966, WAQY eventually reinstated the Beatles to its playlist. Ignoring hits like "Eleanor Rigby," "Yellow Submarine," "Strawberry Fields Forever," "Penny Lane," or "All You Need Is Love" was commercial suicide for a one-thousand-watt Top 40 station with more powerful competitors. The ban that had got Tommy Charles and Doug Layton so much publicity at the time soon became an albatross around their necks.

"When the Beatles first came to America," says Layton, "the parents were shocked by these wild, long-haired, crazy people. So, when we started our campaign they said, 'Look! Somebody's gonna save us.' However, the kids didn't think so. It was one of those weird things that happened. It was a period we were in. We did it and . . . I don't know. It would probably have been better if we hadn't done it."

A casual remark, "said in passing to a friend," as John put it, would have a significant impact on the shape of the Beatles' career. In a 1971 interview with the radical left-wing British magazine *Red Mole* he said that it was "the second political thing I did," the first being to say (against the advice of Brian Epstein) that he didn't approve of the Vietnam War. "It really broke the scene. I nearly got shot in America for that. . . . Up to then there was this unspoken policy of not answering delicate questions, though I always read the papers. . . . The continual awareness of what was going on made me feel ashamed that I wasn't saying anything. I burst out because I could no longer play the game any more. It was just too much for me." In his posthumously published book *Skywriting by Word of Mouth*, John wrote: "I always remember to thank Jesus for the end of my touring days. If I hadn't said that the Beatles were 'bigger than Jesus' and upset the very Christian Ku Klux Klan, well, Lord, I might still be up there with all the other performing fleas! God bless America. Thank you, Jesus."

But there was a punch line he hadn't anticipated. The Jesus comment and the atheism expressed in his 1972 song "Imagine" were two of the things that brewed in the mind of Mark David Chapman, a mind that had already been affected by LSD, propelling him to New York in the winter of 1980 on a mission to end John's life. He thought that the ex-Beatle had overstepped the mark and the time was right for him to pay for his sins.

"The record burning was a real shock," said John in 1966. "The physical burning. I couldn't go away knowing that I created another little bit of hate in the world. Especially with something as uncomplicated as people listening to records and dancing and playing and enjoying what the Beatles are. Not when I could do something about it."

Chapter Three

In My Life

Religion just doesn't do anything for me, really.
—Ringo Starr, 1965

Ninety-nine percent of the people who go to church on Sunday think
that if they don't go, God will get them.
—George Harrison, 1965

I don't profess to be a practicing Christian although I think Christ was
what he was and anybody who says something great about Him, I
believe.
—John Lennon, 1966

We all feel roughly the same. We're all agnostics.
—Paul McCartney, 1965

*M*r. Lennon," queried one journalist at the Chicago press conference, "are you all Christians?" There was a pause. "We were all brought up . . . ," John began, then suddenly changed track, referring only to himself. "I'm not a practicing Christian like I was brought up to be. But I don't have un-Christian thoughts." He had clearly been on the verge of saying, "We were all brought up as Christians" or "We were all brought up in the church" but had then thought better of it. Why?

It wouldn't have been for fear of embarrassment. Days later he gladly told Leroy Aarons of the *Washington Post* of his religious background, defining it as "normal Church of England, Sunday school and church." The most likely reason for the hesitation was the fact that although all four Beatles had been christened—he and Ringo as Anglicans, Paul and George as Roman Catholics—only he could have been said to have been "brought up" in the church. The rest of them had periods of contact with organized religion but were under no family coercion to follow the Christian path.

Paul and George were born to Catholics who had married Protestant agnostics. They were raised in homes where religion played no significant role. Harry Harrison and Jim McCartney shared the traditional northern workingman's suspicion that the church was used by the rich and powerful to control the common people. Ringo's mother belonged for a while to the local Orange Lodge (a sectarian Protestant organization), and he went to Sunday school at the Low Church evangelical St. Silas's on High Park Street in Toxteth Park until 1952 when it was closed and then demolished. "I went because it was a place where you could play with blocks and paint," he once admitted. In a similar spirit he later joined the choir because it paid well.

Although their religious backgrounds differed in detail they had all lost interest in the church by their mid-teens. None of the men in their immediate families had been religious, and so there were no role models. Christian virtues such as humility, obedience, and sacrifice seemed incompatible with the demands of masculinity in working-class Liverpool. Church was for the elderly (who needed comfort), women (who needed emotional succor), and children (who needed guidance).

However, Paul was right to qualify their agnosticism as only "roughly" the same. Their feelings toward religion had been shaped by what they knew of it thus far, and it was in their knowledge that they differed. John, who had spent more time in church than the other Beatles, was irritated by the wishy-washiness of sermons, something that didn't appear to concern the others. He felt that the clergy either sidestepped the big issues or dealt with them in language that was bewilderingly obscure.

In his 1965 book *A Spaniard in the Works* he parodied *Epilogue*, a five-minute late-night religious program well known in Britain, which consisted of a well-meaning homily from a church leader. In John's sketch a clergyman begins by saying that someone had recently asked him for a definition of sin, "And, you know, I couldn't answer him!" This was John's dig at the church's reticence to say what it meant, either because it was no longer certain of what it believed or because it was afraid of being seen as out of touch with modern thought.

The clergyman then interviews an African who asks why there is so much poverty, disease, and starvation in the world if God is a God of love. Unable, or unwilling, to give a direct answer, the vicar offers parables of men traveling on trains and an irrelevant metaphor of people being like bananas swaying in the wind, "waiting as it were . . . to be peeled by his great and understanding love." John was parodying the evasion that was so often passed off as theology. "I was being heavy on the church," he later admitted.

George didn't attack the Catholic Church for being spineless but for being manipulative. He believed people attended mass because of fear of damnation rather than out of love for God and that this fear, once instilled in children, was hard to shake off. A maxim attributed to the Society of Jesus (the Jesuits) was that if it could have a boy until the age of seven, it could show you the man. "This is the Catholic trick," said George. "They nail you when you're young and brainwash you, then they've got you for the rest of your life."

George's sister, Louise, who moved to America in 1954, was educated at a convent school, but reacted to the faith in a similar way. "It's just a fear thing," she says. "When we were little enough to be ruled by fear we did what we thought we'd better do because we thought we'd fry somewhere if we didn't. But once we got old enough to make our own minds up we decided that this wasn't our god. This was a crazy god, a nasty old fellow in the sky who's zapping everybody with thunderbolts. So we both got right away from that."

Their father, a bus driver who became a union leader for Liverpool transport workers, encouraged a skeptical view of authority figures which George and his sister would both inherit. "He taught us to think for ourselves," she says. "He taught us to treat people the way you would want to be treated. You don't have to go around falling in front of the mighty, and nor do you have to go around lording it over the lowly."

Paul rarely criticized Christianity, perhaps because he hadn't experienced enough of it to develop a grudge. Unlike John and George, he didn't feel let down or involuntarily indoctrinated. He just felt no need of religion. His life was too full and interesting to accommodate its demands. "I don't feel I have to be religious," he told Maureen Cleave in 1963. "I may need it as I get older to comfort me when I die. But now, as far as I'm concerned, I can rot." (Presumably a reference to the well-known statement made by the atheist philosopher Bertrand Russell in 1925: "When I die I shall rot, and nothing of my ego shall survive.")

His negative characterization of the church in "Eleanor Rigby" was based more on received wisdom than personal experience. As he started to write a song about loneliness, the story of a priest and a spinster rose up from his subconscious. It wasn't intended as an analysis of the state of contemporary religion yet betrayed his assumption that it was moribund. When journalists at the "Jesus" press conference wondered whether it was a veiled attack on Christianity, Paul seemed surprised. "It was just a song about one lonely person who happens to be this priest who's darning his socks at night, you know," he answered. "That's all there was to it."

That may have been "all there was to it," but his automatic association of church with lonely spinsters, death, ineffective priests, empty pews, and ignored sermons betrayed his presuppositions. There is an atmosphere of decay about the church he describes. People are going through the motions of religion, but the force that once inspired it has long since left the building. Father McKenzie's "sermon that no one will hear" and Eleanor's "face that she keeps in a jar by the door" are both disguises that conceal an underlying emptiness. The final line of the song is literally damning: "No one was saved." (Paul may have taken this from Chaucer's "No one was converted" in *The Miller's Tale*, a book he studied for English at school.)

Ringo, typically, was neither hostile toward nor disinterested in the church. He was just unsure. He felt that there was an unexplained spiritual power but lacked the confidence to declare it to be God as described to him by the Church of England. Weren't our beliefs a result of early conditioning? How could he know that the truth taught to him as a child happened to be the absolute truth? At the same time, even his agnosticism might have been a result of conditioning. "I'm agnostic because I honestly don't know if there's anything up there or down there," he said in 1965.

It wasn't only their teenage loss of faith that was colored by their Liverpool upbringing but their pursuit of other faiths in later years. One of the first things that John did when he was "working it out about God," as he later described it, was to research Christianity, the belief of his early years. He described meditation as worshiping in his own inner temple and read the Bible throughout his life. "I was brought up as a Christian," he said just before his death in 1980, "and I only now understand some of the things that Christ was saying in those parables anyway—when I got away from the interpretations that were thrown at me all my life. There is more to it."

Jesus remained a figure against whom John measured himself. "He viewed the Bible as a universal symbolic drama that was enacted daily in front of our eyes," said Frederic Seaman, his personal assistant during the late 1970s. "In particular, John was fascinated by the life of Jesus Christ." It was as though he had imagined he'd thrown off his influence when he became an agnostic but, to his horror, discovered that Jesus kept returning. His provocative comments were his way of dealing with what the poet Francis Thompson called "the hound of heaven." "The Beatles are more popular than Jesus" was a way of asking "Why are the Beatles more popular than Jesus?" or "Should the Beatles be more popular than Jesus?" or "Jesus—why are the Beatles so popular?"

George, who was also fond of quoting Jesus, was so hard on his Catholic past that he presented his conversion to Eastern religion as though it was a complete break. However, it was what he saw as weaknesses in Catholicism that made Hinduism appear so attractive. His major quarrel with the church he was baptized into was that its followers weren't spiritual enough. They were observant, yet once they had taken the sacraments they carried on with their lives as though none of it was really true. There was a gap between their spoken confession and the beliefs that motivated their day-to-day behavior.

"The thing with religion is that it's something you're forced to do on a Sunday morning," he reflected at the age of twenty-two. "It means very little to a lot of people. Even if they do go to church they still don't get a great feeling from it. As I see it, religion should be how you handle yourself, how you act among other people, and what you give to other people. It's not what you receive. That's why religion is all screwed up. People think that you go to church on Sunday and God sees you going and that's it. All is forgiven. But you know that's not it. People think that after Sunday they can go back to doing what they were doing before they went. So it's all back to normal, and they don't alter the way they act."

By contrast, on his first visit to India in 1966 he was impressed that the devoted Hindus he met incorporated their beliefs into every aspect of their lives. Also, it appealed to him that guilt over sin was not a dominant concern. Two things Hinduism had in common with Catholicism were iconography, something that had impressed George as a child when he had been moved by the fourteen Stations of the Cross, and prayer beads. The answer he would give in 1982 to the question, "What helps you fix your mind on God?" would not surprise any devout Catholic. "Just having as many things around me that will remind me of Him," he said. "Like incense and pictures."

Paul's caution about religion originated in his father's liberal agnosticism. The important values in life, according to Jim McCartney, were "toleration and moderation in all things," and these didn't need religious endorsement. In fact, when religion poked its nose in, it usually had the opposite effect. His experience had been that both Catholicism and Protestantism contributed to intolerance and extremism. It was because of this view that neither Paul nor his brother Mike were sent to church schools (as was most common in Liverpool) and, in 1956, when Paul was fourteen he was even withdrawn from religious instruction classes at his secondary school.

The McCartney home was based on northern working-class values reinforced by experience and family ties rather than dogma and church membership. Mary McCartney didn't abandon her core beliefs in Catholicism, but her lack of churchgoing suggests that Jim influenced her more than she influenced him. The boys attended Sunday school for a time, and this pleased her because she thought it provided a good start, but there was no coercion to continue when they gave it up. "We didn't do much else in the way of religion," said Paul.

Like John and Ringo, he sang in a church choir for a while (at the Protestant St. Barnabus, close to the Penny Lane roundabout), but the attraction was the music, not the belief system. In 1953 he even auditioned for the choir of

Liverpool Cathedral but wasn't picked, mainly because over ninety boys applied that year and he couldn't sight-read music. His choir singing familiarized him with hymn tunes. "When I started writing, I remember asking people, 'What does this sound like? How do you like this song?'" said Paul. "They'd say, 'Well, it sounds a bit like a hymn.' It was one of the damning things people said about some of my early numbers."

The Beatles grew up in a city suffused with religion. In terms of church attendance Liverpool was the most religious city in England during the 1940s and 1950s (over 60 percent of its Catholics attending mass each week), yet the religious culture was markedly different from that of Birmingham, Alabama. It was dominated by the Catholicism brought over by Irish immigrants in the nineteenth century (half of all England's Catholics still live in the diocese of Liverpool), but there was also a quietly liberal homegrown Anglicanism and some Calvinism from the Welsh chapels and the Scottish churches.

The taboos associated with American fundamentalism were rare. There was dancing, drinking, and smoking in the Catholic social clubs, and the Anglican youth clubs were among the first places to host skiffle and rock 'n' roll. The archetypical church leader on Merseyside was not a hellfire preacher denouncing the evils of the jungle beat but a red-nosed priest with a bottle of whiskey in his hip pocket or a rosy-cheeked vicar eating cucumber sandwiches on the lawn with a group of neatly dressed parishioners.

The Beatles were aware of religion's power and symbolism. They heard the verbal jousting of the Protestant and Catholic preachers who denounced each other as heretics to the delight of crowds at the Pierhead and were aware of the sectarian battles between Protestants and Catholics on their annual marching days. They saw the many statues of Jesus, Mary, and the saints. They were familiar with the smell of incense and the sound of church bells, the sight of priests and nuns. Even the swearing and joking frequently had a religious flavor. When Cardinal John Heenan visited in 1957 to conduct a service on the site of the soon-to-be-built Catholic Cathedral, a crowd of forty thousand worshipers attended.

The Anglican Cathedral, with its 331-foot spire, started in 1904 and still under construction in the 1960s, towered over the Liverpool Institute where George and Paul were students and the art school attended by John. The second largest church building in Europe, it housed the largest organ in Britain and had the loudest bells. When Paul premiered his *Liverpool Oratorio* there in 1991, he recalled sleepovers at John's flat in nearby Gambier Terrace, where "the cathedral would loom at you through every window of the flat. You couldn't escape it."

Celtic lore from Ireland, Scotland, Wales, and the North of England was also present. David Ashton, a childhood friend of John's, believes that this was often embodied in the most orthodox forms of Christianity. "Despite the layers of Calvinism, Catholicism, and earlier Celtic Christianity there's an understanding of life that permeates Liverpool that I would call matriarchal nature religion," he says. "It has to do with second sight, visions, the evil eye, witchcraft, ghosts, fairies, and the belief that other supernatural beings exist."

Although at this time there were not significantly large communities of Muslims or Hindus, Liverpool's connections with the rest of the world through its shipping meant that tales of exotic cultures and exotic beliefs were brought back home by sailors. Mo Best, owner of the Casbah Club, where John, Paul, and George played frequently as the Quarrymen, had been born in India and would tell them stories of life in Bombay. She had a large stone statue of Buddha in her hallway and a painting of a Chinese dragon on one of the walls of the club.

John had the most interesting religious pedigree of all the Beatles. His paternal grandfather, Jack Lennon, was a Dublin-born Catholic who married a Liverpool girl named Mary Maguire. Her family believed she had rare psychic abilities, and she spoke of premonitions and ghosts. Jack's brother studied to be a priest at Maynooth College in County Kildare, Ireland. After ordination he came to Wallasey, Cheshire, where he was rumored to have been defrocked for having an affair with his housekeeper. Jack and Mary's first two children were baptized Catholic but as both of them died in infancy Mary superstitiously had the rest of her children, including John's father, Alfred, baptized as Anglicans.

Despite the Irish connection and the priest in the family, the Lennons were not religious. Alfred's second wife, Pauline, who wrote his biography based on an unpublished manuscript he left behind on his death in 1976, summed up their beliefs: "None of the family attended church," she wrote, "and her [Mary Lennon's] true religion was that of fatalism—she staunchly accepted everything she was dealt in life without a trace of bitterness or self pity."

The maternal side of John's family had been devoutly Protestant. His great-grandmother, Mary Morris, known for her absolute sense of right and wrong, belonged to a Welsh-speaking Calvinistic Methodist Chapel. She was scornful of Catholics. Her daughter Annie married George Stanley, a shipping agent, and had six children, one of whom was John's mother, Julia. When George was away at sea, Mary would exercise control over her daughter's household, making sure that the girls read their Bibles, attended church, and didn't play games or read books on the Lord's Day.

The Stanley family was Anglican, a social step up from the Morris's Methodism. When they came into some money and moved to Huskisson

Street in the center of Liverpool, they attended the Cathedral (still under construction, but the Lady Chapel had been completed and opened for worship in 1910, four years before Julia was born), and two of their children who died young, Henry and Charlotte, were buried in its grounds.

Despite their strong Anglican roots, none of the Stanley girls went to church as adults. However, each of them made sure that their children grew up to be God-fearing. This was not unusual in the 1950s: although only 10 percent of English adults attended church regularly, 50 percent of them sent their children to Sunday school. Religious education was still assumed to be morally beneficial. It kept youngsters out of trouble and taught them virtues such as kindness, honesty, respect, and obedience. It gave them a good start in life and enabled them to become useful citizens. According to left-wing historian E. P. Thompson, author of *The Making of the English Working Class*, it was "one of the main agencies of transmission of bourgeois values to the working class."

John's mother, Julia, had relationships with several men after Alfred Lennon walked out of her life in 1943, eventually moving in with John "Bobby" Dykins, with whom she had two daughters, Julia and Jacqueline. Her sister Mimi Smith didn't think it appropriate for John to be living in a small flat with an unmarried couple, and so at the age of five he went to be with her and her husband, George. Mimi was a total contrast to Julia. Whereas Julia was modern and carefree, Mimi was old-fashioned and strict. Julia played the mandolin and knew the words to bawdy Liverpool songs like "Maggie May," whereas Mimi disapproved of anything that she thought was "common."

Mimi had strong middle-class aspirations. She wanted an identity that separated her from the working-class folk who lived in terraced houses, drank beer, played bingo, and spoke with a scouse accent (the English dialect spoken in Liverpool). Mimi sipped gin, played bridge, and had what was considered to be a "cultured" manner. Her house was semi-detached and although sited on a main road was in the desirable suburb of Woolton, a favored area for rich industrialists in the nineteenth century and one that still had the feel of a country village. It even had a name, *Mendips*, that distinguished it from houses that had only a number.

Her cultural aspiration had a beneficial effect on John because it introduced him to the world of ideas. The Book of the Month Club she joined supplied volumes of Oscar Wilde, F. Scott Fitzgerald, Honoré de Balzac, Edith Sitwell, and Edgar Allan Poe that graced the shelves beside the living room fireplace. She earned extra money by taking in student lodgers, most of them training at Liverpool University to be vets and chemists. They would discuss art, science, literature, and contemporary events among themselves while John listened. He later spoke of the value of having been exposed to "eighteen-year-old intelligent minds" at such an impressionable age.

One of the lodgers, John Cavill, who lived there for a year starting in September 1949, gave John his first lessons in guitar picking. "I played the piano but Mimi had very little in the way of furnishing and had no piano so I bought a guitar," he says. "John and I used to play tunes together. I hadn't discovered chords, believe it or not. My father had a violin and I had learned to play *pizzicato* on it, so when I got the guitar I played tunes on the strings and John did the same."

It would have been in character for Mimi to have joined a church. Social status was still attached to Anglican membership, especially if you were involved in organizing social activities. However, no one who lived at *Mendips* can remember her attending a service. Michael Fishwick, a biochemist who spent seven years as a lodger (1951–1958) and slept in the bedroom next to John, says that although she was culturally Anglican, "You wouldn't have really known except that John was sent to St. Peter's church."

John's half-sister Julia agrees. "She was stalwart Church of England. My mother and Mimi were Anglican equivalents of 'cradle Catholics,' but neither of them ever went to church. I think the war had changed things for them. We children were all sent to Sunday school, and there was no way we could get out of it."

For Mimi, like many of her aspiring contemporaries, the church promoted a belief system that helped perpetuate the best values associated with being English: decency, fair play, endurance, courage, service, selflessness. This was the version of Christianity that John would come to know best and which would lead to his final rejection of it. He couldn't separate Christ and his teachings from this particular expression of it. As he rebelled against the bourgeois way of life, so he rebelled against the faith that he believed encouraged and supported it. "Respectability," as historian Geoffrey Best pointed out, "was the outcome of a vulgarisation and perhaps secularisation of established Christianity."

Mimi's religion could be summarized by a stanza she had framed on her wall:

However black the clouds may be
In time they'll pass away
Have faith and trust and you will see
God's light make bright your day.

This was God as a divine tonic, his principal role in our lives being to brighten things up. The verse stayed with John, and inspired a parody version in his short story "Sorry Norman," published in *A Spaniard in the Works*. The same year he also adapted it, and secularized it, for a verse of "Tell Me What You See," a track on the *Help!* LP.

> Big and black the clouds may be
> Time will pass away
> If you put your trust in me
> I'll make bright your day.

While Mimi remained at home on Sundays preparing the roast dinner, John went to St. Peter's parish church in Woolton where he was in turn a student at the Sunday school, a chorister, and a member of the Bible class. For a period he was attending events at the church on at least four days of the week, making it the hub of his early teenage social life. Among his fellow church members were those who would have a significant influence on his adolescence: girlfriend Barbara Baker, future Quarrymen Pete Shotton and Rod Davis, first manager Nigel Walley, Paul McCartney's friend Ivan Vaughan, and Geoff Rhind, who took the first photograph of John as a performer. "Religion was never forced on him," Mimi told Hunter Davies, "but the inclination was there."

St. Peter's, Woolton, a red sandstone perpendicular-style building with a ninety-foot bell tower, looks like an archetypal fifteenth-century English village church, although when John began attending it was barely sixty years old. Financed by four wealthy local merchants in the late Victorian era because the existing church had become too small, it had stained-glass windows by Charles Kempe and could seat five hundred. Such philanthropy wasn't unusual at the time because captains of industry accepted that religion encouraged a view of life that prepared employees to be honest, industrious, and reliable. Christianity was not just good for saving souls; it was good for business.

The official residence of the Anglican bishop of Liverpool was in Woolton, making St. Peter's his local church. During John's childhood, Clifford Martin—"Bish Martin" to the boys—was the bishop. He would preach at least four times a year, and his wife and daughters attended morning prayers regularly, always giving the boys in the choir appreciative smiles.

Within a few yards of the church was the gravestone of an Eleanor Rigby ("The Beloved Wife of Thomas Woods") that may have been the subliminal inspiration for the song. She died on October 10, 1939, at the age of forty-four, five years before John joined the Sunday school. It's likely that there were people in the congregation who knew her. Beyond the churchyard was the field where the Quarrymen would perform on July 6, 1957, and across the road was the church hall where John would meet Paul for the first time, after the Quarrymen's performance.

Ecclesiastically, St. Peter's was "broad church." This was traditional Anglicanism that was neither "Low Church" (evangelical) nor "High Church" (Anglo-Catholic) and represented the most familiar and acceptable face of the Church of England. Its supporters believed its strength lay in its ability to embrace almost all shades of belief and doubt. Its critics, both secular and Christian, considered it so tolerant it was afraid to unambiguously declare its beliefs for fear of causing offense. In avoiding both the strict adherence to doctrine that characterized Catholicism and the emphasis on personal salvation that defined Evangelicalism, it ran the risk of being no more than a society for the promotion of decency.

The rector, Morris Pryce Jones, was a Welsh bachelor in his mid-thirties, valued more for his fund-raising ability than for his preaching. A 1929 graduate of the London College of Divinity, he'd served in the Liverpool parishes of Edge Hill and Norris Green before taking over at St. Peter's in 1941. The previous rector had been knocked off his bicycle in Menlove Avenue during a wartime blackout and had died from his injuries.

Despite his shortcomings in the pulpit, Pryce Jones was an effective organizer and motivator, and by the mid-1950s St. Peter's was at the heart of Woolton village life. There were not only three services each Sunday (Holy Communion, Morning Prayer, Evensong) but activities almost every night of the week: an adult fellowship on Mondays, a youth club on Tuesdays, choir rehearsal on Thursdays, and a teenage dance and social on Saturdays. The Cubs, Scouts, Brownies, Guides, and Rangers also met at the church.

There was an annual Sunday school outing that John enjoyed. At a time when few people traveled abroad for holidays, it was a huge treat to go by rail to Southport from Gateacre station or to sail by steamer ship from Liverpool to the Welsh seaside town of Llandudno. In Southport there would be a visit to the funfair, a picnic in the Floral Gardens, a walk on the pier, and tea at Holy Trinity church. In Llandudno they played on the beach, swam in the sea, and had tea at a hotel where Pryce Jones knew the manager.

The importance of the church to the community in Liverpool can be judged from the *South Liverpool Weekly News* of the period, in which religious news was far more important than the activities of celebrities. In one random edition from 1955 there are three such stories on one page: "Student Pastor as Guest of Honour at Woolton," "Twenty Years as a Church Organist," and "Church Warden's Appointment." The arrival of a new vicar, a Sunday school prize giving, or a guest speaker at a fellowship group would make headlines, as would the pronouncements of a church spokesperson on moral decline.

In December of that year, St. Peter's youth club, then 170 members strong, was the subject of a feature article (John would have joined two months previously on his fifteenth birthday). Among the regular activities mentioned were chess, draughts, table tennis, billiards, gymnastics, darts, and netball. The church even had a football team that played in the Liverpool Combination League. Some members were working on a project to build new radios from parts of broken sets. Every two months there was a special youth service, and regular discussions and debates took place in the church hall.

John's point of entry was the popular Sunday school that met in various rooms in the church hall. "We had the Scripture Union notes and we'd sit and discuss the Bible portion for that week," says David Ashton, who always sat next to John in the choir. "We would talk about what it meant. Sometimes we would make things. I've got my membership card for 1956, and it lists all the scriptures for that year. For example, on January first we were studying the book of Peter."

Most of the boys attended because their parents wanted them to. Christian doctrines seemed abstract to them, but they enjoyed being with friends. "I went along not because my family were desperate believers but because it was just the normal thing to do," says Rod Davis. "It would probably have been seriously abnormal if I hadn't gone. None of us was deeply religious, there's no question about that. We were shallowly religious."

John discovered he could sharpen his wit at St. Peter's. The reverence of a church service was an ideal atmosphere in which to make others laugh. David Ashton can recall opening his Boy Scout diary during a service at which Pryce Jones was preaching. John took it away from him and with his pen changed the law "A Boy Scout is thrifty" to "A Boy Scout is fifty." "We got our choir pay docked for talking in a sermon," says Ashton. "It was yet another example of John's creative mind."

Another time when their teacher Miss Davies was talking about the evils of the scribes and Pharisees, John raised his hand and announced that, if what was said about them in the Gospels was true, they must have been Fascists. Miss Davies got angry with John, telling him that Fascists were far worse than scribes and Pharisees, and sent him and David Ashton to Pryce Jones for a caning that was administered on their upturned hands with a parishioner's umbrella that happened to be laying nearby

The church's musical director, Eric Humphriss, who had a day job as a chemist with a local milk company, was a novelty to John and his fellow choristers because, although he had a passion for religious music such as John Stainer's *Crucifixion* and Handel's *Messiah*, he was an atheist. Occasionally he would shock the boys by casting doubt on a fundamental Christian teaching or questioning the authenticity of a date in the church calendar. "He didn't agree with religion at all," says David Ashton. "He thought it was barmy. I think John might have been influenced by some of his ideas."

John was in the choir from around 1948 until 1954, and this involved rehearsing on each Thursday evening, singing at Morning Prayers and Evensong on Sundays, and performing at weddings and funerals. The pay for weddings and funerals was exceptional. At a time when weekly pocket money could be as little as one shilling, they would earn two and a half times that amount for one wedding. Ashton can recall one Saturday when they had three weddings. They wore white surplices over black cassocks, which had to be taken home every Easter and Christmas to be washed.

Humphriss was a dedicated choirmaster who grounded his boys well in both words and music. He explained musical terms such as *crescendo* and *pizzicato* and would share the stories of the hymn writers, illustrating how their personal experiences of tragedy informed their writing, in order to equip the choristers to invest each word and phrase with the appropriate emotion. This would have been John's introduction not only to the breadth of musical vocabulary but to the biographical nature of lyrics. "Eric Humphriss often discussed death with us," says Ashton. "Many of the hymns had been written by people who had lost loved ones or who had faced difficult times. Early death was quite common in those days. I had a school friend die and Eric spoke to us about it, and I remember that evening we practiced Sir Arthur Sullivan's 'And God Shall Wipe Away All Tears.'"

For "All in the April Evening," by Hugh Robertson (music) and Katherine Tynan (words), which Humphriss explained to them was based on a Celtic folk tune, they were taught four-part harmony. He played Welsh dance tunes on his harmonium during breaks in choir practice, told the boys that the hymn tune "Cwm Rhondda" was the Welsh equivalent to "La Marseillaise," and pointed out that the English weren't very good at producing stirring songs. "Rule Britannia" he found vulgar and blatant. Elgar's "Pomp and Circumstance" had no national emotion behind it, he said. He encouraged them to sing with what the Welsh called "hwyl": a deep feeling that grips the heart. "Everyone join in. No mumbling," he would say. "Open your mouths and let it go!"

The one disadvantage of being in the choir, from the perspective of the boys, was sitting through Pryce Jones's sermons. As nice a man as he was—and no one seems to have a bad word to say about him—his sermons were dull and uninspiring. What's more, he had a habit of repeating them. The only times the boys sat up was when he preached about Robert Louis Stevenson's novel *Dr. Jekyll and Mr. Hyde* or, for some unknown reason, denounced psychopaths.

A flavor of his antiquated and long-winded style is captured in his monthly letters in the parish magazine. In October 1950 he wrote about the "deterioration of character, conduct and standards of which so many have complained." He went on: "There is a serious lack of feeling as to why your particular action, provided it gives pleasure, should not be taken, even though it may not be, morally, particularly respectable. 'Why shouldn't I?' Such is the unspoken question. But there is an answer; and it is one which may be particularly noticed at harvest time. For there is a parallel between the life of a man and a harvest. What we do, what our actions are, however secret and private they may be, brings forth its consequences as surely as seed planted in the ground brings forth as in the old parable, well or ill." Satirical echoes of this style would later emerge in John's book *A Spaniard in the Works*.

In 1955, at the age of fifteen, John was confirmed, "of his own free will" as Mimi later proudly told the Beatles original biographer Hunter Davies. This meant renewing the promises made on his behalf at his baptism, "ratifying and confirming" in public that he accepted the teachings of the church and would "reject the devil and all rebellion against God," "renounce all the deceit and corruption of evil," "repent of the sins that separate us from God and neighbor," "turn to Christ as savior," "submit to Christ as Lord," and "come to Christ, the way, the truth, and the life."

Confirmation classes were led by Pryce Jones. The usual way of teaching was study of the catechism, but Pryce Jones took a more liberal approach. "He said we didn't need to bother to learn it," recalls David Ashton. "His favorite thing was to say that the world was like a picture book that teaches us about God's love. He was more concerned to teach us how to hold our hands when we received the bread at communion than he was to ensure we understood Christian doctrines."

It's uncertain exactly when and where John was confirmed. There are no detailed church records from this period. He was prepared in the same class as David Ashton and Rod Davis, who were confirmed on December 13, 1955, but they both believe John was confirmed personally by Pryce Jones at a later date because he and Shotton had missed too many of the required confirmation classes to be declared ready.

Whenever and wherever it took place, his confirmation certificate would have been the same as David Ashton's: "Confirmed . . . and signed by the cross in baptism, strengthened by the Holy Spirit in confirmation and sent to be Christ's soldier and servant and to live and work for him. Jesus said, 'Go ye, and lo I am with you always until the end of the world' (Matthew 28 vv 19–20)."

The resolution, signed by the confirmed person, was: "With the help I receive in confirmation I will always try to do my duty to God and my neighbour and especially I intend to pray to God every day, worship in church every Sunday and be a regular at communion and witness to others by word and by deed that they too may come to accept Jesus as their saviour and their Lord." At the bottom of the certificate, beneath the signature, was the verse: "I can do all things through Jesus Christ who strengthens me (Phil. 4:13)."

Formally welcomed into the church, John and his friends were now eligible for the Bible class that met in a side chapel in the church. This was taught by youth club leader Jack Gibbons, a tall, broad-shouldered man with large ears and the face of a friendly giant. The boys liked him because he had a sense of worldliness about him. He was more like the men they knew in their families. He had been an aircraft fitter for the Royal Air Force at Biggin Hill during the Battle of Britain and was now a foreman bricklayer. "Jack really did believe in God," says Ashton. "I think that he assumed that we believed in God as well. I don't think we disbelieved, but I don't think that we knew what it was about."

As a child John had experiences he would later interpret as mystical. He had no explanation at the time and thought only that he was somehow different from his friends. The first hint he had that others might have experienced something similar was reading the work of Lewis Carroll, especially *Alice's Adventures in Wonderland.* Years later, after becoming familiar with surrealist art, he decided that he belonged "to an exclusive club that sees the world in those terms. Surrealism to me is reality. Psychedelic vision is reality to me and always was."

The first experience was of looking into a mirror and seeing his face going through changes, "becoming more cosmic and complete . . . the eyes would get bigger and the room would vanish." When he spoke of this in 1980, he named it "trancing out in alpha," referring to the relaxed condition when the brain-wave pattern is eight to twelve cycles per second, which is believed by biofeedback practitioners to be the most creative and dreamlike state of consciousness. He said he was aged "twelve or thirteen" at the time.

The second experience was nature mysticism. His mother's sister Elizabeth lived in Edinburgh, and when John was between the ages of nine and fifteen, he would spend part of his summer holiday with her and her husband, Bert. They had inherited a Highland croft—a house with a small enclosed plot of land attached—in the rural community of Durness on the remote northern tip of Scotland, and John would go there for a few days to walk and fish. In an interview his cousin Stanley Parkes recalled: "It was completely wild countryside with moorland hills, peat bogs and no commercial buildings. It's the last natural wild, rugged section of Scotland left."

On one of his mountain walks with Aunt Elizabeth he was overwhelmed by a feeling of completeness that was beyond description. "I thought, this is what they call poetic . . . when I looked back I realize I was kind of hallucinating. You know, when you're walking along and the ground starts going beneath you and the heather, and I could see this mountain in the distance, and this kind of *feeling* came over me. I thought, this is *something*. What is this? Ah, this is the one they're always talking about, the one that makes you paint or write."

William James had dealt with such feelings in *The Varieties of Religious Experience* (1902), where he compared them to what can be experienced under nitrous oxide and ether as well as in religion. One of the most common findings was a blending of opposites. All dualities—up and down, right and wrong, subject and object—disappear, and everything seems to be one. This leads to the feeling that all conflict, inner and outer, is over. There is nothing to worry about because there is no competition. The remaining question is whether the world of opposites is an illusion or whether this experience of unity is an illusion.

After experimenting with nitrous oxide James famously concluded, "Our normal waking consciousness, rational consciousness as we call it, is but one special type of consciousness, whilst all about it, parted from it by the flimsiest of screens, there lie potential forms of consciousness entirely different. We may go through life without suspecting their existence; but apply the requisite stimulus, and at a touch they are all there in all their completeness, definite types of mentality which probably somewhere have their field of application and adaptation."

George claimed to have had similar feelings. He said they left him feeling terrified as a child because he couldn't understand them. It was only during meditation later in life that he drew comparisons between them and the meditative state. His experience was of feeling simultaneously small and insignificant yet huge enough to embrace everything that exists. "It was like being two completely different things at the same time," he said. "This feeling would vibrate right through me and start getting bigger and bigger and faster and faster. Before I knew what was happening it was going so far and so fast it was mind boggling, and I'd come out of it really scared."

George ignored his experiences at the time, but John took his to mean that he was gifted in a special way. This was the back story to "Strawberry Fields Forever," where he chose a Salvation Army children's home in Woolton as the locus of his experience just as the poet William Wordsworth had chosen Tintern Abbey for his poem about "the joy / Of elevated thoughts; a sense sublime / Of something far more deeply interfused." The song described the dream state where nothing was real. There was nothing to get "hung about" because when all is one, there truly is nothing to bother about. Good and evil, pleasure and pain, past and future, heaven and hell—they all unite.

He rooted the song in a childhood memory, even though he'd had similar experiences on drugs in many different locations since. He explained: "The line [in the song] says 'No one I think is in my tree, I mean it must be high or low.' What I'm saying, in my own insecure way, is 'Nobody seems to understand where I'm coming from. I seem to see things in a different way from most people.'" In his original draft he had written, "No one I think is on my wavelength."

Strawberry Field (John pluralized it in the song) was a huge, imposing Gothic building built for a wealthy Victorian shipowner but bought by the Salvation Army in July 1936. It stood on six acres of land, half of which were given over to gardens, pine trees, and lawns. At the opening ceremony the Reverend Canon J. H. Jordan had given thanks "for Christ's revelation of the value of children and their nearness to the Father of all." When Evangeline Booth, Salvation Army general and daughter of founder William Booth, first visited Strawberry Field, she said: "There is something else, not of this world, already in the place. The wings of the Almighty, promised to gather over the heads of those who save the little ones, are already here."

At the summer garden parties John was there with Mimi, and on weekends he would sneak in and walk around the grounds. The beauty of the surroundings and the mystery of the building gave him the sense of an alternative reality. "There was a high sandstone wall around it with a peak on top but you could climb over," says David Ashton. "Inside there were rhododendrons, brambles, Cypress trees, and exotic plants. To grow up in Woolton was a near religious experience in itself because there were just so many beautiful things around us."

John made no connection between his experiences and religion and never discussed them with friends at the time, although at the age of eight or nine he did tell Mimi that he'd just seen God. When she asked him what God was doing, he had answered, "Oh, just sitting by the fire." Mimi humored him, telling him that maybe God was feeling a little cold. David Ashton can remember a period during which he, John, and their friends thought they heard voices in their heads. "I told them to go away and they did," he says. "I don't know whether we dreamed that up or whether it really happened."

If Ashton's memory is reliable, John's ideas about religion were idiosyncratic even when he was a child. Once the gang of friends was playing in a den they'd built in Woolton Quarry, and one of them claimed that the beauty of the butterwort, which had just begun to flower, was an expression of God. John cut in to say that it was to do with "spirituality," not God. Ashton had never heard the word before.

Another time they were at the church hall fooling around on the Scout band's drums, pretending that the gods were speaking to each other through the beats. The Scouts' bass drummer, a boy called Bertie, took the opportunity to announce that he didn't believe in the gods or indeed any god at all. "John then said that in German the word for God was the same as the word for good," says Ashton. "He said that he didn't believe in God, but he believed in good. I'd never really thought about it. I wasn't sure." (John was wrong on the language point. The German for good is *gut*. God is *Gott*.)

If true, this would date John's agnosticism back to 1951 or 1952. In his unsophisticated way he was making an argument that Ludwig Feuerbach made in his 1842 essay *Preliminary Theses on the Reform of Philosophy*, which was that religion was no more than a projection of human nature. There was nothing real "out there." Humans had created gods and angels, devils and demons, to give shape to otherwise amorphous hopes and fears that swirled around within the consciousness. It was a thesis later developed by Freud, among others.

Paul came to a similar conclusion after hearing Catholics and Protestants hectoring each other from their podiums. "I developed my religious philosophy at the Pierhead," he said in 2000.

> It was like Speakers' Corner. . . . The Protestant would say, "What my friend over there is telling you is all wrong. There is no such thing as mortal sin. You're not born a sinner." Then the Catholic guy would start up: "My friend over there doesn't know that there *is* such a thing as mortal sin, and that if you don't get rid of your guilt you will burn in hell and damnation." They couldn't get it together, even though they were Christians. . . .
>
> I was exposed to so many religious arguments on the pier head, and I came to the conclusion that "God" is just the word "good" with the "o" taken out, and "Devil" is the word "evil" with a "D" added. Really, all that people have done throughout history is to personify the two forces of Good and Evil. And although they've given them many names—like Jehovah or Allah—I've got a feeling that it's all the same.

John's doubts about orthodox religion coupled with his mystical bent would provide the foundation for his subsequent ideas. His quest was to find a framework that could contain both his skepticism and his spiritual awareness. As he said in 1980, "People got the image that I was anti-Christ or anti-religion. I'm not at all. I'm a most religious fellow. I'm religious in the sense of [admitting there is] more to it than meets the eye. I'm certainly not an atheist. There is more that we still could know. I think this 'magic' is just a way of saying 'science [that] we don't know yet' or we haven't explored yet. That's not anti-religious at all."

In common with many of their generation, John and his friends didn't suffer crises of faith and then sever their ties with church. They just drifted away as other activities crowded into their lives. In this respect the explosion of television ownership that started when Britons bought sets to watch the 1953 coronation of Queen Elizabeth did more to empty the churches than the combined works of Darwin, Nietzsche, Freud, and Bertrand Russell. For David Ashton going to work marked the cutoff point. For Rod Davis it was when his father bought a car, and Sunday became the only day for "motoring" into the country. For Nigel Walley it was when girls became more interesting than Bible stories. For John it was when rock 'n' roll squeezed his heart.

Chapter Four

Think for Yourself

Once I heard rock 'n' roll and got into it, that was life. There was no other thing.

—John Lennon, 1975

We were baptized in Hamburg.

—Paul McCartney, 1997

We were suddenly getting a lot of arty types. Existentialists; the lot.
—George Harrison, 1968

Let your inside fill out until your stomach and brains are so bloated with pain and strife and despair, till your pores weep tears of blood, till your eyes sing a song of glass and splinters. . . .
—Stuart Sutcliffe, 1960

*H*earing rock 'n' roll music for the first time was the real conversion experience for John. It happened in May 1956 when he heard "Heartbreak Hotel" played on Radio Luxembourg, one of the few stations transmitting to Britain at the time that played the latest American music. He hadn't yet seen a photo of Elvis Presley and didn't know the roots of the music, but the attitude behind the performance connected with something inside him. It chimed with all his feelings of resentment toward prim and proper Britain.

A year before, his Uncle George had died suddenly of a hemorrhage after collapsing on the staircase at *Mendips*. He was only fifty-two years old. John was on holiday in Scotland with his cousin Leila and didn't hear the news until he arrived home. The loneliness that Elvis sang about was of a broken love affair, but it could have struck an emotional chord with John. He hadn't lost his "baby," but he'd effectively lost his father and now his beloved uncle. You could live in a well-kept suburban house and still feel as though you were down at the end of Lonely Street.

Elvis looked the way he sounded. Everything from the long, greased-back hair to his white shoes confronted the postwar conformity recently satirized in *The Man in the Gray Flannel Suit*. His shirts seemed feminine, his jackets came from a Memphis store that was a favorite of Beale Street pimps and blues singers, and his hair was partly inspired by southern truck drivers. To the British, the oversized jackets and long sideburns made him look like a Teddy boy (an English teenage subculture associated with antisocial behavior), the latest teenage outlaw to terrorize the respectable.

John said of his church, "there was actually nothing going on," but Elvis, he explained on another occasion, was "what was happening." At church, "nothing really touched us," but rock 'n' roll, when it hit, made him sit bolt upright. It was "the only thing to get through to me." The church spoke in obscurities whereas rock 'n' roll was honest and direct; "rock 'n' roll was real." The church stressed the need to extinguish sinful thoughts before they gained control of the body, but "rock 'n' roll put . . . minds and bodies together through the music." Elvis transformed John's life in a way that Jesus never had.

Elvis and his music gave shape to John's aversion toward refined culture. He was already bucking against school discipline, seeing teachers as people to outwit rather than respect and obey. His report for Christmas 1955, the last before rock 'n' roll came into his life, was reasonably good. "The best report he has had for a long time," wrote the headmaster, Mr. Taylor. "I hope this means that he has turned over a new leaf." After rock 'n' roll, his behavior worsened. Most of his teachers saw him as an intelligent boy, but one who lacked determination and fooled around too much in class. The headmaster concluded: "He has too many of the wrong ambitions and his energy is too often misplaced."

His energy was increasingly directed toward the King of Rock 'n' Roll. "Elvis was bigger than religion in my life," he said, and this was truer than he perhaps realized. Once his head was filled with music, he stopped going to Jack Gibbons's Bible class, and all attachment to St. Peter's was ended. "I shuffled it very well in those days," he later said of his childhood beliefs. "I was cynical about religion and never even considered the goings-on in Christianity." Mimi had wanted him to become a doctor or a vet like her nice student lodgers, but John already had an inkling of an alternative future that would require less effort and would bring greater reward. "I worshiped Elvis the way people worshiped the Beatles," he once said.

Interviewed in 1985, Mimi admitted, "I couldn't understand it. Here was a nicely spoken boy attending church three times on Sunday of his own free will, in the church choir, suddenly taken to twanging a guitar. I told him it was awful and that it was distracting him from his studies."

Shortly after John heard "Heartbreak Hotel," a school friend, Mike Hill, played Little Richard's "Long Tall Sally" for him. "When I heard it, it was so great I couldn't speak," John later remembered. "You know how it is when you're torn? I didn't want to leave Elvis. We all looked at each other, but I didn't want to say anything about Elvis, even in my mind." He was put out of his quandary when he discovered that Little Richard was black. The fact that he was that different meant that John could admire him without feeling disloyal to Elvis.

Little Richard was about as far removed from the British idea of a decent sort of chap as it was possible to be in 1956. Not only was he black but he was bisexual and highly camp, and he got away with singing about male prostitutes and adulterous liaisons because he used hip ghetto slang that eluded white audiences. His piano playing was frantic, his singing sometimes ascended into high-pitched screams, and he invented phrases ("awopbopaloobam") that sounded like a secular form of speaking in tongues. Little Richard didn't make records to be appreciated or even whistled along to. He made records to ravage the senses.

Rock 'n' roll was the sound of a generation slipping free from the restraints of the past. The music rarely articulated what it was against. Its values were primarily communicated through its spirit. In a nutshell, rock 'n' roll was about rediscovering the primal urges and chipping away at the encrusted values of Western civilization. The teenagers who went wild in the aisles, or who tore up cinema seats and started fights, weren't responding to inciting messages in the lyrics. They just knew instinctively that rock 'n' roll was encouraging them to let loose.

The enemies of rock 'n' roll were coldness, inhibition, and lifeless conformity. Its friends were passion, spontaneity, individuality, and imagination. "When I started, rock 'n' roll itself was the basic revolution to people of my age and situation," John once said. "We needed something loud and clear to break through all the unfeeling and repression that had been coming down on us kids." It was commonly assumed that the church was on the side of lifelessness and inhibition because lifeless, inhibited people made better, more docile followers. Passion and imagination were found among outsiders, those who had no significant stake in society—blacks, petty criminals, delinquents, deviants, hoboes, gypsies, junkies. Rock 'n' roll was largely forged by such outsiders—poor whites like Elvis, Carl Perkins, and Jerry Lee Lewis; blacks like Chuck Berry and Little Richard; punks like Gene Vincent.

The spirit of revolt that John recognized in rock 'n' roll was more pervasive than he was aware of as a teenage schoolboy in the north of England. The same month that "Heartbreak Hotel" entered the British charts, twenty-five-year-old Colin Wilson published his philosophical enquiry *The Outsider* and twenty-six-year-old John Osborne premiered his breakthrough play *Look Back in Anger* at the Royal Court Theatre in London. The critics dubbed these writers the Angry Young Men, their work seen as symptomatic of a rising mood of dissatisfaction with a lingering Victorianism that stifled ambition, self-expression, and unconventional thought. Rock 'n' roll singers like Elvis generally claimed ignorance of any possible connection between their music and youthful unrest, but the writers weren't so coy. They intended their work to reflect and ultimately change attitudes.

Wilson's book, which examined the theme of alienation in a wide range of literature, was philosophical and mystical. It became hugely popular with students grappling with life away from family influence for the first time. The Outsider, he argued, was the person who saw things as they really were and therefore could never "live in the comfortable, insulated world of the bourgeois, accepting what he sees and touches as reality." It would be a few years before John read *The Outsider*, but it's easy to see its appeal. "The Outsider may be an artist," said Wilson, "but the artist is not necessarily an Outsider."

Osborne's venom was also directed at the bourgeoisie, but he recommended intense living rather than mysticism as the way of breaking free. Britain, in his view, had become backward-looking and inert. Symbolically, most of the play's action takes place on a Sunday with the sound of church bells in the background. His antihero, Jimmy Porter, says, "Oh heavens, how I long for a little ordinary human enthusiasm. Just enthusiasm—that's all. I want to hear a warm, thrilling voice cry out Hallelujah! Hallelujah! I'm alive! I've an idea. Why don't we have a little game? Let's pretend that we're human beings, and that we're actually alive. Just for a while. What do you say? Let's pretend we're human."

Kenneth Tynan, the theater critic who would one day use John's writing in his controversial show *Oh Calcutta!* thought *Look Back in Anger* was the best play of the decade by a young writer. "The Porters of our time deplore the tyranny of 'good taste' and refuse to accept 'emotional' as a term of abuse," he wrote. He feared that it would remain a minority taste but added, "What matters, however, is the size of the minority. I estimate it at 6,733,000, which is the number of people between the ages of twenty and thirty."

John later acknowledged the connection, saying that the rebellion of which he became a part "all really began with *Look Back in Anger*." Colin Wilson was at the celebrated Foyles Literary Luncheon in 1964 where John was guest of honor and expected to give a speech. "Although we were introduced, there wasn't much time to talk," says Wilson. "Christina Foyle came up to me a few minutes later and said that John was too shy to make a speech, and so would

I do it for him? I said 'OK' but to my relief, half an hour later, the comedian Arthur Askey agreed to do it instead. I think John must have read *The Outsider* because some time later my agent asked me if I would be willing to write an introduction to his second book (*A Spaniard in the Works*). I said 'Yes,' but heard no more of this."

Paul's interest in rock 'n' roll developed at the same time but wasn't so inextricably linked to noncompliance. For John it was an artistic expression of the resentment he felt toward the authority of schoolmasters and the twitching net curtains of suburban England, whereas Paul was a popular student who respected boundaries and got on well with both of his parents. Aunt Mimi abhorred rock 'n' roll, which she associated with hoodlums and juvenile delinquency, but Jim McCartney, having once played in a jazz band, was sympathetic to Paul's passion for the music. He could see his younger self in Paul. The biggest trauma in Paul's life came shortly after he'd first heard Elvis, when his mother fell ill with breast cancer. His brother, Mike, found her crying on her bed with a crucifix in one hand and a photo of a cousin who was a missionary priest in Africa in the other. Within a few weeks she died in hospital, rosary beads tied around both her wrists. Paul, fourteen at the time, can remember praying that she would come back to life again. "I thought, it just shows how stupid religion is," he said in 1968. "See, the prayers didn't work when I really needed them to."

By the time the two boys met, in July 1957, their agnostic outlooks, although arrived at through different routes, were similar. John now fronted a skiffle group, the Quarrymen, made up of Quarry Bank school pupils. The washboard player was Pete Shotton, one of his oldest Sunday school friends. Pete's mother ran a shop in Woolton where she overheard a customer discussing the upcoming St. Peter's church garden fete. She suggested that the Quarrymen, largely former Sunday school members, could be a useful attraction.

Skiffle had become popular in Britain immediately before the success of "Heartbreak Hotel," mostly through the records of Lonnie Donegan, who had started off playing guitar in a London-based jazz band led by Chris Barber. Although it drew from the same musical well as rock 'n' roll, skiffle didn't divide the generations in the same way because it was perceived as worthy. The music appealed to many of the same people who liked folk, gospel, country, and traditional jazz and could be appreciated by pipe-smoking men in chunky sweaters as well as jiving teenagers. The songs were frequently as fast as a Little Richard number but weren't usually amplified and tended to avoid sexual innuendo.

It was the vigor of skiffle and the copious American cultural references that appealed to people like John. "Rock Island Line," "Worried Man Blues," and

"Cumberland Gap" spoke of freight trains, railroads, and prison farms, all of which seemed a magic world away from leafy, suburban Liverpool. There was also a suggestion of the forbidden. The characters in the songs tended to live on the edge. They were gamblers rather than bankers, hobos rather than office workers, members of a chain gang rather than a bridge club. They were people who lived outside the law.

Ivan Vaughan, a student at the Liverpool Institute with Paul and, like Shotton, an old Sunday school friend of John's, persuaded Paul to visit St. Peter's summer garden fete specifically to see the Quarrymen. The group played two half hour sets in the church field and then twice more across the road at the church hall for what was billed as the Grand Dance. It was here, in the room where John had spent so many years learning from the Bible, that Lennon and McCartney met each other for the first time, Paul famously impressing John by knowing all the words to Gene Vincent's "Be Bop a Lula" and Eddie Cochran's "Twenty Flight Rock." Three months later, at John's invitation, Paul joined the Quarrymen, and at the end of the year another Liverpool Institute student, George Harrison, came to see them. By early 1958 he, too, was a Quarryman.

John's reputation for cynicism started with the death of his mother in July 1958 just as he was ending his first year at art school. Julia was visiting Mimi, who was in the front room with her lodger, Michael Fishwick. Nigel Walley, the Quarrymen's manager, had just called by to see if John was there. Julia left the house to catch a bus home, but as she crossed Menlove Avenue, she was hit by a speeding car that then kept going. Fishwick, who had heard an "unmistakable bang," rushed over to see what had happened. "She was just lying peacefully on her back when I arrived, but there was blood seeping from her head," he remembers. "She had obviously cracked her skull. She had beautiful red hair. She gave a little death rattle in her throat, and I think she probably died there and then. We didn't know. The ambulance came soon after and took her away. Someone must have made a phone call."

John was out walking in the village but had planned to visit Julia, which is why she was in a hurry to get back. Fishwick went to the hospital with Mimi and then returned to Julia's home on Springfield Road where shocked friends and relatives were already gathering. He'd had to bring Mimi's shoes with him because she was still wearing carpet slippers when she'd gone to the hospital. "All I can remember was going into the main room where everyone had gathered. There just seemed to be sea of faces. John was there. I retired pretty quickly to the kitchen because I was so traumatized. Someone revived me with some whiskey. Life was never the same again for John."

Walley witnessed the aftermath of the collision. He'd accompanied Julia out of Mimi's house and waved to her as she crossed the road while he continued to his home on Vale Road. He heard the noise of the impact behind him. "I turned round and saw her flying through the air," he says. "It's so clear to me. Unbelievable. It was the first time in my life I had ever seen anybody dead, so that was a frightening experience. But to see someone dead who you had only been speaking to a few minutes earlier was devastating."

Julia's death made John tough and callous, Walley believes. It was only after this that he became known for his brutal comments and his aversion to sickness and deformity. The world had shown itself to be a cruel place, and his way of immunizing himself against further pain was to be cruel in return. "John took it very badly," says Walley. "He was always brash on the outside, but he had a lot of time and love for his mother. You had to look hard because he would never want to show you that. But the death really hit him, and he dressed in black for quite a while after. He'd lost his father, his Uncle George, and now his mother. He didn't seem to be having much luck. All his friends, like myself and Ivan Vaughan, had steady home lives with mothers and fathers, and I think it had always affected him to some degree that he didn't have that upbringing."

Julia's death deepened his skepticism about religion, particularly about the notion of a loving God who looked after all his children. It made him more receptive to the atheistic ideas that students in the late 1950s found stirring and liberating. Freud argued that Christianity had corrupted civilization by labeling harmless desires as evil. Nietzsche, another favorite of the time, said in his book *The Antichrist*: "When one places life's centre of gravity not in life but in the 'beyond'—in nothingness—one deprives life of its centre of gravity altogether. The great lie of personal immortality destroys all reason, everything natural in the instincts. Whatever in the instincts is beneficent and life-promoting or guarantees a future now arouses mistrust."

One of those who embraced these ideas was Stuart Sutcliffe, a painting student who became John's closest male friend. He had been through a similar church upbringing: Sunday school as a child, confirmation at fifteen, and choir singing at St. Gabriel's in Huyton, Liverpool, where he was head chorister. His Anglican father and Roman Catholic mother had decided to let the three children make their own choices about religion. The youngest, Pauline, went to a Catholic church while Stuart and Joyce joined the Church of England.

At school Stuart showed exceptional artistic talent and was a precocious reader. As a child he borrowed adult books from the local library and at secondary school had a reputation for advanced tastes. At the age of fifteen his class was told to return from the summer holidays with a list of books that they'd read. "Stuart's list included Dostoevsky, Aldous Huxley, Albert Camus, and people like that," says Ken Horton, a classmate who also went on to Liverpool School of Art. "The rest of us listed people like H. G. Wells and H. Rider Haggard."

At art school Stuart was soon recognized as one of its most promising students, and he seemed an unlikely companion for John, who was going through a drunken, loutish phase. Whereas Stuart was sensitive, deeply committed to his art, and intellectually inclined, John was hard-shelled, casual about his studies, and more likely to be seen reading *The Daily Mirror* than Freud or Nietzsche. Yet each had something that the other lacked. John's creativity was expressed through idle speculation and free association. Stuart had a more systematic, disciplined, and educated approach.

Stuart was the first student John had met who agonized over his art. He made lists of books that he felt he had to read that ranged from Herbert Read's *The Meaning of Art* to fiction by Joyce, Lawrence, Maupassant, Proust, and Turgenev. In notebooks that detailed the development of his thinking about art, he made observations such as, "We owe it to ourselves to cross the threshold of self-knowledge" and "We need to give our souls to our work." He wasn't embarrassed to ask the big questions. "We would talk about this stuff in the pub," says fellow student Bill Harry, who had introduced Stuart to John and would later found the local music paper *Mersey Beat*. "Who am I? Why was I born? Who put me here? Is there a God? We had this interest in psychic phenomena and strange powers of the mind. We were also wondering how mankind would develop."

In embracing high and low art with equal enthusiasm, Stuart was in tune with the emerging pop art movement. To him, Michelangelo and Eddie Cochran, cathedrals and Italian shoes, although obviously unalike, could be treated with the same seriousness. He exhibited this easy flow between high and low culture in his own tastes. He was a studious teenager who nevertheless dressed like James Dean, a fan of European art movies who could rave about Elvis. It was unusual for art students in the late 1950s to be huge fans of rock 'n' roll because the music was "commercial" (and therefore tainted) and it appealed to the culturally illiterate. The preferred music was folk, jazz, or authentic blues.

Like John, Stuart had been converted by "Heartbreak Hotel" and began collecting singles to play on his parents' gramophone. During his first year at art school, while on the intermediate course that provided a foundation in everything from drawing to costume design, he did a painting titled *Elvis Presley* that looked like a stained-glass window created by a cubist and was in keeping with the direction that would be taken by people who created contemporary iconography from pop culture like Andy Warhol in America and Peter Blake in Britain.

For Liverpool art students, who mostly came from northern working-class families, the most exciting ideas in the late 1950s emerged from either America or France. The American impact was visceral: neon signs, wide cars with huge tail fins, skyscrapers, diners, drive-ins, comics, open roads. It was the promise of an extravagant, colorful life that could erase the memory of Britain's fogs, bomb sites, run-down accommodation, and wartime "utility" clothing. The French impact was mostly cerebral; Left Bank cafes, smoky basement clubs, philosophy discussions over glasses of wine, late-night entertainment, and art films in black and white. The Cavern (opened in Mathew Street in 1957 by Alan Sytner, the venue where the Beatles would play 292 times) was based on Le Caveau de la Huchette, a Parisian jazz club Sytner had visited as a teenager.

What these students knew about America came through Hollywood movies, rock 'n' roll, television, and the stories told by merchant seamen traveling regularly to New York. There were also still U.S. soldiers and airmen stationed in Lancashire who would come into Liverpool on weekends to party. Their impressions of Paris came through the songs of Juliette Greco, the stories of art school lecturers like Arthur Ballard who had lived and worked in France, the films of Cocteau, and the existentialist philosophy of Jean Paul Sartre and Albert Camus. Although Sartre and Camus didn't invent existentialism, they had become the poster boys for the philosophy and had been lionized by the media in the postwar years.

Existentialism posited that with God out of the picture our individual existence was the only true absolute. There had never been any tablets of stone containing unchanging laws nor was there any book recording our every thought and action to be opened on a judgment day. Our behavior, and the value we put on life, were entirely a matter of choice. Consequently, Sartre argued, we are free to act in any way we choose. "It is nowhere written that 'the good' exists, that one must be honest or must not lie, since we are now upon the plane where there are only men," he wrote in *Existentialism and Humanism*. "Dostoevsky once wrote 'If God did not exist, everything would be permitted'; and that, for existentialism, is the starting point."

This conclusion didn't necessarily make Sartre happy. The relief of being free from judgment was diminished by the prospect of being alone in the universe. There was no divine anger, but neither was there divine love. There was no justice, but neither was there mercy. After quoting Dostoevsky, Sartre added: "Everything is indeed permitted if God does not exist, and man is in consequence forlorn, for he cannot find anything to depend upon either within or outside himself. He discovers forthwith, that he is without excuse."

In the form in which it filtered down to the average art student, existentialism was more about a license to live without regard to rules than a chill wind of alienation. The student heard Sartre speak of freedom but not that "Man is *condemned* to be free" (italics added). Thelma McGough (née Pickles), who was John's girlfriend during his first year at art school, remembers that in her case existentialism simply supported the atheism she'd been left with after rejecting the church. She didn't study it firsthand in books but absorbed it from films, magazines, and conversations with older students.

"It was breathtaking," she says. "It just seemed so right that you should live for the day, live for the moment. That's what we tried to do. The problem was that most of us were constrained by rules both at home and at school. The default position was that you went to church and said your prayers. It was as if they were embedded in the program, and it was difficult to escape from these constraints. Existentialism was a new way of thinking and living, and we envied those who lived in Paris and sat in cafes on the Left Bank. Stuart might have intellectualized it, but I don't think John did. We just took it at face value and thought it was wonderful."

To Stuart, who was also moved by the power of religious art, the idea of a godless universe was not unqualified good news. He loved the fifteenth-century cathedral frescoes of Fra Filippo Lippi and well as the twentieth-century expressionist paintings of the French Catholic Georges Rouault. If religion was no more than a mass delusion, where did its capacity to inspire and transform originate? Such questions led him to study the Christian existentialism of Kierkegaard and Berdyayev. "He gave me *The Journals of Kierkegaard 1834–1854* to read," says his sister Pauline. "He wanted to explore the idea of being a religious existentialist. I think he was always trying to integrate polarities, and that's something you can see in his painting."

Unlike Stuart, John didn't leave behind lists of books that he'd read as a student. Bill Harry is certain that John read Allen Ginsberg's poem *Howl* and Colin Wilson's *The Outsider*. He thinks he may also have read other Angry Young Men such as John Braine. An art school friend, Margaret Duxbury, remembered lending him a copy of J. D. Salinger's *The Catcher in the Rye* that he never returned. He later told her that it was his "favorite book." Some who knew him believe he didn't read a lot at the time, and that his ideas were gained through conversations with those who did. "It was Stuart who nurtured an interest in John to want to know more about things than he knew," said lecturer Arthur Ballard. "In other words, he was educating him. Lennon wouldn't have known a Dada from a donkey."

Everyone agrees that John behaved as though existentialism were true. "He lived his life the way he wanted to," says Thelma. "He didn't give a sod about anything or anyone else." Bill Harry agrees. "To me it seemed as though he didn't really care about anything and he didn't have a conscience. For example, when we collected for Panto Day, I'd be interested in getting the money for charity whereas he'd be interested so he could take the collection box, go into the toilet, open it up, and use the money to buy beer. If he was ever taught any religious principles he certainly threw them all away."

John also liked to expend the least effort in return for the greatest reward. Thelma remembers that part of his rebellion was to go to the cinema or walk down to the docks when he should have been in class. "We were the first spoiled generation," says Tony Carricker, another of John's close circle of art school friends. "We were the ones not to have to go to war and the first ones not to have to do National Service. I can remember John saying to me, 'I'm not gonna work. I'll play me guitar in pubs, but I'm not gonna work.' That was a revolutionary statement."

All of the Beatles had a similar wish. They saw rock 'n' roll as a potential means of avoiding the numbing work routine that had been the lot of their fathers (ship's steward, bus driver, docker, cotton salesman). Without it Paul would probably have become a teacher and George an electrician. "I came into this to get out of having a job, and to pull birds," said Paul in 1989. "And I pulled quite a few birds, and got out of having a job." Two years earlier George had said much the same thing, "Our original intention was just to be in a band as opposed to having a job."

Although Paul and George were still students at the Liverpool Institute in 1958 and 1959 and John at art school, they rehearsed, played at local events, and started writing their own material. By the end of the 1950s their repertoire consisted of almost ninety songs, the bulk of which were from Elvis, Buddy Holly, Carl Perkins, Chuck Berry, Lonnie Donegan, Jerry Lee Lewis, Gene Vincent, and Little Richard. However, fifteen of the songs were their own.

The songs that survive, such as "Hello Little Girl," "Like Dreamers Do," and "The One after 909," were emulations of what was popular at the time rather than individual expressions. The points of view they adopted were determined by what they thought was required rather than what they personally felt. For example, despite being sexually promiscuous, when writing songs they would adopt the attitude of you're the only girl for me, I'll love you forever and would die if you ever left me.

The song that came the closest to expressing their "live for the moment" approach was "I'll Follow the Sun," written in 1959 but not released until the *Beatles for Sale* album in 1964. Far from swearing fidelity and undiminished love, Paul warned a girlfriend that he wouldn't stick around if times got hard or passion waned. He was in a relationship for the good times alone. If rain should come, he was off—to follow the sun. This might have been the first time that a Beatle wrote an honest song.

In January 1960 John invited Stuart Sutcliffe to join the group now known as Johnny and the Moondogs. Stuart seems to have anticipated the time not very far in the future when rock would be hailed as an art form and art students like Jimmy Page, Eric Clapton, Ray Davies, and Pete Townshend would found seminal bands. What was eventually to separate the Beatles not only from the rock of the past but from their contemporaries was their belief that their work had something in common with the painting of Picasso and the poetry of Dylan Thomas as well as with the songs of Broadway and the blues of the Delta.

Earlier rock 'n' rollers had limited education, usually having left school around the age of fifteen and worked in humdrum jobs before being discovered. John and Paul continued their studies, albeit reluctantly, and learned about the creative process in art and literature. Paul read the poetry of Chaucer, the drama of Tennessee Williams, and the fiction of John Steinbeck while John not only became familiar with the history of art but viewed the latest European films at the college film society and read Beat writers such as Jack Kerouac and Lawrence Ferlinghetti. In the autumn of 1960 the university literary magazine, *Sphinx*, ran a section called "The Beat Scene—A Sort of Anthology" with photos of Kerouac and a cover designed by Bill Harry and his girlfriend Virginia Sowry.

The Beat generation writers were as mad at postwar America as the Angry Young Men were mad at postwar Britain. As an antidote to sterility, conventionality, and narrowed expectations they celebrated passion, movement, and irrational experience. Kerouac's love of those who were "mad to live, mad to talk, mad to be saved, desirous of everything at the same time" would have struck a chord with John. Bill Harry can specifically remember John reading *The Time of the Geek*, an extract from Kerouac's first novel *The Town and the City*, when it was anthologized in a 1960 paperback, *Protest*, edited by Gene Feldman and Max Gartenberg. Introducing the extract, the editors wrote:

> It was Kerouac who named his generation "beat". In two novels, *The Town and the City* and *On the Road*, he gave it also its Creed—DIG EVERYTHING—and its Trinity: Poet, Hoodlum and Junkie—an interlocked trio fused by a continuing dialogue. Kerouac's characters are not impinged upon by the society around them. They have fully succeeded in making their own world with places to go, things to do. And when they're not on the move, there's always the big kick: the jazz combo whose beat is beyond mind or reason, the hell-bent party that promises there'll be no end, or the stick of tea that will bring one back to the lap of God.

This impatience and hunger for excitement chimed with the aspirations of John and his circle of friends. Royston Ellis, Britain's own teenage pundit, pop journalist, and Beat poet visited Liverpool in June 1960 at the invitation of Tony Barrell, the editor of *Sphinx*, to read at a late-night "Beatnik session" during the university arts festival. He also gave an afternoon lecture on "Jazz and Poetry."

At the Jacaranda coffee bar, he met Stuart, discovered that he was a musician, and subsequently persuaded the Silver Beetles (as they were by then known) to back his poetry with improvised music at an informal rehearsal. At the evening event, attended by John and Stuart, he performed to gramophone records. Back at the Gambier Terrace flat that Stuart and John shared with art students Rod Murray and Rod Jones, Ellis showed the Silver Beetles how to disassemble a Vicks inhaler, remove the Benzedrine-soaked strips, and chew them to get a mild high. It was a trick that Kerouac had learned in 1940s New York.

Ellis stayed at Gambier Terrace for a week and can remember John pumping him for information on "drugs and queers and the bohemian/beat lifestyle." He believes that he was instrumental in helping John decide to strike out as a musician and leave behind the "phony life of art school" that he'd become accustomed to. "I remember he was doubtful about trying to survive without some sort of educational qualification, and I told him that was middle-class nonsense and that he should follow his heart."

More controversially, Ellis claims that he had a hand in renaming the group. A news item published in *Record Mirror* on July 9, 1960, headlined "The Rock 'n' Roll Poet," said that Ellis had been called "The King of the Beatniks" and mentioned that "for the past few months Royston has been invading clubs and dance halls with readings of his own poetry to a rock accompaniment." At the close of the story the writer noted that he was "thinking of bringing down to London a Liverpool group which he considers is most in accord with his poetry. Name of the group? '*The Beetles*'!" The writer of the news story had seen the beet/beat connection.

Ellis comments: "I still maintain it was the result of a conversation I had with John and George that led to the name change. When I asked them what they were going to call themselves they said the Beetles. I asked how they spelled it and John said 'Beetles' because he liked the Volkswagen car popularly known as the Beetle. I didn't think much of that and said that because I was a beat poet and they were going to back me, and also because they played beat music, why didn't they call themselves Beatles?" It was a connection that Jack Kerouac himself would later note with pride.

Four years later Ellis fictionalized his visit to Gambier Terrace in his Beat group novel *Myself for Fame*.

> The hallway was stacked on both sides with canvasses, easels, lumps of rock and clay chipped into weird shapes. The wallpaper was splattered with splodges of oil paint. Thanks to the destructive enthusiasm of a wild group

of beatniks who evidently lived here, the luxury of this particular flat was a myth. . . . There were three mattresses strewn about the bare boards of the floor. . . . The only light came from a red bulb stuck high up in the ceiling. As though to make the ceiling lower, someone had draped gauze from wall to wall, and this filtered the light to almost total darkness. Piles of books and paintings were everywhere. In the far corner, running alongside one wall was a cupboard-like piece of furniture which turned out to be two home-made bunks. A clothes line tacked along the other wall supported various hangers with the limited, but entire wardrobe of the four inhabitants of this room.

Two months after Ellis's visit the flat was at the center of an exposé in the British Sunday scandal sheet *The People*. As part of a five-week investigation into beatnik beliefs and behavior (beatniks were an "unsavoury cult," in *People* terminology), a journalist, Peter Forbes, had inveigled his way into the building by saying that he was working on a story about the adversity students faced in living on small grants, purportedly for the more reputable *Empire News*. The ensuing story, spread over two pages, was headlined 'This Is The Beatnik Horror," with a subheading, "For though they don't know it, they are on the road to hell." The photographer, Harold Chapman, was well placed to take pictures of the group. He had been based in Paris since 1954 and had lived at the notorious "Beat Hotel" where he had photographed fellow residents such as the Beat poets Gregory Corso, Allen Ginsberg, and Peter Orlovsky and novelist William Burroughs. He captured several flatmates and Jacaranda owner Allan Williams sitting in John and Stuart's bedroom with a poster for a "Big Beat!" show at the Grosvenor Ballroom in Wallasey. The poster, on the wall over the fireplace, featured "Gerry and the Pace-Makers" supported by the "Silver Beetles."

Part of Forbes's article read:

Beatniks, according to the American "teachers" are rebels against conventional society. They do not give a damn for anyone or anything—except themselves. How that works out in practice can be seen from the group that inhabits a three-roomed flat in decaying Gambier Terrace in the heart of Liverpool. There live Rod Jones, Rod Murray and a fluctuating number of their beatnik friends. Jones, 22, is at the local art college. Murray, who is a year older, has just left. The squalor that surrounds these well-educated youngsters is unbelievable. When I visited their "home" the only furniture I saw in their living room was a decaying armchair and a table which could not have been seen for debris. Boxes, newspapers, milk bottles, bits of orange peel, beer and spirits bottles, tubes of paint, cups, plastic beacons from zebra crossings, clothes, lumps of cement and plaster of Paris—these were just a few of the things that lay ankle deep across the floor. In the middle of all the chaos was a magnificent home-built hi-fi record player, blaring the "cool" jazz without which no beatnik "pad"—their slang for home—is complete. Besides Jones and Murray there were four other self-confessed beatniks in the flat.

The section on Gambier Terrace ended with quotes from the inhabitants. Rod Murray said, "At our last place, we burned all the furniture because we didn't have any money to buy coal. We were very lucky. We found a whole cellar-full of furniture belonging to the landlady. So we started burning our way through that, too." Rod Jones added, "We don't believe in work—it's just for mugs. My only interests are girls and poetry." Needless to say, when their parents saw the story, which was heavily plugged on the front page and on news vendors' posters, they were shocked and worried. Their worst fears of what could happen to their teenagers had come to pass. "It was very embarrassing for everybody at the time," says Rod Murray. "My girlfriend's parents were terribly upset. We were all middle-class kids basically pretending to be beatniks. To be like us in those days was to be outlandish. If you had a beard people pointed at you in the street and called you Jesus Christ. If you wore a beret you were a beatnik. Attitudes have changed dramatically since then."

The Silver Beetles had been used to playing to fairly unsophisticated teenagers in Liverpool suburbs, often in church halls that had to be locked up by midnight. In Hamburg, where they first traveled in August 1960 with Pete Best as their new drummer, they were playing to sailors, motorcycle gang members, gangsters, prostitutes, strippers, and tough guys, in clubs that stayed open until daylight. To amuse such jaded clientele they had to excavate the rock 'n' roll back catalogue and learn how to accurately match songs to moods. If the crowd was too lethargic they had to wake them up with barnstorming rock 'n' roll. If they became too riotous they would play show tunes to calm things down. It has been calculated that by the end of 1962 the Beatles (as they were now called) had spent eight hundred hours onstage in four different clubs, a priceless apprenticeship. It was in this milieu that their image, sound, and attitude developed.

Hamburg was important in other ways. St. Pauli, the area where the nightlife was concentrated, was one of the most notoriously liberal districts in Europe. Although Liverpool had its unruly bars and illegal gambling clubs, especially in the dock area, there was enough Welsh and Irish righteous indignation to keep it under control. St. Pauli experienced no such inhibition. Every extreme form of human behavior was tolerated and, in most cases, celebrated. There were male and female brothels and strip clubs, a mud-wrestling venue, transvestite bars, gay clubs, and even peep shows where girls performed with animals. One of the best-known streets, Herberstrasse, could only be entered by passing through iron gates because prostitutes sat semi-naked in shop windows to entice passersby.

The rules of behavior that the Beatles had been raised on seemed not just inappropriate but outmoded. There were no guardians, teachers, landladies, or girlfriends to answer to here. St. Pauli was an enclosed society where all bourgeois values and Christian principles were discarded, and it was made easy to yield to every previously unfulfilled desire. The Beatles loved what they saw. It made their home city seem dull and subdued by comparison. "Liverpool lately means nothing to me, nothing," wrote Stuart to his old friend Ken Horton. "Sick of faces. Fed up with Cathedrals and squares. . . . Tired of seeing so many people jabbering away about nothing."

They quickly became a part of what was going on, visiting the sleazy bars, befriending transvestites, and taking part in group sex, often with off-duty hookers. George, still only sixteen, had sex for the first time. Stuart took a girl's virginity in the shelter of a bombed-out church. John claimed to have "rolled" a sailor, attacking him in a dark street at night when he was drunk and stealing his money. Forbidden experiences beckoned to them from almost every doorway. For the first time songs like "Rip It Up" and "A Whole Lotta Shakin' Goin' On" described their actual lives rather than their fantasies. "We all got an education in Hamburg," said Paul. "It was quite something."

The perfect complement to this reckless life was the drug Preludin. Manufactured as a slimming aid but illegal without a prescription, it was an amphetamine made up of phenbutrazate hydrochloride and phenmetrazine that worked by stimulating the central nervous system. Club owners handed them out to prostitutes, strippers, and musicians to prevent their drowsing during their long nights of work. The pills boosted the energy level, increased confidence, and aided concentration.

Combined with beer, Preludin and other amphetamines would alter the shape and pace of the Beatles' shows. Before Hamburg they had played their two- or three-minute cover numbers in sequence, talking politely between them. In Hamburg the new overflow of energy and heightened concentration encouraged them to stretch and distort the songs. Once they took Ray Charles's then-recent hit "What'd I Say" and made it last for an hour. Another time half their set was composed of Jerry Lee Lewis's "Whole Lotta Shakin' Goin' On." Feeling brave, they would insult the audiences and stage mock fights. John was even known to appear on stage with no trousers or a toilet seat hung around his neck.

"You'd get smashed way in your head somewhere but you didn't fall around if you'd taken Preludin," says Tony Sheridan, the British guitarist and singer they backed on their first studio recording ("My Bonnie," by Tony Sheridan and the Beat Brothers) and played with on stage in Hamburg. "You discovered this feeling where you knew there was a guitar solo coming up in five seconds and you began to plan it. You'd be thinking, 'I'm gonna invent this and it's gonna go this way and it's gonna be a great solo.' This was the attitude. So we did great solos, lengthy solos and developed weird chords. We learned to mess it up. We discovered that it wasn't necessary to copy Chuck Berry or Little Richard or Jerry Lee Lewis. We could do it our own way. We could invent. We could even write songs!!"

On their first visit, while playing at the Kaiserkeller, they came into contact with a group of Germans who were to have a significant and lasting influence on not only their thinking but their looks. Jurgen Vollmer, Klaus Voorman, and Astrid Kirchherr were all art school graduates, dressed mostly in black, and they drew their inspiration from the left-bank bohemians of Paris. Astrid had cropped hair, while the boys wore their hair long and combed forward in a style that was so unusual for the time that they would be insulted in public. To the leather-jacketed rockers who frequented clubs like the Kaiserkeller they were the enemy. They referred to them as Exis, an abbreviation for existentialists, which they meant to sound insulting. The name stuck.

The Exis, like English art students, enjoyed the new jazz by Dave Brubeck or the Modern Jazz Quartet. Rock 'n' roll seemed too mainstream and superficial. However, Klaus had a taste for it, and one night, after a disagreement with Astrid, then his girlfriend, he went out walking aimlessly and found himself in St. Pauli where he heard the sound of music coming from the doors of the Kaiserkeller. Intrigued, he descended the stairs and peered into the murky club. On stage he saw Rory Storm and the Hurricanes, a Liverpool group whose drummer was Ringo Starr. They were soon followed by the Beatles, five young men in black leather jackets. He was so captivated by their performance that he persuaded Astrid and Jurgen to come down the next day.

Jurgen considered himself a typical Exi. He liked jazz and Juliette Greco, read Camus and Sartre and wanted to live in Paris. He had no rocker friends and wasn't a fan of rock 'n' roll. But when he saw the Beatles he felt exactly as Klaus had felt. They embodied his view of life. The existential approach to art was to strip things back to basics—to bare existence—and then to begin rebuilding without concern for absolutes. This was a good description of what the Beatles were doing with music, scraping away the veneer of pop comfort and exposing the naked form. Beneath their tough exteriors he sensed that the Beatles were more like his old art school friends than they were like the working-class rockers in the audience. "They looked like rockers," he says, "but inside they had the spirit of the Exis." As he wrote in his book *The Beatles in Hamburg*, "The songs were all American. At that time there was no other rock music around. Some of the songs I had heard before on the radio but only through the Beatles did I really come to appreciate and love that music. The libidinous long-ings expressed in the lyrics expressed exactly my own sexual desires and those of my generation that had been brought up in the fifties under the anti-sex morals of a restrictive and hypocritical German society."

The Exis had stumbled on the truth that rock 'n' roll, played as the Beatles played it, was a closer approximation of their outlook than the mild and quite polite expressions of modern jazz. Like John Osborne, Little Richard, Colin Wilson, and Jack Kerouac, they were revolting against those who weren't mad to live, who weren't desirous to have everything at the same time. Like Sartre, they thought that religion kept people down. "I went to Sunday school, but I discovered immediately what ridiculous bullshit religion was," says Jurgen. "One of the things I have fought against all my life is the stupidity of religion."

In like manner, the Beatles were attracted to the Exis. Jurgen worked for a well-known photographer, Klaus had studied illustration and was already designing album covers, Astrid was a trained clothes designer who also collected art and took photographs. They had never met a girl like Astrid. She lived in an annex of her family home, drove her own car (a VW convertible), and lived with Klaus with her mother's complete approval. Her sheets were black satin, her ceiling was covered in silver foil, modern art hung between full-length mirrors, and spotlights played on the walls. On her bookshelves were works by Genet, de Sade, Camus, Cocteau, Baudelaire, Villon, and Sartre, which John would question her about so persistently that she would buy him English translations. Her independence and artistry would become a role model for John and Paul when they later came to choose partners. "I saw all Germans as people who were in boxes, and I didn't want that," she said. "I was my own being, trying so hard to be different. I needed to rebel."

She and Jurgen began to photograph the Beatles, capturing for the first time their sensitivity and intelligence as well as the excitement of their performance. Astrid created black-and-white portraits with their faces half in shadow that were more like art photographs in a Parisian society magazine than show business publicity snaps. She took them to a fairground where she took solo shots of Paul and then John, with Stuart as a ghostly figure in the near distance. She photographed Stuart in dark glasses with a black scarf around his shoulders.

Her pictures made the Beatles look mysterious, moody, and introspective. The dark clothing and shadows suggested nighttime and the forbidden. They were never shown leaping or laughing as the London show business photographers would do later on. She made them look like dignified artists rather than eager-to-please entertainers.

Her visual ideas became incorporated into the Beatles' look. After she and Stuart began a relationship they shared clothes, and he would arrive on stage wearing high-collared white shirts, collarless jackets, black waistcoats, and leather jeans. She encouraged him to stop greasing his hair and to comb it forward like Klaus and Jurgen. A new, more sexually ambiguous style was forming. The old rocker image, part Elvis, part Gene Vincent, was being replaced by a bohemian look inspired by Astrid's vision of Paris. "Existentialism was our way of expressing our difference from the old Germany," she said. "Our major influence was France. America was too far away, and it couldn't be England for they were our enemies. . . . We took all our information and inspiration from France—music, writing, art, the looks. I loved Juliette Greco. My hero, and the biggest influence, was Jean Cocteau; the strict black and white, and the way he composed every image."

Stuart's letters back to Ken Horton were full of existentialist angst. Beneath his descriptions of how empty everything was, it was possible to detect the relish of a young man privileged enough to be able to wallow in philosophical despair. "I have no money, no resources, no hopes," he wrote in October 1960. "I'm not the happiest man alive. Six months ago I was an artist. I no longer think about it. I am. Everything that was art has fallen from me." The only redemption, in his view, came from intense living. "The age demands violence," he said, "and we have only abortive explosives." He constantly needed to have his senses shaken to make life worth living. "Passion is too quickly exhausted," he moaned, "and we all fall back on ideas."

John and Paul made their first pilgrimage to Paris in October 1961, financed by a twenty-first-birthday gift from John's aunt Elizabeth. They wanted to experience the fabled Latin Quarter for themselves. Their only Parisian contact was Jurgen, now in the city working for a photographer. He was living at Hotel de Beaune at 29 Rue de Beaune, within walking distance of the Café de Flores and Les Deux Magots where Sartre and Simone de Beauvoir famously wrote and held meetings. "For types like me this was the center of the artistic world," says Jurgen. "I was the first of the Exi group to go to Paris, and I was Paris mad."

Jurgen took them on a guided tour of the Left Bank, pointing out the watering holes of the philosophers, the jazz clubs, and the parks. John and Paul were both enraptured by the bohemian atmosphere. Hamburg had encouraged their raucous, animalistic side. In Paris they felt poetic, artistic, romantic, and philosophical. They wanted to meet girls in berets and fishnet stockings who looked like Juliette Greco or Bridget Bardot. Jurgen took them to the Café Le Royal on Boulevard St. Germain, a hangout popular with artists at the time, but the girls he knew showed no interest in his English friends because they still looked like rockers with their leather jackets and greased-back hair. To look like Gene Vincent was definitely not cool in the 1961 Parisian demimonde.

Jurgen bought his clothes from a flea market at Porte de Clignancourt, and so he took them there to shed their greasy image. "I remember very well that John bought a vibrant green corduroy jacket, and I think Paul did too. Then, they wanted my haircut." Jurgen had been the first of the Exis to wear his hair forward. It started when he was at school, and he left it uncombed after a swimming session. "The teacher was so shocked and he asked me why I didn't tidy it. This made me feel ridiculous in front of the whole class, and it provoked me to be more rebellious. I was always rebellious, and I still am. I never do what the norm is." He took them back to his room at the Hotel de Beaune and cut their hair. "For the rest of the week we were like Paris Existentialists," said Paul. "Jean Paul Sartre had nothing on us. This was it."

Stuart and Astrid had become engaged by the end of the first trip to Hamburg. Rather than return to Liverpool, Stuart stayed in Germany, enrolling in an art school. He and John wrote feverish letters to each other that veered between comic nonsense and Augustinian confessional. It was the first time that John had poured out his feelings of inadequacy, loneliness, and grief, and he was self-conscious about doing so. He was revealing, as he wrote in one letter, part of his "almost secret self." If the letters were seen by anyone else they would "wonder what the hell is going on or just pass it off as toilet paper."

During their second visit to Hamburg, in 1961, Stuart left the Beatles. He knew that his bass playing was inadequate and his relationship with Astrid had become more important to him than any dreams of pop stardom he may have had. His letters home became increasingly morbid and bizarre. He complained of depression and severe headaches. When he wrote to John, he took on the persona of Jesus, and John, assuming it was a joke, adopted the voice of John the Baptist. In April 1962, just before the Beatles' third visit to Hamburg, Stuart collapsed and was rushed to a hospital where he died of a brain hemorrhage.

It was another huge blow to John, who was told the news in Hamburg by Astrid. Stuart was the first friend he'd had whom he not only admired as an artist but with whom he could share his deepest thoughts. "For a long time Stuart was the only person John could trust enough not to have to act the tough anarchist," says Pauline Sutcliffe. "Stuart never betrayed him. They were truly, intimately close. Forget any sexualizing of the relationship. They were close emotionally and spiritually. My sense was that there was nothing John didn't feel he could rehearse with Stuart."

Stuart would live on through the Beatles, for it was his moody, dark-shirted, long-haired look that would soon become the instantly recognizable Beatle image of 1963, and it was Astrid's shadowy Parisian-style photos that would appear on the cover of *With the Beatles*. The spirit of existentialist-period Hamburg would be translated into the live-for-the-moment attitude that characterized the group during the rise of Beatlemania. Astrid said, "The four of them had the same urge as us. We wanted to get it out, all of our emotions and feelings. That's what we all discovered, and that's maybe why we took pills; because they enabled us to leap the hurdles of convention and nationalism and communication as lovers and friends. Ninety percent of people would never be able to jump those barriers."

Chapter Five

Eight Days a Week

We just behave as normally as we can. We don't feel as though we should preach this and tell them that. You know, let them do what they like.

—*John Lennon, 1964*

I'm more worried about personal happiness than I am about world happiness.

—*George Harrison, 1964*

People who are mature are respectable, ordinary, and dull.

—*Paul McCartney, 1965*

We never think of any influence we have. We're not setting examples for anybody.

—*Ringo Starr, 1965*

*I*n the twelve months after Stuart Sutcliffe's death the Beatles were transformed. They met their manager, Brian Epstein, sacked drummer Pete Best and recruited Ringo Starr, signed to Parlophone, began recording with producer George Martin, had their first three hit singles—"Love Me Do," "Please Please Me," and "From Me to You"—and released their debut album, *Please Please Me*. They also graduated from the dance halls and cellar clubs of Liverpool to playing theaters and prestige venues such as London's Royal Albert Hall and the ten-thousand-capacity Empire Pool at Wembley.

Although still virtually unknown in America, they were being tipped in Britain as the next big thing. By March 1963 their popularity was so huge that when they toured as a support act to the American stars Chris Montez ("Let's Dance") and Tommy Roe ("Sheila"), they had to be briskly moved to the top of the bill. By May they had their own BBC radio show, *Pop Goes the Beatles*.

During these early days their revolutionary nature wasn't to be found in the words of their songs but in their attitude: how they dressed, the way they behaved, the energy they created on stage, what they said during interviews. They didn't sing specifically about personal liberation, yet everything about them from their style of hair to their surrealistic answers to journalists' questions implied that boundaries were to be challenged and that personal freedom began with being true to oneself.

They were something new in pop because they appeared to be without pretense. Elvis had always been deferential to journalists, addressing them as "sir" or "ma'am," and when faced with controversy over his hip-shaking performances, he expressed disbelief that anything he did on stage could be construed as provocative or lewd. The Beatles gave facile answers to facile questions, never addressed their interlocutors formally, and, with the exception of the Jesus controversy, never retracted statements. It's impossible to imagine Elvis saying of the influential columnist Walter Winchell, as John did in a press conference in America, "He's stupid because he just lies and writes a lot of trash."

The message that came across was, "Get real. Be yourself. Don't pretend." They championed a new frankness and honesty that contrasted with the old show business promotional strategy where the star was portrayed as perfect in every area of life and lines were fed them by press agents. Years later John would write a song titled "Give Me Some Truth," a slogan that was a précis of the Beatles' approach to almost everything. Although they came to have one of the most instantly recognizable images in popular culture, there was no trickery. There wasn't a huge difference between the public's impression of the Beatles and who the Beatles were in private.

Being committed to the pursuit of truth didn't mean that their behavior was always exemplary, simply that they endeavored to be open with their public. Initially it was shocking that they smoked during press conferences and admitted that their favorite drink was Scotch and Coke rather than orange juice or milk. Questions were asked in 1964 about the appropriateness of the unmarried Beatles vacationing abroad with their girlfriends. Their attitude was that they wouldn't pretend to be other than what they were. "It's good fun being a Beatle," said Ringo in 1965. "We're not restricted in what we say or do. We have a lot of freedom, and we're not ashamed that we drink and smoke and swear." Paul said, "In the old days we never used to believe it when we opened a magazine and it would say that so-and-so doesn't drink, doesn't smoke, and doesn't stay out late."

Their regional accents were a perfect complement to this frankness because it made them sound "natural," not the product of elocution lessons. The voice of officialdom was the clipped upper-class tones bequeathed by an expensive private education whereas the voice of authenticity was found in such regional accents as Cockney (London), Geordie (Newcastle), or Scouse (Liverpool). In England there had been a history of working-class performers changing the way they spoke in order to win acceptance and respectability. Cliff Richard, for example, who was Britain's biggest pop star at the time that the Beatles started recording, was raised on a council estate in Cheshunt but sounded almost posh. He had what Nik Cohn would call a "noncommittal accent." The Beatles, however, had no intention of changing. It wasn't an act of defiance. It was an assertion of pride in their origins.

In 1963 Edward Heath, then Lord Privy Seal, later prime minister of Great Britain, complained that when the Beatles spoke they were unintelligible to him because they didn't seem to speak the Queen's English. John's response was to point out that many of the people who had elected Heath as an MP didn't speak the Queen's English either. In October 1963 when the Beatles were due to perform before the Queen and Duke of Edinburgh at the Royal Variety Show in London, a journalist asked Paul if they'd be "losing some of your Liverpool dialect" for the event. "Are you kidding?" he responded, sounding genuinely taken aback. "No. We wouldn't bother doing that."

These small gestures had a significant effect in that they gave dignity to those outside the powerful South-Eastern elite who controlled the British establishment. "The whole embarrassed thing about being a provincial is different now," said Paul in 1965. "We always felt funny when we first came to London about the North Country accent." Indeed, it was so effective that it soon became a disadvantage to come from a privileged background. A posh pop star was suspected of being fraudulent. John's old girlfriend Thelma McGough remembers: "When I was a girl and went away to camp with the Guides in Wales my mother used to say that if anyone was to ask me where I was from, I wasn't to tell them that I was from Liverpool. It wasn't until the Beatles were accepted that it suddenly became OK to have an accent and admit that you came from Liverpool."

Although the Beatles defied these conventions, they didn't immediately challenge the convention that a successful pop song had to be between two and three minutes long and about love. Every track they recorded during their first two years was about love, and three quarters of them contained the word "love." As they later admitted, they rarely wrote from personal experience during this period and had no thoughts of persuading or educating anyone. At times they used real people and events as a stimulus, but their goal was to entertain rather than inform. As Paul said in 1964, "Our lyrics aren't more intelligent than others have been, but we always try to say something different in the way that a song should say it."

Motivated more by craftsmanship than self-expression, their worldview nevertheless naturally informed the songs. Even when tackling the same assignments, John and Paul would reveal the imprints of their different backgrounds. Paul was always unstintingly optimistic. His home had been happy and secure. His father encouraged him to believe in himself. In his songs he always knew that he could get the girl if he chose to make a move, and he was equally confident that she would fall in love with him. He didn't anticipate complications.

John, on the other hand, revealed a guardedness in his songs. He wanted to dance with the girl, but was unsure that she'd want to dance with him. Even if she did dance with him, he would worry that that's all she'd do with him ("I'm Happy Just to Dance with You"). His father's desertion and the deaths within six years of his mother, uncle, and best friend had caused him to build a defense system of jokes, put-downs, and withering comments. Every time he allowed himself to become vulnerable, he paid for it in tears. It was easier just to expect the worst. As he mournfully explained in 1965 to the American columnist Phyllis Battelle, "The things that I look forward to usually turn out lousy."

The archetypal early Beatles love song was "I Saw Her Standing There," written mostly by Paul in 1962 and used as the opening track on *Please Please Me* in April 1963. Like many of the early songs they wrote, the words were scribbled in a Liverpool Institute exercise book and the music was completed at Paul's family home in Forthlin Road, Allerton. In most instances a song was well on its way to completion by one of the partners before being shown to the other, who would change words, make suggestions, and possibly add the contrasting "bridge" section that in a traditional pop song went between the second and third verse.

In the case of "I Saw Her Standing There," Paul had opened with the couplet "She was just seventeen / Never been a beauty queen," and John had objected to the mention of a beauty queen because he knew it had been shoehorned in to provide a rhyme. It added nothing to the story. In fact, it diverted interest from the main theme because the tempting image of a teenage girl in the first line is immediately neutralized. It also raised too many questions. Had she placed second in a beauty pageant, or was she just plain? To declare a girl to be "no beauty queen" is usually a polite way of saying that she's ugly.

John's solution was inspired. He suggested "You know what I mean?" an apparent throwaway line which was in fact an injection of innuendo. Sixteen was the age at which it was legal to have sexual intercourse (hence the number of pop songs about sixteen-year-olds), and so to be "just seventeen" was to be fair game: not too young to be borderline but certainly not too old to be rejected. The difference between "beauty queen" and "know what I mean" was the difference between Paul and John. Paul's natural inclination was to play it safe and rely on pop clichés. John's inclination was to subvert and make use of double meanings.

Although the song didn't purport to be of great philosophical significance, it embodied the Beatles' existentialist outlook. They grew up in an era that still promoted the concept of courtship. The only girls who went "all the way" on a first or second date were "slappers" or "scrubbers" who weren't considered good wife or mother material. But the courtship model required self-control and a belief in delayed gratification, neither of which seemed consistent with a live-for-the-moment philosophy.

In "I Saw Her Standing There" there are no preliminaries. He sees her, she sees him, and the next step is that they're dancing "through the night," which, like "holding each other tight," is usually a euphemism for sex in Beatles' songs. For Paul there was rarely a delay between seeing and taking. Things didn't backfire. Jealous boyfriends didn't pursue him. Reticent girls didn't slap his face. In this song he only has to walk across the room for all his dreams to come true. His heart goes "boom," but an accelerated heartbeat or a minor palpitation is a small price to pay.

The contraceptive pill had become available by prescription in Britain by December 1961, nine months before Paul wrote this song. The religious grounds for abstinence already held less sway over an increasingly lapsed generation, and now one of the final barriers to guilt-free sexual promiscuity—the fear of getting a girl "into trouble"—had been lifted overnight. The pill, Paul admitted, "was a very handy thing. Suddenly, women were prepared to sleep with a fella with no great risk of pregnancy. Now we could all have some fun." In his book *Magical Mystery Tours*, Tony Bramwell, a childhood friend of George's who later worked for Brian Epstein in various capacities, makes the claim that the eager acceptance of the pill was made possible by the spirit that the Beatles promoted. "If the Beatles hadn't happened," he said, "I don't think the Pill would have been so widely used and accepted so fast. There would have been some kind of social embarrassment or embargo, which would have slowed down the pace of change."

Two other events that illustrated the pace of social change in Britain were the 1960 trial of Penguin Books over the publication of D. H. Lawrence's novel *Lady Chatterley's Lover* and the March 1963 publication of *Honest to God* by the then bishop of Woolwich, Dr. John Robinson. The *Chatterley* trial was not just about more permissive attitudes toward sexual behavior but about the right of the ruling powers to control the private artistic consumption of the population. A question put to the jury—"Is this a book you would like your wife or even your servant to read?"—emphasized the gap. *Honest to God* was the first time that a senior Anglican churchman had publicly cast doubt on the orthodox beliefs of the church. In an attempt to make the church relevant to the "modern" and "scientific" age Robinson suggested letting go of our age-old conceptions of God, heaven, and morality and developing a new understanding that would be more readily accepted by people with no time for the miraculous. It went on to sell a million copies.

Instant gratification was a signature of the new era as Britain emerged from post-1945 austerity. Members of the older generation who had lived through two world wars, a financial depression, high unemployment, and rationing were used to "scrimping and saving," "making do," and "saving for a rainy day." They had learned through hard experience how to make a little go a long way and were fond of cautionary sayings such as "waste not, want not," "neither a borrower nor a lender be," and "marry in haste, repent at leisure." Increasingly young people didn't want to live by such belt-tightening attitudes. The world of installment-plan purchasing, the Pill, and disposable products implied that there was no virtue in waiting. Additionally, the prospect of nuclear annihilation (then still relatively new) made it imperative to get your wild living done while there was still time.

This attitude had already affected the Beatles in their choice of career. Although John, Paul, and George had been given the educational advantages that could have got them to university, none of them considered it. They were reluctant to postpone the good times. John fooled around in school and got into art school only through Mimi's persuasion and a reference from his art master. George became an apprentice electrician. Paul's father wanted him to become a teacher. "I never cared much about a career and a future and all that stuff," Paul said in 1964. "But I had a bit of a conscience towards my dad."

It could also have predisposed them to their choice of drug. By providing an instant high through accessing nervous energy, amphetamines promised to deliver pleasure without having to endure pain. It seemed to be a sign of progress that where previous generations had expected moments of elation in return for effort expended, science was now able to short-circuit the process.

The only thing they couldn't conjure up in an instant was love. Sex, yes. Love, no. Even money couldn't buy you love. In the early songs of the Beatles the major obstacles to happiness were loneliness, boredom, and depression, and the solution was invariably sexual companionship. The right girl would wipe all your blues away ("Thank You Girl"), bring you companionship ("It Won't Be Long"), and make you feel all right ("A Hard Day's Night"). Feeling all right was very important to the Beatles. This was the litmus test of any relationship—when they held their baby tight, usually all night, did it make them feel "so good"?

This fixation with love as an antidote to lack of fulfillment was standard pop fare, but in their real lives it was easier for them to have brief sexual encounters than deep relationships because they were constantly moving. John had married Cynthia in 1962 but saw her less after the marriage than he had done before, when the group was relatively unknown. "I know from Hamburg that all of them had been at it in one way or another," says Cynthia. "I had no illusions about what was going on when they were on tour because girls were throwing themselves at their feet."

Five years after "Love Me Do," with "All You Need Is Love" as their current hit, Paul reflected on the continuity of the love theme. He suggested that although "Love Me Do" was musically and lyrically primitive, it contained the essence of what the Beatles believed in. "You get to the bit where you think if you're going to write great philosophy, it isn't worth it," he said. "'Love Me Do' was our greatest philosophical song. 'Love, love me do / You know I love you / I'll always be true / So, please love me do.' For it to be simple and true means that it's incredibly simple."

The emphasis on love and freedom had a unique resonance in the early sixties. Their impact in America is frequently explained as a response to the assassination of President Kennedy. Just as the country was coming to terms with the loss of a young leader who represented hope and idealism (November 1963) the even younger Beatles came along and uplifted spirits (February 1964) with their version of hope. It was also the time of the escalating American involvement in Vietnam, the Cold War, and bloody clashes over civil rights.

During such a time of uncertainty the Beatles represented the best of what people longed for. They represented laughter rather than tears, hope rather than despair, love rather than hatred, life rather than death. Not that they commented directly on social issues at the time. If asked questions on war, poverty, or the A-bomb during 1963 and 1964, they would either shrug their shoulders or make flippant comments. They gave the impression that they were so busy enjoying themselves that they didn't have time to think about global problems. "If an atom bomb should explode I'd say 'Oh, well,'" said Paul in 1963. "No point in saying anything else, is there? People are so crackers. I know the bomb is ethically wrong, but I won't go around crying." John said that he didn't "give a damn" about the future. "It's selfish, but I don't care too much about humanity. I'm an escapist. Everybody's always drumming on about the future but I'm not letting it interfere with my laughs, if you see what I mean." Asked about the war in Vietnam, George said, "It's not worth brooding about, is it? It's not worth brooding about anything really." For Ringo, it was "youth that matters right now. I don't care about politics."

Faithful to their essentially existentialist outlook, the Beatles weren't concerned about the past or the future. They believed in extracting the greatest pleasure from the moment they were living in without bothering about the way things had always been done or the possible consequences of their actions in days yet to come. George was typical in saying, "I don't think too much about the future. I never think more than a week or so ahead."

The Christian view was that life should be lived carefully and soberly in light of an eventual judgment. Christianity encouraged reflection, self-examination, confession, and consideration for others. But if there was no judgment and no all-seeing God, why be careful? Why continue to act as if something were true if it was false? As Paul told American journalist Michael Lydon: "One thing that modern philosophy—existentialism and things like that—has taught people is that you have to live now. You have to feel now. We live in the present. We don't have time to figure out whether we are right or wrong, whether we are immoral or not. We have to be honest, be straight, and then live, enjoying and taking what we can."

This was a subtle yet significant change. Even though their parents' generation (born in the Edwardian era) had largely lost the religious certainty of their grandparents (born in the mid- to late Victorian era), there was still an adherence to general Christian principles. "Do unto others as you would have them do unto you" was accepted as the Golden Rule. John's mother, for example, would always say "God bless" as she tucked her children in bed at night, and she told them that God made the sun, moon, and flowers. There was a vague belief in an afterlife that was determined upon how you behaved in this one. Even unbelievers refrained from washing the car or trimming the hedges on the Sabbath. Yet there was now no vibrant faith underpinning this conduct. They were habits developed in a former age and held on to because there was no sufficient reason to replace them.

The new generation thought there was sufficient reason to replace them or, at least, no reason to continue with them. Traditionalists argued that although conventional morality wasn't grounded in eternal truth, as previously supposed, it served a purpose in restraining excess and rewarding good behavior. The existentialist position was that the Christian worldview, being untrue, was inhuman. It subdued and inhibited us. It made us fearful of discovering our full potential. There was no implicit virtue in holding back and no implicit vice in letting go. "Christianity should not be beautified and embellished," argued Nietzsche. "It has waged deadly war against this higher type of man; it has placed all the basic instincts of this type under the ban."

Although in their songs prior to 1965 the Beatles didn't speak explicitly of freedom, everything that they did and said implied a belief in it. The leaps in the air, the high-pitched screams, the irrepressible force of the music, the celebratory cries of "Yeah, yeah, yeah"—all of it communicated a joyous release from previous restraints. Although they had derived "Yeah, yeah, yeah" from previous rock 'n' roll recordings it was significant that they would be identified with such positivism. Following an era of caution and prohibition they represented a fresh attiitude that said "Yes" to new experience rather than "No," "Hold on," or "I'm not sure." It was reminiscent of Dean Moriarty, Jack Kerouac's hero in *On the Road,* who expressed his hunger for life by constantly muttering "Yes! Yes! Yes!" In the Britain of their childhood there had been a network of tacit agreements about appropriate dress, speech, manners, and general codes of behavior, many of them with roots in Victorian Christianity. Long hair on men, for example, or clothes that were sexually ambiguous were taboo, and the only people who would break these rules would be outsiders: gypsies, homosexuals, transvestites, tramps, artists, eccentrics, or hermits. "In America they were all getting house-trained for adulthood with their indisputable principle of life: short hair equals men; long hair equals women," said Paul. "Well, we got rid of that small convention for them."

Simply by wearing different clothes and brushing their hair forward the Beatles tested this convention. Their implicit message was that you could only take control of your life if you stopped allowing outside agencies—whether school, church, the BBC, the police, or government—to dictate on personal matters. "We've always taken the line that what happened in the '60s was about an astonishing movement that came at the end of the Second World War, the end of all that repressive Victorian thought," said Paul in more recent years. "We just happened to become leaders of whatever cosmic thing was going on."

Devin McKinney, in his book *Magic Circles: The Beatles in Dream and History,* makes the point that whereas Christianity redirected adolescent anxieties and desires, the Beatles never sought to quell them. "What made them diferent from any religion before or since was that, rather than redirecting those energies in the service of doctrine, they gave the fan free reign to explore them, intensify them, take them anywhere. Speaking in the cliché of the '60s, the Beatles were from the church of Do Your Own Thing; granting their accomplishment the respect it deserves. We recognize that they preached a faith of complete and open possibility that was by its very innocent nature a transcendent vision."

A key agency in guaranteeing conformity in British boys was National Service. From the end of the Second World War in 1945 until December 31, 1960, every male over eighteen and not in full-time education had to spend two years in the armed forces. Besides putting Britain on a permanent war footing it introduced boys of all classes and abilities to an identical standard of discipline, deportment, fitness, grooming, and personal hygiene. All individual desires had to be subordinated to the demands of the service. All conscripts wore the same basic "short back and sides" haircut. The older generation regarded time in the forces as an indispensable rite of passage.

Typically it meant that youthful rebellion was nipped in the bud. National Service made men out of boys. It turned surly adolescents into valued citizens, proud of their country and ready to settle down. The Beatles thought that the army had been responsible for destroying all that was unique and powerful in Elvis, turning him from a rebellious rocker into a marketable all-around entertainer. When, in 1977, John was informed of Elvis's death, he was quoted as saying: "Elvis died the day he went in the army." Three years later he expanded: "That's when they killed him, and the rest was a living death." For Paul, the end of National Service was the beginning of freedom in Britain. "Not just for me, for anyone of a certain age. Without that, there could have been no Beatles. To me, that was like God opening the Red Sea for Moses and the Israelites to come pouring through. It was like God decreed that there would be no National Service. . . . It meant that we were the first generation for so many years that didn't have that 'We'll make a man of you' threat hanging over them. We weren't going to be threaded through the system like so many before us."

With no compulsory growing-up period or shouldering of the burden of national defense, teenage fashions and attitudes no longer had to end on the parade ground of a military barrack. Youth could be prolonged indefinitely. The Beatles wore their hair the way that schoolboys wore it when they were too young to use a comb properly and be concerned about looking smart. It was the haircut of Tom Sawyer and Huck Finn or William Brown from Richmal Crompton's novels whose hair was described as looking like "a neglected lawn" (John was a big fan of William). It was the haircut that symbolized the carefree nature of living outside the adult world with its concerns about impressions, status, and the idea that "cleanliness is next to godliness."

The idealization of childhood would be important to the sixties revolution, and the Beatles played a part in its promotion. The thesis was that we are most natural in childhood—full of potential, wonder, and hope—but then, as William Wordsworth put it in his ode "Intimations of Immortality":

> Shades of the prison-house begin to close
> Upon the growing Boy

As parents, teachers, and priests begin the job of civilizing us, so the thinking went, we develop inhibitions and fears that prevent our natural growth. John's songs "Strawberry Fields Forever" and "In My Life" didn't express a yearning to be back living with Mimi and attending Quarry Bank School but a belief that he was most liberated when he was a boy. In a letter to Stuart, probably from 1962, he wrote in the form of a poem:

> I remember a time when
> Belly buttons were knee high
> When only shitting was dirty
> And everything else
> Clean and beautiful

Several years later in "She Said She Said" he would write in a similar spirit that when he was a boy, "Everything was right."

At the time, the Beatles probably weren't directly motivated by the Romantics of the nineteenth century, but they were discovering a view that had been important to these writers. Poets such as Wordsworth and Blake felt that the rationalist thinking of the Enlightenment left no room for the imagination, so they treasured children, among others, as people whose minds had yet to be corrupted by this outlook. John believed that creative ability was generally stifled in the same way. "All kids draw and write poetry," he told *International Times*. "Some of us last until we're about 18 but most of us drop out at 12. That's when some guy comes up and says, 'You're no good.' That's what we're told all our lives, what our limitations are. People are limited into thinking that they can't run their own affairs. What we're trying to say is that you're unlimited. You're all geniuses."

George expressed similar ideas to Maureen Cleave in 1966. "Babies when they are born are pure," he said. "Gradually they get more and more impure with all the rubbish being pumped into them by society and television and that; till gradually they're dying off, *full* of everything." In an aside Cleave described this as "a Wordsworthian view of the evils of urban society," referring to the poet's idea expressed in "Intimations of Mortality" that babies enter the world "trailing clouds of glory" but are then gradually corrupted. This ran counter to the prevailing Christian idea that we were each "born in sin."

Sixties fashions would pillage childhood for inspiration, from the baby-doll and Twiggy-thin looks for girls during the time of "swinging London" to the ripped jeans and dungarees of the Woodstock era. Growing up was something that the Beatles never liked to think about. In 1965 Paul said that he thought the word "maturity" was a description of people who were stuck "in a rut." The older generation had been responsible for laying down the rules from which young people were now trying to escape. "It's best for people to come of age and then decide what they want to believe in rather than having it forced on them by the older people," said George. They referred to the elderly as "crocks." John admitted, "The thing I'm afraid of is growing old. I hate that. You get old and you've missed it somehow."

By the time they arrived in America, in February 1964, they were a well-established unit that had been playing together for six years. Their welcome in New York was unprecedented, and when they appeared on *The Ed Sullivan*

Show, they attracted the largest television audience to date. Some commentators thought they were a breath of fresh air while others thought they would prove to be a short-lived craze. The evangelist Billy Graham broke the habit of a lifetime to watch them on television on a Sunday and concluded that their performance was symptomatic of "the uncertainties of the times and the confusion about us." *Newsweek*, on the other hand, called them a "band of evangelists" whose gospel was "fun."

As the Beatles hardly spoke on *The Ed Sullivan Show*, the conclusions of *Newsweek* and Billy Graham can only have been based on their singing "All My Loving," "Till There Was You," "She Loves You," "I Saw Her Standing There," and "I Want to Hold Your Hand." What they both detected from the Beatles' appearance, performance, and sound was that they were cutting loose. Their mind-set differed from the prevailing orthodoxy. Graham interpreted this as "confusion," a loss of the old certainties, while *Newsweek* saw it as "fun," a celebration of freedom.

The scenes at Beatles concerts where girls wept, screamed, and fainted were a topic of constant analysis in papers and magazines. What was the trigger? What did it symbolize? The Beatles had no clue. They knew it wasn't the music alone because they'd played similar sets just twelve months before to polite applause. Something was let loose around the end of 1963 that the British press dubbed Beatlemania, and it appeared to spread by replication. The more film and photographs of the mayhem that girls saw, the more they wanted to be a part of it.

The call to freedom that came from the Beatles led these girls into a state of abandon. For the duration of the concert they could completely ignore society's rules for appropriate conduct. They could shout, swoon, and wail. They could jump and writhe. They could mess their hair up and cry until their mascara was ruined. It didn't matter because, for that short period, breathing the same air as their idols, enveloped by the sound of screaming and the voices of their fellow fans, they were transported into a state of consciousness where "normality" seemed irrelevant. Some people drew parallels between their behavior and that of celebrants in a Pentecostal church "overcome by the Spirit" or participants in a shamanistic ritual.

Vance Packard, author of *The Hidden Persuaders* and an expert on techniques of persuasion and mass manipulation, wrote a piece for the *Saturday Evening Post* in 1964 in which he examined the effect of the Beatles. He wrote: "The subconscious need that they fill most expertly is in taking adolescent girls clear out of this world. The youngsters in the darkened audiences can let go all inhibitions in a quite primitive sense when the Beatles cut loose. They can retreat from rationality and individuality. Mob pathology takes over, and they are momentarily freed of all of civilization's restraints. The Beatles have been particularly adept at giving girls this release."

University of Massachusetts professor Nick Bromell puts forward a convincing argument that during Beatlemania it was the girls who surrendered to their passions who were a greater force for change than the Beatles themselves, because when John, Paul, George, and Ringo lost self-control it was usually with the help of drugs or alcohol and done in private. The girls used no artificial stimulants and didn't care who saw them. He suspects that the Beatles were embarrassed to be upstaged in such a way. "Their passion swelled into a force that made the lads from Liverpool look suddenly like little figurines of themselves," he wrote in *Tomorrow Never Knows*. "Acting for adolescents everywhere, they seized and made a world, taking power and space away from the control of adults. In creating Beatlemania, they were demonstrating the force of an impulse—leaders of the New Left would call it 'direction action' [*sic*]—that would drive young people just a few years later to seize university buildings and city streets."

It was virtually impossible to hear the Beatles speak during their concerts. When the public did get to hear them it was usually in a broadcast from a press conference. They rarely spoke about the burning issues of the day, mostly because they were hardly ever asked. To these show business reporters the Beatles were simply the latest Frank Sinatra, and Beatle-maniacs were bobby-soxers for the 1960s. Questions were inevitably limited to their hair, marital status, success, or first impressions of a new city. What did they think of New Orleans / Detroit / Pittsburgh? How different were Japanese / French / American fans from British / German / Australian fans? How long did they think they would last? No one asked them how they wrote their songs, what their words referred to, or what they believed.

Yet the way they handled the questions spoke volumes about their approach to life. What journalists would refer to as their "refreshing" or "irreverent" approach to interviews was frequently an exercise in surrealism. Their collective thinking refused to be bounded by traditional protocol or even logic. Asked "Does every city look the same?" John answered, "No. Some have trees. Some don't." Told that a psychiatrist in Detroit had said that the Beatles were a menace, George responded, "Psychiatrists are menaces too." When he was asked, "As you're confined to your room all day, what do you do?" George answered, "Oh, tennis and water polo." Once John was asked what he thought a bald-headed Beatle would look like. "Well," he said, "he'd look like a fella with no hair, wouldn't he?"

Those performances owed a lot to the humor of *The Goon Show* which, when it was first broadcast on BBC radio in 1953, was seen as a reaction to the stuffiness of postwar Britain. Spike Milligan, the scriptwriter, specialized in leaps of imagination, entertaining nonsense, engaging wordplay, and an abhorrence of clichés. He later considered his work to have been the "break out" that set the tone for the sixties and said that the sixties could be summed up as the decade when Victorianism finally ended. "The next group to come after us was the Beatles," he said in 1988. "Fortunately they were into music which was more universal than comedy. I think we started the whole thing." John had already agreed with him, saying in 1971, "We were the sons of *The Goon Show*. We were of age. We were just the extension of that rebellion, in a way."

The Beatles' humor was liberating because it was so unstuffy. It exposed shallow questions for what they were and showed that they would only play the press game on their own terms. "It's pointless trying to answer an idiotic question in a serious way," said George. "So we answered them humorously." They challenged the process of rational inquiry by picking up on unintended meanings in questions. The inference was that the irrational might yield more interesting results. After all, creative inspiration often came not by the application of relentless logic but from chance, mistakes, or previously unconsidered connections.

> **Question:** The French have not made up their minds about the Beatles. What do you think of them?
>
> **John:** Oh, we like the Beatles. They're gear. [slang for "great"]
>
> **Question:** Do you like topless bathing suits?
>
> **Ringo:** We've been wearing them for years.

They took the same spirit to the studio. In 1962 EMI ran Abbey Road like a military installation. Producers were its equivalent of commissioned officers; they dressed like executives and were referred to as Mr. This or Mr. That. Engineers wore white coats. There were even rules about the volumes at which instruments could be recorded. Great concern was expressed if it was thought likely that a phonograph stylus could jump when playing an EMI record because the sound was too loud. To the Beatles this rigidity was the antithesis of the spirit of rock 'n' roll and, gently at first, they challenged the rules. The answer to the question, "Why are things done this way?" was usually "Because they've always been this way," and for them that was an insufficient answer.

Their progressive leaps as writers and recording artists were generally the result of ignoring convention. It wasn't that they wanted to expunge the past—Paul in particular admired the songwriters of the 1920s and 1930s—but they had a vision far broader than what was considered permissible at the time. Why couldn't a song begin with a chorus ("Can't Buy Me Love"), a crashing chord ("A Hard Day's Night"), extended feedback ("I Feel Fine"), or a fade-*in* ("Eight Days a Week")? Why couldn't Ringo thump on a packing case ("Words of Love") or George play on an African drum ("Mr. Moonlight")? Why did singles all have to be less than three minutes long and be featured on current albums?

Fortunately, George Martin, although appearing to be an orthodox EMI career producer—military service, posh accent, correct posture, smoothed-back hair, necktie—was every bit as adventurous as the Beatles and as hungry for success. He'd produced albums for the Goons and had worked with experimental music but was also a trained musician (Guildhall School of Music, London) who knew his Bach from his Elgar. He was able to convert what they imagined into recorded sound. "I think we just grew through those years together, him as the straight man and us as the loonies," said George Harrison. "He was always there to interpret our madness."

By the end of 1964 the Beatles seemed to have everything that four young men could want. They were rich beyond their wildest dreams, had achieved their aim of outshining Elvis, were respected by their peers, and had all the drugs, drink, sex, cars, and gadgets that they could possibly want. Besides success the only other thing they had ever wanted was financial security, and now this was easily within their reach.

At this time they weren't looking to religion to inject a fresh sense of purpose. In October 1964, while touring Britain they told an interviewer from *Playboy* that they were "more agnostic than atheistic." John said, "If you say you don't believe in God, everybody assumes that you're antireligious and you probably think that's what we mean by that. We're not quite sure *what* we are. . . ." Ringo thought it was better that they admit to agnosticism than be hypocritical. According to John the first time they had mentioned their lack of faith, people "went potty. They couldn't take it."

John had a blasphemous streak, presumably because Christian teaching had played a larger role in his life than it had in the others. Ridiculing religion was his form of exorcism. Thelma McGough, John's girlfriend at art school, remembers that that when Pope Pius XII died on John's eighteenth birthday he made a cruel caricature of him begging to be let into heaven but being refused entry. Letters written from Hamburg to a fan named Lindy Ness in 1962 included cartoons of the crucifixion. One showed an electric guitar nailed to a cross. Another showed Jesus with God looking down at him with the caption: "God larfing, thinking 'Oh Christ!'"

Tony Sheridan, who had emerged from a fundamentalist Christian upbringing in Norwich, England, to play rock 'n' roll for a living, remembers John spying a pile of dried-up vomit in Hamburg when they were sharing a flat in

1961 and planting a cross made from the balsa wood of a matchbox on its summit. "He turned it into a Calvary," says Sheridan. "He liked to shock. He was grateful for attention of any kind. He could be cruel about anyone that he thought was weak or vulnerable. He just knocked them, but in a way I think he was knocking himself."

On the road they would invent sacrilegious verses to well-known hymns, and there is a recording of them in a hotel room in 1963 with Gerry Marsden of Gerry and the Pacemakers reading the Bible in slurred and deranged voices to gales of laughter. Together they recited the entire seventeenth chapter of 1 Kings, presumably from a bedside Gideon's Bible. They then sang comic versions of Psalm 23 ("The LORD is my shepherd") and Psalm 24 ("The earth is the LORD's, and the fulness thereof").

They knew very little about world religions but felt that their instincts were inimical to Christianity, at least to what they knew of Christianity from rudimentary lessons at school and differing degrees of church attendance. They didn't express hostility to the church. When clergymen came backstage to speak to them on British tours, perhaps in their capacity as theater chaplains, the Beatles would encourage them to update their music and recommend listening to American gospel. One vicar, Rev. Ronald Gibbons, even made national headlines by inviting the Beatles to record "O come, all ye faithful yeah! yeah! yeah!" because, he reasoned, "The Beatles cult can be the very shot in the arm that the Church needs today."

"I've tried Christianity," said Ringo. "I've read the Bible. I've prayed. I've sung hymns. I've done everything our religion talks about, but I really feel about vicars and priests the same way that I feel about politicians. None of them give me any confidence that they're right. I'm not saying the Bible doesn't mean all it says, but it doesn't mean all that for me."

In July 1964, just after the London premiere of *A Hard Day's Night*, Derek Taylor was quoted by *Saturday Evening Post* writer Al Aronowitz as saying,

It's incredible, absolutely incredible! Here are these four boys from Liverpool. They're rude, they're profane, they're vulgar, and they've taken over the world. It's as if they've founded a new religion. They're completely anti-Christ. I mean, I'm anti-Christ as well, but they're so anti-Christ that they shock me, which isn't an easy thing.

But I'm obsessed with them. Isn't everybody? I'm obsessed with their honesty. And the people who like them most are the people who should be outraged most. In Australia, for example, each time we'd arrive at an airport it was as if [French President] De Gaulle had landed, or, better yet, the Messiah. The routes were lined solid with people. Cripples threw away their sticks. Sick people rushed up to the car as if a touch from one of the boys would make them well again. Old women stood watching with their grandchildren and, as we'd pass by, I could see the look on their faces. It was as if some savior had arrived and people were happy and relieved, as if things somehow were going to be better now.

What Taylor meant by saying they were "anti-Christ," and why he would boast such a thing to a representative of a mainstream American magazine, was baffling. The quote would live to haunt him, being repeatedly brought up by those who thought the Beatles were an evil influence on the young or even that they were agents of communism. After all, this wasn't some wild-eyed religious fanatic saying that the Beatles were anti-Christ. This was one of their closest friends, someone with a journalistic background who treasured words.

Twenty years later, in his book *Fifty Years Adrift*, Taylor offered a partial explanation. "I was often called in on this quote, not by Brian or the Beatles, but my own conscience. If I did say it, I didn't mean it, because not one of us— Brian, Beatles or I—was really anti-Christ. We *were*, however, uncommitted and this is what Al must have picked up on. His piece was nevertheless warm and generous, long and detailed, and established him as one of our gang."

Aronowitz would prove to be a pivotal character in their development. He was different from the journalists they were used to meeting. He was hip. In the past he had been immersed in jazz, folk, and the writing of the Beats. He had met Jack Kerouac, hung out with Miles Davis, and had Bob Dylan as a house guest. The Beatles appealed to his Greenwich Village, bohemian, poetry-loving, establishment-hating spirit. He would become the vital link between their party-making, scream-inducing existentialism and the reflective, dream-like mysticism that would turn them into shamans for their generation.

Chapter Six

Nowhere Man

I don't want to be fiddling round the world singing "It's been a hard day's night" when I'm thirty, do I?
　　　　　　　　　　　　　　　　　　　　—John Lennon, 1964

Personally I'm a bit fed up of touring.
　　　　　　　　　　　　　　　　　　　　—George Harrison, 1964

At first we wanted to make money. Now we've got it. We've got a fantastic platform of money to dive off into anything.
　　　　　　　　　　　　　　　　　　　　—Paul McCartney, 1965

See, when you start putting out messages people start asking you "What's the message?"
　　　　　　　　　　　　　　　　　　　　—John Lennon, 1970

*I*t's remarkable in retrospect how soon the thrill of Beatlemania subsided for the Beatles. The full-blown phenomenon is usually dated to November 1963 when they appeared at the London Palladium and were met by a level of fan hysteria that hadn't been seen before in Britain. Three months later they received their unprecedented rapturous welcome in America. Yet, by the end of 1964 they were already weary of being Beatles. What had started as a way of avoiding work had itself become work, with its own timetables, uniforms, responsibilities, employers, and employees.

As a nonwriting member, Ringo was under the least pressure. His happy-go-lucky attitude, extremely endearing to the fans, was hugely important in keeping his colleagues sane. Paul enjoyed being a Beatle and rose to the challenge of dealing with the press, officialdom, and fans. At press conferences he was always the one to avert potential controversies and to offer coherent answers when the others were peddling amusing nonsense. If a misunderstanding could be avoided by adding an explanatory note, he was the one to do it. He approached his job as a Beatle with a sense of responsibility and pride.

George and John were the most disappointed by fame. Although their backgrounds differed, they were the most naturally rebellious of the Beatles. They both resented authority, hated the fuss that came with success, and were skeptical of the worship they were receiving. George had always been intense about his craft as a guitarist. He studied records, invested in new instruments, and wanted his breaks and riffs to be appreciated. For him, the screaming was an insult to his musicianship. What was the point of performing for thousands of fans if the sound you were making could barely be heard? "The more fame we got the more people came to see us," he said in 1966. "Everyone was making such a noise that it got to a point where nobody could hear us. So, over the last two years nobody has heard us on stage. Consequently our performances have deteriorated to such an extent that our stage shows are terrible. They can't hear it and we can't hear it. That's why it's terrible."

He was also the most ruminative of the Beatles and was known as "the quiet Beatle." It wasn't that he had nothing to say but that he enjoyed contemplation. In 1964 he was only twenty years old, and the frenzy around the Beatles had overwhelmed him. He complained in June of that year to *Rave* magazine that the Beatles were being treated as if they were just things, not human beings. "I only asked to be successful," he once told Maureen Cleave. "I didn't ask to be famous." The attention he was getting seemed out of proportion to his actual achievement. Only two years before he could happily walk the streets of Speke without being accosted and be treated as plain George by his friends. Now he was regarded as an object of fascination, as though he were a being with mysterious powers.

"George didn't understand why he, George Harrison, was famous," says Pattie Boyd, his ex-wife, who first met him on the set of *A Hard Day's Night* in 1964. "He wanted the answer to that. It was a permanent question in his mind. He couldn't grasp what had happened. As a group the Beatles had something major to offer, but it always confused him. He didn't understand. He just saw himself as the boy from Liverpool. Because he was also extremely humble, what he couldn't recognize was that he was so talented. He was a great guitarist with a most beautiful voice who could write fabulous songs. He dismissed that. He couldn't see it."

The issue of fame and recognition didn't bother John as much. He'd always been arrogant about his talent, believing that he was an undiscovered genius even when he was a child. In one interview he said that when he was a teenager he used to read reviews of great artists and wonder why he hadn't been mentioned, even though he hadn't yet created anything. He told Mimi that she'd regret throwing out his early drawings and poetry because one day he was going to be famous. When he received poor reports at school, he believed that this was the fault of the teachers who weren't smart enough to see his gifts.

What did concern him was that he'd become a Beatle in order to be free, to avoid having to socialize with people he didn't like. Now, precisely because he was a Beatle, he'd lost that freedom and had to be polite to dignitaries, socialites, politicians, and businesspeople. He was free to take part in orgies, spend large amounts of money on adult toys, and order room service at any time of day, but he wasn't free to walk the streets without a disguise, make ordinary friends, or take time off whenever he wanted to. The demands of being a Beatle were becoming greater than the demands of being a head teacher or a Member of Parliament. There were schedules to keep, albums to deliver, and shareholders to please.

John would later explain his position like this: "The idea of being a rock 'n' roll musician sort of suited my talents and mentality, and the freedom *was* great. But then I found I wasn't free. I'd got boxed in. It wasn't just because of my contract, but the contract was a physical manifestation of being in prison. And with that I might as well have gone to a nine-to-five job as to carry on the way I was carrying on. Rock 'n' roll was not fun anymore."

He said that being a Beatle was like living in "a moving hothouse." The environment of flashbulbs, screams, spotlights, microphones, and camera lenses seemed artificial. The outside world had become something the group could only glimpse from hotel windows or on TV. A change was bound to come. "We've been mushroom grown, forced to grow up a bit quick," said John. "It's like having 30- to 40-year-old heads on 20-year-old bodies. We had to develop more sides, more attitudes. If you're a bus driver, you usually have a bus driver's attitude. But we had to be more than four mop-heads up on a stage. We had to grow up or we'd have been swamped."

Discontent began to creep into the Beatles songs. The album *A Hard Day's Night* had showcased the Beatles as vibrant, youthful, and optimistic, the essence of the swinging sixties, but, by contrast, *Beatles for Sale*, released at the end of 1964, was downbeat. The title itself, although intended as irony, hinted at diminishing reserves. If you sell yourself, you become a servant of your buyers. "We're money makers first," John had told *Playboy*, "and entertainers second." The group looked drained of energy in the cover photograph. Wrapped in heavy dark coats and surrounded by an autumnal haze they stared at the camera without the flicker of a smile on their faces.

Of fourteen songs on the album only eight were Lennon-McCartney originals, and the mood was unusually bleak, rescued only by Paul's optimism in

"Eight Days a Week" and "Every Little Thing." Each of John's songs was either about being stood up, let down, or cheated on. The only genuinely fifty-fifty composition, "Baby's in Black," was about a girl still fixated on a past boyfriend. The rest of the album was filled with rock 'n' roll tracks that they'd first heard as teenagers and which they'd used in their sets back in Liverpool and Hamburg.

The biggest artistic influence on their work over the past twelve months had been the songs of Bob Dylan. They'd been given the album *The Freewheelin' Bob Dylan* while in Paris and were gripped by it. Although Paul had been the first Beatle to hear Dylan, it was John who most closely identified with him. He admired his facility with language and the raw honesty of his observations. Beatles' songs up to now, as John was well aware, were not windows into their souls. They didn't openly declare their fears and ambitions. They didn't touch on wider social issues. Dylan's songs, on the other hand, revealed his passions. His approach to songwriting was closer to that of the artists that John had studied at college and the playwrights and novelists that Paul had read at the Liverpool Institute than it was to the skilled tunesmiths of New York's Brill Building, who wrote hits during normal office hours and customized their material for particular artists and audiences.

The earliest songwriting heroes of both John and Paul were people like Jerry Leiber and Mike Stoller, who had hits with the Coasters, the Drifters, Ben E. King, and Elvis, or Gerry Goffin and Carole King, who had hits with the Shirelles, the Chiffons, and Little Eva. They even admired older writers like Rodgers and Hammerstein. Although they would often write autobiographically, these writers were not trying to disclose the contents of their souls. Their guiding principle was not "Is this song an authentic expression of where I am in my life?" but "Will this song work? Will it sell? Will it relate to the experience of the audience?" Dylan was different. His roots were in mountain ballads, blues, union songs, spirituals, and work hollers rather than in vaudeville or Broadway. He used imagery, allusion, and metaphor. He wrote about love but it was mature, adult love rather than teenage obsession. *Freewheelin'* included such Dylan classics as "Masters of War," "A Hard Rain's A-Gonna Fall," and "Don't Think Twice, It's All Right."

The Beatles must have felt that their songs were infantile in comparison. Their current single when they discovered him was "I Want to Hold Your Hand," whereas his was "Blowin' in the Wind." There was a serious side to Dylan's songs but also a counterbalancing humor, whereas Beatles songs, up to this point, had been neither overly serious nor hilariously funny. There was also a moral and spiritual dimension to Dylan's work. His songs took place in a world of moral absolutes where angels kept guard and death was not the end. It was a world that John, in particular, recognized.

Buoyed up by his experience of Dylan's music, John was encouraged to explore his own emotions with greater candor. While promoting his book *In His Own Write* in March 1964, he'd been interviewed by the English journalist Kenneth Allsop for the BBC TV program *Tonight*. Before the interview, Allsop, the program's long-serving anchor, had spoken at length to John about his work and had pressed him to explain why there was such a disparity between his books and his songs. The stories revealed his anger, humor, and love of wordplay whereas these passions weren't exhibited in his lyrics to date. In Allsop's view, they were just revised versions of the same old story about me loving you and her loving him.

Although a generation older than John and a veteran of World War II, Allsop had a better understanding than most of his mind-set. In 1958 he had written a book about the changes that were then taking place in Britain: *The Angry Decade: A Survey of the Cultural Revolt of the 1950s*. He also wrote poetry and had worked on national newspapers. What he said to John had a significant effect. It led him to appreciate that he was avoiding self-disclosure in his songs by projecting himself into fictional situations. He started to write more from, and for, himself. Years later he told his confidante Elliot Mintz that "In My Life" marked a significant turning point in his writing life.

"I would just try to express what I felt about myself, which I had done in my books," said John. "I think it was Dylan who helped me realize that. I had a sort of professional song writer's attitude to writing pop songs, but to express myself I would write *A Spaniard in the Works* or *In His Own Write*, the personal stories which were expressions of my personal emotions. I'd have a separate songwriting John Lennon who wrote songs for the sort of meat market and I didn't consider them, the lyrics or anything, to have any depth at all. Then I started being *me* about the songs."

The first fruit of the new approach to songwriting was "I'll Cry Instead," written in May 1964, with its admission "I've got a chip on my shoulder that's bigger than my feet / I can't talk to people that I meet." It was a brutally direct song in which he admits on the one hand to shyness and a fear of vulnerability and on the other to a cruel streak that gained pleasure from hurting women. It was a bold move at the time for a pop star to admit to having a chip on his shoulder. His later confessional material such as "Jealous Guy," "Crippled Inside," and "Isolation" was a continued exploration of this fundamental discovery.

Two months after recording "I'll Cry Instead" he recorded "I'm a Loser," the title not only meaning "I'm someone who has just lost someone that I love" but "I am a failure in my life." The song originated in the phrase that he'd first heard in America and developed into one of his most intimate and revealing pieces of writing. This was John, the renowned tough guy, shedding tears.

When the song was released on *Beatles for Sale* it was not recognized as a cry from the heart. There was no reason that it should have been. After all, John appeared to be simply telling the story of someone who had lost the woman he loved. This couldn't be autobiographical because John was happily married and had a lovely baby son. Yet, as we now know, he was inching further toward full disclosure. Whenever John was asked which of the songs he wrote as a Beatle he still admired he would always mention "I'm a Loser."

The song's premise was that he was playing a character. The public view of him was incomplete. Although the Beatles had always been honest about themselves, they were only honest up to a point. They didn't lie, but they rarely revealed themselves in any depth. Secretly John thought that if all his inadequacies, fears, and failures were made known, he wouldn't be held in such high affection. As Beatle John he was duping people, producing fan mania through withholding the full truth. His work after this point would be characterized by a growing need to expose himself as he really was to see how much undiluted Lennon people would tolerate. Would the public still need him, would it still feed him, if it could see all his weaknesses? Would it love him with spectacles? Would it love him naked?

He detested having to be affable. Whereas Paul accepted that it went with the territory of being a show business star, John felt that it was insincere and therefore fraudulent. His inclination was to let his feelings show, just as he was likely to confess the truth in interviews when what was required was a tactfully evasive reply. In October 1964 Ray Coleman reported for *Melody Maker* from backstage at a Beatles concert. His article opened with John looking "mournfully" into a mirror and applying stage makeup. "I wish I could paint a smile on too," he told Coleman. "Don't think I'll manage one tonight. Sometimes I wonder how the hell we keep it up."

It was inevitable that the Beatles and Dylan would one day meet. The day came on August 28, 1964, in New York. Al Aronowitz, the broker of the meeting, prided himself on fashioning connections between the worlds of hip and pop, believing that pop would be better if it was hipper. Earlier in the year he'd taken Dylan to meet Allen Ginsberg, a fortuitous meeting that resulted in a lifelong friendship between the poet and the musician as well as work collaborations such as Ginsberg's appearance on the Rolling Thunder Tour and his inner sleeve notes for *Desire*. "Bob and the Beatles *deserved* to know one another," said Aronowitz.

John was fascinated by Aronowitz's knowledge of the Beats and quizzed him about it when he came to Liverpool in July 1964 to write a second story for the *Saturday Evening Post*. He also wanted to know about marijuana, the Beats' drug of preference.

There has always been controversy over whether the Beatles had encountered pot before this time. If what they told Bob Dylan's road manager Victor Maymudes is true they had. "They had tried it, but they didn't get high," said Maymudes. "They didn't have the experience. It was cheapo or whatever. And they knew about hash and stuff like that, but they never got the rush. They had never laughed until tears came out of their eyes."

Aronowitz had been turned on in San Francisco in 1959 by Beat poet Michael McClure and his then-wife, Joanna, and believed that it had transformed his life, making it possible for him to ditch many of the values he'd inherited rather than chosen. "It was as if someone had taken a filter off my vision," he says. "Suddenly I saw how stupid everything was, especially the law against marijuana. All of the values of my middle-class upbringing suddenly disappeared."

From that point on he became an evangelist for pot, considering it to be a wonder drug that would bring about a new society of justice, freedom, and everlasting highs. He surmised that if the Beatles were to turn on, they too would have their filters removed and would, like him, become "Johnny Appleseeds wanting to tell the world about marijuana." He saw himself as part of an apostolic succession. McClure, who'd turned him on, had hung out with Kerouac and had read poetry at the celebrated Six Gallery reading in San Francisco in 1955 when Ginsberg premiered his epic poem *Howl*. Now he could pass on that gift to these people who had the potential to evangelize more people than the Beats ever had access to with a message that was not dissimilar.

Aronowitz liked John but considered him a "pill-head." He tried to discourage him from using manmade chemical cocktails such as amphetamines to get high. Using branded drugs made by the pharmaceutical giants was to be manipulated by an industry that had an unspoken interest in developing dependency. Marijuana, he argued, was natural. It was the drug used by Indian mystics and Native American shamans. The Beatles at the time regarded pot as a dangerous drug. "They sort of considered pot smokers to be in the same category as junkies," said Aronowitz. "Like the DEA, they put grass in the same category as heroin. Finally John said he would try some if I brought it to him."

That opportunity came after the Beatles had played a concert at the Forest Hills Tennis Stadium in Queens. Aronowitz invited Dylan to come to the Delmonico Hotel at 502 Park Avenue, where the Beatles were staying, and it was in their suite with Brian Epstein, Neil Aspinall, Derek Taylor, and Mal Evans in attendance that Aronowitz introduced Dylan and Victor Maymudes to the Beatles, and then Dylan, who was already drunk, took a bag of grass and rolled a joint for them. They retired to a bedroom, lit it, and shared it before Maymudes, an expert at the craft, rolled joints for each of them. Their first reaction to the drug was to burst into hysterical laughter. The second reaction was similar to the one that Aronowitz had felt five years previously. As Paul put it, he felt that he had "discovered the meaning of life."

Paul recalls that he felt that his mind had literally been expanded. Everything immediately fell into place. All his anxieties were swept away. "I suddenly felt like a reporter . . . ," he said. "I wanted to tell my people what it was. I was the great discoverer on this sea of pot in New York." He wrote down his revelation on a piece of paper and gave it to Evans for safe keeping. The next morning Evans handed Paul the paper and written on it were four words: "There are seven levels."

At first he thought this was hilarious but later found that great spiritual significance is attached to the number seven. In Jewish thought it is the number that denotes perfection in creation—seven days of the week, seven colors of the rainbow, and seven notes on the musical scale. Christianity has the Seven Deadly Sins and the Seven Holy Virtues. More pertinent to his experience were Buddhism's seven levels of consciousness (physical, emotional, creative, devotional, dissolved ego, pure awareness, and nirvana) that roughly correspond with the seven chakras of Hindu meditation (rod, sacral, solar plexus, heart, throat, head, and crown).

In an unpublished manuscript left behind after his death in 2001 Victor Maymudes recalled that when they met up the next day Paul gave him a huge hug and said, "It was so great. It's all your fault because I love this pot." Maymudes commented, "He had great thoughts about music and felt it was just magical. He really got into it more than the other guys. He was full of what pot had done for him and what a great night he'd had."

Apart from the fleeting rhapsody John and George had experienced as children, the drug had given the Beatles the closest thing any of them had had to a mystical experience. William James, in his classic study *The Varieties of Religious Experience*, claimed that the four marks of mysticism were ineffability (an experience beyond words), noetic quality (insights into depths of truth that can't be plumbed by the intellect), transience (can't be sustained), and passivity (a feeling of being overtaken by a superior power). James concluded that while mystical experiences were transitory, the effects were long-term. "Some memory of the content always remains, and a profound sense of their importance. They modify the inner life of the subject between the times of their recurrence."

Ringo was so impressed with the experience that he asked Maymudes if he'd have to smoke pot for the rest of his life to maintain the feeling. Maymudes told him that it wouldn't stay with him. He'd have to keep smoking. "Ringo asked me about pot in depth," Maymudes wrote. "He asked me about smoking it, how much it cost, where it was grown, and things like that. Paul talked about how he'd never be the same again. Each one of them had a different approach to the subject."

Hemp and its products, cannabis and hashish (pot, weed, reefer, grass), played a part in some forms of mystical religion. According to the historian of religion Mircea Eliade, ancient Iranians and Scythians used hemp to bring about states of ecstasy in their shamanistic rituals, often when combined with music. Some historians of religion believe that the plant "soma" referred to in the ancient Vedic hymns of India may be hemp. The drug-induced visions of a few could supply the basis of a religion with succeeding generations of followers trying to evoke the original vision through such natural means as music, dance, chant, sensory deprivation, and meditation.

Aronowitz believed that pot would change the Beatles and thus their music. As the music changed, the listening world would get the message, and the gospel of liberation through marijuana would spread more rapidly than ever before. "This was a marriage made in heaven," he said. "I knew I was stage-managing a major event, certainly in the history of pop and maybe even in the overall history of culture. . . . In some vague sense I was helping Hercules divert the mainstream, which would soon eddy in pop's psychedelic era."

The immediate effect of the drug on the Beatles was to give them a feeling of freedom. The explosion of laughter at the Delmonico Hotel was a release from the constraint of stardom. As Beatles they were restricted to hotel suites, dressing rooms, concert halls, recording studios, and private clubs, but with marijuana they could mentally slip away, wherever they happened to be. They could be day-trippers. As Paul would put it in his hymn to pot, "Got to Get You into My Life," smoking was like taking a ride to an unknown destination. You didn't know what you would discover there.

The long-term effect was that it made them question boundaries. Their agnosticism had led them to the conclusion that, as far as it was possible to determine, the material world was all that there was, but their marijuana experience suggested other dimensions to reality that couldn't be appreciated by the normal waking consciousness. Maybe there truly was more than meets the eye. Seven levels, even. "Dope puts your mind into a different sphere, and it opens up the consciousness a bit more," says Pattie Boyd.

To claim that it opens the consciousness assumes that normal consciousness is inferior to the state produced by marijuana, that the mind in its natural condition is closed. An equally credible explanation would be that pot allows the brain to be deceived or provides an illusion of freedom by inhibiting its rational centers. What can't be disputed is that the drug affects the consciousness and changes perceptions. It has been used in religious ritual, most blatantly by the Rastafarians of Jamaica, and by others who think that it reveals truths or even that it enables them to commune with God.

The Beatles' answers to questions they were asked about religion changed after they began smoking pot. In 1964 when a reporter asked, "Would any of you care to give any of your views on religion or politics?" John answered, "We're not interested in either," but by 1965 the indifference was giving way to cautious conjecture. "I believe in the supernatural," said Paul at a press conference in Chicago. He even made the surprising admission that he'd "got hung up on séances and the tarot." At the same conference John said he didn't know what he felt about religion, but "I'm no atheist, that's true. I believe in something that is. I'm not the godless sort, but neither am I saintly." Even Ringo had moderated his position. "You can't say there's nothing up there because you don't know," he said. "Atheists are as bad as those righteous types. . . . But if I had visions, I'd take up churching."

Musicians who regularly use marijuana claim that the drug alters the way they hear music and thus they way they create it. Time appears to slow, allowing more attention to details that otherwise would have been overlooked. These details then tend to be imbued with extraordinary significance. The sensual aspects of music are enhanced, and there is a heightened sensitivity to the quality of sound. Music stimulates both mind and body. It was after his discovery of pot that Paul began playing bass guitar as a lead instrument and developed the heavier, more enveloping sound of "Ticket to Ride" and "Drive My Car," tracks, which when played loudly had a more physical impact than past recordings.

Under the influence of pot, bizarre associations between sounds are made, and a freedom to draw from a wider variety of musical idioms opens up. The partitions in the brain's normal filing system are temporarily removed. As one pot-smoking jazz musician says, "You access more of your total musical memory to solve musical problems." Paul was now living in the West End of London at the family home of his actress girlfriend, Jane Asher. When smoking pot here late at night, Paul would listen to esoteric music supplied by Barry Miles, a friend of Jane's brother Peter, most of which he would previously have dismissed as too cerebral or unexciting: electronic music by Luciano Berio, John's Cage's *Indeterminacy*, Albert Ayler's *Bells* and *Spirits Awake*, the jazz of Pharaoh Saunders, Ornette Coleman, and Sun Ra, and a Folkways double album released in 1959 *The Way of Elheiji Zen-Buddhist Ceremony*, one track of which consisted of a bell being rung once a minute. *Rubber Soul* was the first Beatles album to draw not only from the English past but from other cultures. George Martin played baroque piano on "In My

Life," a sitar was used on "Norwegian Wood," and the guitar on "Girl" imitated the Greek bazouki.

John Dunbar, another friend of Peter Asher who used to smoke pot with Paul, says, "It opened them up to other things. When you smoke pot your old prejudices die off and you become interested in other stuff. Your ears are opened. I think they became much more thoughtful all round. They went from a boozy culture to a much more intellectual one."

Pot made the Beatles more reflective. Prior to late 1964 they didn't think a lot about the big questions, but starting in 1965 they pondered more on the purpose in life beyond good times and financial security. Asked about making money in April 1965, John said: "I want no more from being a record star. I'm not disinterested, but there is more now than to make good records and sell them." At the end the year *New Musical Express* editor Alan Smith reported: "One thing that struck me backstage—the Beatles have become much quieter of late. There's a calm, mature atmosphere about them. It isn't all jokes and drinks and living it up."

It may be significant that it was only after pot that death came into their songs. The first mention, in "No Reply," was used as an overstatement ("I nearly died") but in "In My Life," John's poignant song of nostalgia for his Liverpool childhood, the reference is an intimation of mortality. After Paul had written the verses to "We Can Work It Out," John added a couplet about life being too short for fussing and fighting.

Yet death was no longer such a sobering thought. It was, to them, just another transition. In "Rain" John suggested that there was no difference between sunshine and rain. The crucial factor was not the weather but our attitude toward it. There is no good or bad weather, just convenient and inconvenient. With a transformed consciousness we could be equally happy in either condition. This fit in with later comments he made about death being no more than going from one bus to another. It was nothing to get hung up about. Reality was in your head. Rain? "It was just a state of mind."

Pot introduced a more laissez-faire attitude to the Beatles, according to Paul. It was an antidote to the pressure of fame. When they filmed *Help!* in 1965, it caused them to break into fits of mirth so often that much of what was shot was unusable. In his book *John, Paul, George, Ringo and Me*, Tony Barrow says that one reason the Bahamas was chosen as a location was because there was more opportunity for the group to openly smoke joints without fear of arrest. Paul has said that it introduced surrealism and abstraction to their work. A different state of consciousness promoted unconventional trains of thought. "It's this not conforming and wanting to do something different which keeps our music different," he said.

One of the most-cited examples was when John took "Rain" home to review in his music room. As John later explained he was high that night. His impaired dexterity meant that he fed the tape in wrong to the take-up spool and as a result part of the track played backward. (George Martin disputes this version of events, claiming that he made the suggestion while in the studio.) To John in his stoned state this sounded beautiful, and the next day he asked Martin to add a section of reversed vocals to the end of the song. The eerie, distorted sound was unlike anything that had been heard on a pop single before. "That one was the gift of God," he said in 1980. "Of JA actually, the god of marijuana. So JA gave me that one."

The Beatles became alert to the creative possibilities contained in mistakes, appreciating that they can often offer an escape from the restrictions of logic. Thus the feedback created by a guitar left leaning against a speaker led to the introduction to "I Feel Fine," a misread line in "You've Got to Hide Your Love Away" turned "two foot tall" into "two foot small," and a malapropism that Ringo uttered when extremely tired ("It's been a hard day's night") became not just the title of a song but a movie.

The studio became a laboratory where things were discovered rather than a factory where products were manufactured to a predetermined design. "Eight Days a Week," recorded in October 1964, was the first song that they had taken to the studio unfinished and worked on until they achieved a version that pleased them. This marked a changed approach to recording, illustrating their willingness to extend their querying of convention.

"I think that pot made them concentrate a lot more on music just as they would notice more details if they were studying paintings," says Barry Miles. "It certainly gave them a very different high. Instead of being a front brain depressant, like alcohol, it expanded their consciousness. It made them more reflective. Paul was very into it."

One of the first tracks written after the night at the Delmonico with Dylan was Paul's "She's a Woman," an experimental sound that included their first use of drug slang, a reference to being turned on, and which was the first Beatles song to exceed three minutes. *Help!* was the first complete album written and recorded after pot; it didn't show any obvious signs of change except on the title track. It's now generally known that the song was a genuine cry from the heart by John, but there appears to be a subtext that refers to drugs.

The song is about a life crisis. He was once self-assured, independent, and secure but something has happened that has destroyed his confidence and left him needing help. The effects are mentioned, but not the event that changed everything. It could be that his experience of marijuana had momentarily destabilized him. The line "Now I find I've changed my mind," rather than meaning "Now I've altered my choice," could mean "Now I've altered my state of consciousness"—exchanging the unenlightened mind for the enlightened mind—which would then make sense of the next line, "I've opened up the doors," perhaps a reference to Aldous Huxley's book *The Doors of Perception*, first published in 1954, detailing the exiled British writer's experience of mescaline. (Huxley's title, later to inspire Jim Morrison's group, the Doors, was itself taken from William Blake: "If the doors of perception were cleansed everything would appear to man as it is, infinite").

Such a reading of the lyric would make sense of a lot of otherwise unfathomable lines. It would explain why his life had changed "in oh so many ways" and also why he needed someone to put his "feet back on the ground." The drug experience could be as bewildering as it was exhilarating, particularly to someone like John who suffered from a frail sense of worth and was in constant need of reassurance. Of course, in the context of the nutty movie the song didn't alert its listeners to psychic disturbances and crises of identity. It was just another fun Beatles song. Pete Shotton, his old friend from Woolton, had a hunch that the song was addressed to him.

The real turning point was *Rubber Soul*. The cover was similar to *Beatles for Sale*. The four of them stood facing the camera in exactly the same line-up—George, John, Ringo, and then Paul—and there was foliage in the background. But this time the leaves were green rather than brown, and the boys, although still not smiling, didn't look burned out. They looked cool and slightly detached. Instead of looking at us directly, as they had done on the cover of *Beatles for Sale*, they looked down on us, although only John made eye contact. They were above us.

But the most instantly recognizable difference was that both words and image were distorted. The Beatles stretched diagonally across the cover so that George was in the bottom left corner and Paul was in the top right. The lettering looked as rubbery as the title sounded, the lower halves of each letter bulging out as if the words had been printed on a balloon and then inflated. It was the sort of typeface that would soon become familiar on psychedelic posters and doodles in student notebooks.

The choice of portrait was indicative of the pot-inspired creativity. This was the first cover that they had a free rein in designing—the choice up to them had been made by the record company—and photographer Robert Freeman was projecting transparencies of his session with them onto a piece of white card for the Beatles to make a choice. The card bent, causing the picture to distort, and they seized on this image as the way they wanted to look. Previously they would have waited for the card to straighten, but now they embraced such accidents. They asked Freeman to reproduce this distortion for the finished artwork because it had the same dreamlike quality as the songs and suggested an altered state of consciousness.

Rubber Soul was a transitional album between the physical "beat music" of *Help!* and the more cerebral music of *Revolver*. There are elements of the old Beatles in Paul's songs "Drive My Car," "You Won't See Me," "I'm Looking through You," and "Michelle," but even these are different from the standard fare of the early days. "Drive My Car" is about a powerful woman who controls her man, "I'm Looking through You" about a threat to a girlfriend who has changed too much, and "You Won't See Me" about a broken relationship. "You could almost smell the pungent smoke on the album," said former NEMs employee Peter Brown in his book *The Love You Make*. "There was no doubt about it; Dylan had given them the key that opened a door to a new dimension in pop music, and they took the youth of the world across the threshold with them."

"Norwegian Wood" and "Drive My Car" were both intended to be humorous, perhaps partly inspired by Dylan's flights of fancy on songs like "I Shall Be Free" and partly by the hilarity that pot produced. Paul told *New Musical Express* that they'd written "some funny songs," and just prior to the release of *Rubber Soul* he said, with reference to "Norwegian Wood," "It's something new for us. It's just that we're a bit sick so we thought we'd write something funny."

"The Word," by contrast, was serious. In his 1971 interview with *Rolling Stone* John told Jann Wenner that he regarded it as his first message song. Although to fans at the time the love it advocated probably sounded no different from the love of "From Me to You," it was the first time John had written about love in the universal, spiritual sense, rather than the personal, erotic sense. Rather than linking love with feeling good, he links it with freedom and enlightenment. This is transformative love, the selfless *agapē* of the New Testament, the love he'd previously read about in the "good and the bad books" but which he has only recently understood.

It was the love that he had felt when smoking. This was the first song that he had composed with Paul under the influence, and they decorated the lyric sheet in bright colors to reflect the drug-hazed feeling of the moment. He was writing about love as the primal energy of the universe, often hidden from us because of our dominant egos. He now believed that these impediments could be removed. "The Word" was the prototype of "All You Need Is Love," "Within You without You," and "The End."

In the Christian theology that John was familiar with, "the word" was another way of saying "the gospel" or "the word of God." In the parable of the Sower and the Seed in the Gospel of Mark, for instance, the sower sows "the word." Contemporary evangelists speak of "speaking the word." John clearly intended "The Word" to convey two meanings: "a unit of speech or writing" (i.e., 'love' is a word), and "the gospel as embodying divine revelation" (i.e., love is the message of salvation).

It was the first taste of John's style of preaching. "Say the word and be like me" is a command. He was establishing himself as an enlightened person qualified to guide others. "Now that I know what I feel must be right / I'm here to show everybody the light." What could be more evangelistic? "It could be a Salvation Army song," Paul admitted at the time. "The word is 'love,' but it could be 'Jesus.' It isn't, mind you, but it could be." It was also a testimony. He had been in the darkness; now he was in the light, and the key to his transformation was to have understanding, an understanding made possible by drugs.

> In the beginning I misunderstood
> But now I've got it, the word is good.
> —"The Word"

What was his misunderstanding? It could have been his agnosticism, which had ruled out the mystical. It could have been his early nominal Christianity that didn't allow him to see the truths behind the memory verses. Or it could have been his normal waking consciousness that didn't appreciate the intricacy of reality—the "eyes closed" he would later refer to in "Strawberry Fields Forever." Whatever he was alluding to, he was recognizing a break with the past and the development of a new vision.

Amphetamines and alcohol, their drugs of choice so far, had made them energetic, outgoing, and often aggressive. They were drugs that encouraged communal experience, letting off steam, and dancing. Pot had the opposite effect. It made them feel mellow, introspective, and peaceful. It quietened them down and led them to appreciate that music could have effects other than making people want to twist, shake, and scream. "Cannabis makes people peaceful," said Ringo. "We're all saying peace and taking peaceful drugs."

Three weeks before recording "The Word," the Beatles had recorded "Nowhere Man," a song that John had written quickly after five unproductive hours searching for his muse. The moment he abandoned his quest, both the words and music came to him fully formed. It could have been the frustration of trying to write that suggested the subject matter. A composer with writer's block feels like a nowhere man who knows not where he's going to.

Another philosophical song, it provided great material for literary critics who saw parallels with characters in plays by Harold Pinter and Samuel Beckett, for sociologists who thought it was a condemnation of modern-day ennui, and preachers who thought that, in a style evocative of Ecclesiastes, the Beatles were admitting that their fabulous life of kicks had led to despair and emptiness. But the nowhere man with no point of view was not John. John was addressing an unenlightened person, beseeching him to discover what he'd been missing. Before John turned on, he misunderstood, and he refers to the nowhere man as blind because he only sees what he wants to see (like the unenlightened person in "Strawberry Fields Forever" whose eyes are closed).

The song built like a sermon. The question at the end of the opening stanza, "Isn't he a bit like you and me?" had a rhetorical flourish similar to that used by vicars, reticent to cast the first stone at sinners. The chorus ("please listen") begs the nowhere man to regain his senses. If he responds to this altar call from the Beatles he will have the world at his command. The nowhere man's root problem, blindness, also has a biblical ring.

John's experience with drugs had affected his self-assurance as an agnostic. Not only was he not as confident about dismissing the idea of the evidence of spiritual realms, but his cosmic awareness and his reawakened sense of love made him want to reevaluate the religion he had been raised in. He bought theological books and began rereading the Bible. This exploration had an effect on the writing of "Girl," which he explained was "trying to say something or other about Christianity . . . I was just talking about Christianity in that—a thing like you have to be tortured to attain heaven. . . . I was talking about 'pain will lead to pleasure' in 'Girl' and that was sort of the Catholic Christian concept—be tortured and then it'll be alright."

Paul played "Girl" to Francis Wyndham for the interview with *London Life* in December 1965. "John's been reading a book about pain and pleasure, about the idea behind Christianity that to have pleasure you have to have pain," he said. "The book says that's all rubbish. It often happens that pain leads to pleasure but you don't *have* to have it. All that's a drag. So we've written a song about it with, I suppose, a little bit of protest."

It's likely that the book in question was *Masochism in Modern Man* by Theodor Reik, a former pupil of Freud who took the view that the teachings of Christ appealed to a masochistic tendency. He suggested that the command to love our enemies and pray for those who persecute us was "a translation of masochistic behavior modeled into a religious format." Likewise the idea that suffering is a means of grace (1 Pet. 2:20) and a gift of God's love (Heb. 12:5ff.). "The dying Saviour had found a new way of enjoyment," he wrote. "The steps of suffering became rungs of the ladder to heaven. The warrior-ideal is by and by replaced by the ideal of the saint or martyr. The late Jewish prophets and the Christian faith bring the glorification of masochism. But behind the pleasure of suffering there appears the triumph. The greatest of all sufferers, who drank the cup of sorrow, who was humiliated and crucified, was the one to conquer the world."

In John's hands those ideas led him to question whether the "girl" had been raised to believe "that pain would lead to pleasure." He followed these lines with a jibe at the Protestant work ethic, alluding to the consequence of the fall when God says to Adam: "In the sweat of thy face shalt thou eat bread, till thou return unto the ground: for out of it wast thou taken; for dust thou art, and unto dust shalt thou return" (Gen. 3:19). Did the girl believe those who told her "that a man must break his back to earn his day of leisure"?

Although the Beatles were changing, their concerns remained the same. They still represented a spirit of freedom but were dealing with inner freedom as much as outer freedom. They still wrote about love but were interested in the idea of cosmic love as well as sex and companionship. They still wanted their music to bring ecstasy but not necessarily hysteria. There were ways for art to elevate the spirit that didn't involve screaming and shouting.

"The Beatles had basically moved from the school classroom to the Cavern and then the concert circuit," says Tony Barrow. "A lot of what they did after 1964 with drugs and all the rest was a sort of belated adolescent experimentation of one sort or another. Stuff that they would otherwise have read earlier they were only just catching up with. I remember John and George in particular expressing almost adolescent surprise at discovering different things in books. They had never had a chance to discover this in their late teens because they were too busy doing lunchtime gigs."

Chapter Seven

All You Need Is Love

God is in everything. God is in the space between us. God is in the table in front of you. For me it just happens that I realized all this through acid.

          —Paul McCartney, 1967

Everybody is potentially divine. It's just a matter of self-realization before it will all happen.

          —George Harrison, 1967

God isn't in a pill, but LSD explained the mystery of life. It was a religious experience.

          —John Lennon, 1970

Drugs made a lot of difference to the type of music and the words. It gave everyone more scope and more things to talk about.

          —Ringo Starr, 1967

Although pot disturbed their agnosticism, it was LSD that started the Beatles talking about having experienced "God" and would soon steer them toward religions of the East. It's unlikely that they would have been transformed from skeptical, worldly Liverpool boys who only believed what their eyes could see into peace-loving mystics speaking of karma, nirvana, and the coming golden age, if it hadn't been for this chemical catalyst.

Their approach to life was more visceral than intellectual. They didn't generally arrive at conclusions through examination of evidence and evaluation of claims. They had been, as *Newsweek* said of them, "four iconoclastic, brass-hard, post-Christian, pragmatic realists." They acted on feelings more than facts, altered perceptions rather than rational argument, intuition rather than dogma. Whereas Christianity spoke of a peace that "passeth understanding" and a few saints and mystics claimed to have been caught up into the heavens, drugs could guarantee you peaceful feelings and a sense of other dimensions without all the palaver of holy living. George summed up his approach as, "Don't believe in nothing [*sic*] until you've witnessed it for yourself."

LSD came to them unexpectedly but at a time when they were ready for a major change. Their lives had been turned upside down over the past three years, and they were wondering what came next after wealth, fame, possessions, and enough critical respect to last a lifetime. As writers, they needed new perceptions to keep their songs sounding fresh. "I feel as though it's an interesting time," said Paul in 1965 before he'd taken a drink from the special cup, "because something's got to happen. There's got to be some kind of change."

The hallucinogenic power of lysergic acid diethylamide, later known as LSD-25 or "acid," was discovered in 1943 by a Swiss chemist, Dr. Albert Hoffman, who had for the past five years been experimenting with compounds related to a fungus (ergot) which grew on rye and other grasses. His first "trip" came through accidental exposure but, realizing its potential, he then deliberately investigated these previously unknown properties. "I was overcome with fear that I was going out of my mind," he wrote of one of his early experiences. "Occasionally I felt as if I were out of my body. I thought I had died. My ego seemed suspended somewhere in space from where I saw my dead body lying on the sofa. It was particularly striking how acoustic perceptions such as the noise of water gushing from a tap or the spoken word were transformed into optical illusions."

After World War II research began on the therapeutic potential of the drug. It was thought that it could be useful in unearthing the origins of traumas and helping those with unusual psychological conditions. Then, in the 1950s, American military scientists took a close interest in its power. Initially they thought it could be the "truth drug" they'd long dreamed of that would transform interrogation procedures, but after discovering that it distorted views of reality they switched to thinking it could be swallowed by their own agents if captured as it almost guaranteed that whatever was said under duress would be nonsensical. Eventually they entertained the idea that it could confuse and disorient enemy troops if spread in the form of a spray or introduced into water supplies. During this time a steady stream of paid volunteers was being turned on in the cause of military-funded scientific research, and many of them not only enjoyed the trips but found their perceptions altered.

The British author Aldous Huxley took LSD in 1955. The respected scholar and former Episcopalian priest Alan Watts took it in 1958 under the guidance of Keith Ditman, the psychiatrist in charge of LSD research at the Department of Neuropsychiatry at the University of California, Los Angeles. These writers saw the drug not as therapeutic or mind-bending but as an aid to increase spiritual awareness. They drew parallels between what they had

felt and the experiences of mystics through the ages. Huxley started corre-
sponding with a British psychiatrist working in Canada, Dr. Humphrey
Osmond, who encouraged doctors to take LSD in order to understand schiz-
ophrenia. In one of these exchanges Huxley said that drugs like mescaline and
LSD should be called "phanerothymes." Osmond suggested "psychedelics"
(which, like phanerothymes, was based on Greek words for "to show" and
"soul" or "mind"), and after he introduced the word to the New York Academy of Sciences in 1957, it came into popular usage.

The story of how John and George were unsuspectingly initiated into psychedelics when they were slipped the drug by a dentist in 1965 has been retold
many times since George told *Melody Maker*, in September 1967, that "somebody just shoved it in our coffee before we'd ever heard of the stuff." John
gave a more detailed explanation in his 1970 interview with *Rolling Stone.*
However, the full details have never been told, and this has led to inaccurate
information being published about where the drug came from, why it was supplied, and under what circumstances it was taken. Albert Goldman, in his controversial 1988 biography *The Lives of John Lennon*, gave the fullest account
so far, and this has been copied by Beatles' biographers ever since.

Goldman dated the event to 1964 and claimed that the LSD had come from
a supply brought to London by British-born Michael Hollingshead, one of the
earliest proselytizers for the drug and the person who turned on the future
"high priest of LSD," Timothy Leary, who had then passed some to Victor
Lownes, the director of *Playboy* magazine's expanding empire of clubs. "The
go-between was a cosmetic dentist, whose girlfriend was the supervisor of the
Playboy Bunnies and hence in a position to ask Lownes for some acid to turn
on the Fab Four," wrote Goldman. "Glad to be of service to the kings of pop,
Lownes upped with six hits."

This story turns out to be wrong on almost every count. The trip took place
in 1965, not 1964. From all the evidence available, the most likely date is
Thursday April 8. If this was the day it would be additional proof that "Help!"
was a drug song, because it was written over that weekend and recorded on
Tuesday April 13. The key figure was a cosmetic dentist, but his girlfriend was
not then involved with the Playboy Club (it didn't open in London until July
1966 when she did then become its independent public relations representative), and Michael Hollingshead wasn't the source of the LSD.

Hollingshead didn't arrive back in England from America until the fall of
1965, although it's true he came with five thousand doses of the drug made in
Czech government laboratories in Prague and the intention of introducing
what he called "a drug-based religion" to influential British cultural figures.
By the time Hollingshead became a face on the London scene John and

George were well and truly turned on, so much so that Timothy Leary wanted to involve them in the evangelization process. "The idea was to rent the Albert Hall for a psychedelic jamboree," wrote Hollingshead in his memoir *The Man Who Turned on the World*. "We would get the Beatles or the Stones to perform, invite other artists, and, as the climax of the evening, introduce Tim [Leary] as the High Priest."

John and George's first trip happened in fairly mundane circumstances. The dentist—the "wicked dentist" as George jokingly referred to him in *The Beatles Anthology*—didn't believe LSD could transform the world and hadn't been influenced by Leary's talk of starting a new psychedelic religion. John Riley was an affluent thirty-four-year-old South Londoner, the son of a Metropolitan Police constable, who found himself at the heart of the new "Swinging London" by virtue of his high-profile clients. Having studied cosmetic dentistry at Northwestern University Dental School in Chicago, he had returned to London as one of Britain's most accomplished cosmetic dentists and quickly became first choice for actors, models, and singers. He later supplied the teeth for Roman Polanski's 1966 film *The Fearless Vampire Killers* and, as an actor, had a fleeting role as a cowboy the same year in *The Texican* alongside Audie Murphy and Broderick Crawford.

George had become a patient at Riley's private practice on Harley Street in London's West End. The two men had become particularly friendly, and George would drop by his ground-floor Bayswater apartment on his way back to Esher after a day recording at Abbey Road. When the Beatles were filming the beach scenes for *Help!* in the Bahamas in February 1965 Riley flew out to be with them. He was a good-time guy with a charismatic personality. "He was the sort of man that if he walked in the room, you'd feel his presence even before you saw him," says one friend.

According to Cyndy Bury, his twenty-one-year-old girlfriend at the time, and later his wife, his interest in LSD was purely that of a fashionable Londoner of the period who'd heard about the drug and was curious about its effects. "It was nothing to do with getting 'turned on,'" she says. "It wasn't really anything to do with 'drugs' as such. It was totally innocent. I was a really straight girl who just liked my alcohol and cigarettes. My only 'drug' was a little glass of champagne at the end of the day. We didn't have the idea that you can take this and it'll widen your horizons. Nobody knew what it would do. Nobody knew."

The drug had hit the streets, mainly in America, three years previously. It was hip enough by November 1963 for *Playboy* to run an account of a trip taken by the novelist and Beat associate Alan Harrington. A friend of Riley's in the building trade knew of a chemist who was manufacturing the drug, still legal in Britain, at a farmhouse in Wales. He organized the purchase on Riley's behalf and had the supply delivered to his London home.

What is disputed is whether Riley had discussed the drug with the two Beatles before the dinner party. Pattie Boyd says there was no preparation and that George hadn't heard of the drug at the time. George's later comment to *Melody Maker*—"I'd never even heard of it then"—confirms this memory. Cynthia Lennon says there was talk about it over dinner, but just as a topic of general interest, not in anticipation of a trip. "It was just a discussion about what people were doing at the time," she says. "When you go to dinner with a dentist you don't think a professional man is going to do something as stupid as that." This fits with John's comment that they "didn't know much about it" beforehand and that they certainly hadn't been told about "the horrors of LSD." Cyndy, however, believes that there was an agreement between them. John and George, she says, expressed interest in taking a trip but had said that they didn't want to know that they'd been given it. They wanted to be taken by surprise.

The occasion was an evening meal at Riley's two-bedroom apartment at 2 Strathearn Place, near the northern edge of Hyde Park. The three couples first ate a meal in the dining room and then retired to the large living room where the LSD-soaked sugar lumps were popped into their after-dinner coffees. Only Riley knew what was happening. For the rest of them it was initially a disturbing experience, with furniture apparently shrinking and elongating before their eyes and colors burning with a violent intensity. Cyndy, who felt that time had stopped, repeatedly shouted, "The *Bismark* is sinking! The *Bismark* is sinking!"

"It was the most bizarre feeling," says Cynthia. "I was sitting in this room and suddenly it became as huge as the Albert Hall. I was sitting next to John, and Pattie and George were sitting opposite, and they started disappearing into the distance. We looked at each other and thought, 'What is happening?' We must have all felt the same thing at the same time. Then we said, 'We've got to get out of here.' That's how frightening it was. We didn't give a second thought to our host and hostess. We just ran out, and they chased after us. All we could see was these monsters coming to get us."

They escaped to George's car to drive to the Pickwick Club on Great Newport Street where the trio Paddy, Klaus, and Gibson was playing in the newly opened basement club, known as Downstairs at the Pickwick (this was Paddy Chambers, Klaus Voorman, whom they had first met in Hamburg in 1960, and Gibson Kemp). Riley, realizing that his guests would be hallucinating by now, tried to prevent their leaving his apartment, but they misinterpreted his keenness as an invitation to an orgy and pushed their way out.

Their ignorance of the drug and its effects made them feel that they were going insane. "I didn't know what was happening to me," says Pattie. "The most frightening thing was that I thought I was going to be like this for the rest of my life. We couldn't tell anyone what was happening to us because we didn't know. When we tried to leave his place he [Riley] said he'd given us LSD, but we thought, 'So? What's that?'"

After Downstairs at the Pickwick they went on to the Ad Lib on Leicester Place, close to Leicester Square in the heart of London's West End, a fourth-floor club accessible only by elevator. As they ascended they had the impression that the building was on fire and feared that they were on their way to hell. Once in the club their anxieties subsided although their experiences varied. Pattie became mischievous and playful. John was stunned, finding everything "terrifying but fantastic," as he later said. George felt consumed by a feeling of love. "I felt in love," he said, "not with anything or anybody in particular, but with everything. Everything was perfect, in a perfect light, and I had an overwhelming desire to go around the club telling everybody how much I loved them—people I had never seen before."

As the new day dawned, they left the club and slowly drove the nineteen miles to Esher in George's Mini, stopping every now and then to play football by the roadside. John began drawing furiously. In one of the drawings four heads blended together and jointly announced, "We all agree with you." When they arrived at George's bungalow everyone but John went to bed. He stayed up, under the impression that the building was a submarine and he was the captain. Cynthia was panicking in the bedroom, fearful that she would never again be normal. "I'll never know how we got home," says Cynthia. "Thank God George was a good driver. We were just floating."

John Riley and Cyndy had followed John and George to the Pickwick but left after a while and took a taxi back home. They were by now so out of it that they lay on the floor of the cab and asked the mystified driver to make several circles of Hyde Park while they gazed up at the overhanging trees and the stars beyond. They only took LSD twice after that night—two half doses. They never again saw John or George.

They didn't speak to each other about the potential effect on the music of the Beatles. "We never considered the significance," says Cyndy. "It was just something that we'd done at the time, for fun. We never thought about tomorrow." The fact that the Beatles didn't contact them again was not because John and George didn't like LSD—they frequently heaped praises on the drug—but because they felt that Riley had been irresponsible in giving it to them without their knowledge. "When you go for dinner with your dentist you don't imagine a professional man would do something like that," says Cynthia. "He could easily have killed us, I'm sure."

For George and John it was a perception-changing experience. LSD dissolves the normal sense of ego that allows one to distinguish between self, others, and inanimate objects. The tripper feels united with all things: "I am he as you are he as you are me and we are all together," as John would later put it in "I Am the Walrus" (possibly a paraphrase of the mystic Gurdjieff's "I am Thou. Thou art I. He is ours. We both are his"). On returning to normal waking consciousness, the tripper sees ordinary life with its distinctions and divisions as a charade. Colors gain in intensity, concepts such as "past" and "future" seem irrelevant, and the tripper feels goodwill toward all. "Reality is God alone," said George in 1967. "Everything else is illusion."

George said the effect on him was "devastating" because it felt as though his body, mind, and ego had been separated with a knife. "It was shattering. It's as though someone suddenly wipes away all you were taught or brought up to believe as a child and says, 'That's not it.' You've gone so far, your thoughts have become so lofty and you think that there is no way of getting back." A fragment of an uncompleted song written by George on the back of a letter dated September 13, 1965, gives an insight into the shock that he felt: "I didn't ask my life to change / But it's changing / I thought I'd always be the same / But I've changed / It worries me / It worries me."

Those who have tripped out—the turned-on people, beautiful people, heads, freaks—then feel part of an enlightened elite who have seen beyond the facade. The lives of the unenlightened—the straights, squares, normals, gray people—are based on false perceptions: what they call "real" is an illusion, and what they dismiss as illusory—the vision of the hallucinogenic drug taker—is reality.

Michael Hollingshead, who first took LSD in 1960, was one of those who thought that LSD had brought him salvation. Initially, the experience destabilized him because he felt caught between the world of illusion (he was employed by the Institute for British American Cultural Exchange in New York) and "this Other World whose existence alone seemed to disclose the nature of reality." He explained, "In the former [world] I was a stranger to myself, a puppet of rote-consciousness, a cipher on the face of existence, an object furnished with a label and a price tag. . . . In the other I was not a dot but a species in the great evolutionary experiment, a conscious agent in the cosmic process called life."

The next time the two Beatles took LSD was in August 1965 at a rented house in Benedict Canyon, Los Angeles. This time Ringo joined in, as did

David Crosby and Roger McGuinn of the Byrds. The actor Peter Fonda was with them. As a child Fonda had accidentally shot himself with a .22 pistol that damaged his liver and his left kidney. While being operated on his heart stopped three times. He used his memory of this experience to calm George, who was concerned that he might imagine his own death while tripping. "I know what it's like to be dead," Fonda had said, reassuring him that the fear was a result of his mind playing tricks. "John Lennon came over to where we were seated," said Fonda. "'Who put all that crap in your head?' he asked angrily. 'You're making me feel like I've never been born.'" This provided the core of John's song "She Said, She Said" with its lines "She said, I know what it's like to be dead."

Earlier in the month John had discussed LSD with Art Unger, the editor and publisher of *Datebook*, later to play such a key role in the "more popular than Jesus" controversy. Unger's brother, the psychologist Sanford Unger, had been introduced to the drug as a Harvard student by Timothy Leary and went on to conduct clinical research into its effects. When Unger was interviewing Paul in a dressing room before one of the concerts John came up and said to Paul, "Watch him. He'll try to sell you LSD." This exchange was duly reported in *Datebook* in what must have been the first story to quote a Beatle mentioning LSD.

Always the least reckless of the Beatles, Paul still refused to trip. Recreational drugs whose effects wore off in a few hours he could handle. He now thought of them as being roughly in the same category as the socially acceptable alcohol. But a drug that could potentially alter your outlook forever, and one that had reportedly brought about mental collapse in some cases, was one to be careful about. He wanted to bide his time. His father's words about toleration and moderation were still a guiding principle.

Paul's caution caused a temporary division in the group. John and George felt that they had an edge on him; that they had been initiated into mysteries that he couldn't understand. Although Paul was a regular pot smoker by the time of *Revolver*, it was still John who was coming up with freaky tracks like "I'm Only Sleeping" with its backward guitars by George while Paul was doing tender love songs like "Here, There and Everywhere." It's possible that John's "And Your Bird Can Sing," originally titled "You Don't Get Me," was a sly dig at Paul for his reticence.

When *Revolver* was being recorded, John and George were reading literature that interpreted the LSD experience in a Buddhist or Hindu framework. One of Michael Hollingshead's specific goals in Europe was to promote what he called "the methodology of taking LSD in positive settings." By this he meant having people guided through their trips by the aid of religious read-

July 6, 1957: The Quarrymen play at the annual garden fete held by St. Peter's Church in Woolton. Lennon and McCartney would meet for the first time later that day in the church hall. (Sotheby's Picture Library)

Strawberry Field, the Salvation Army home near John's house on Menlove Avenue. The spacious grounds provided a place for childhood reveries that would later inspire a Beatles' song. (Salvation Army International Heritage Centre)

GARDEN FETE
ST. PETER'S CHURCH FIELD

WOOLTON PARISH CHURCH   Rector: M. Pryce Jones.

Saturday, 6th July, 1957
at 3 p.m.

ADMISSION BY PROGRAMME:
CHILDREN 3d.

PROCEEDS IN AID OF CHURCH FUNDS.

The program for the garden fete offered two outdoor sessions with the Quarrymen plus a "Grand Dance" with them and the George Edwards Band at the church hall in the evening. (Steve Turner Collection)

This grave to an Eleanor Rigby stands within yards of St. Peter's Church. John and Paul certainly walked past it. Did it inspire the Beatles' song about a church and a burial? Although Paul can't remember seeing it, he has acknowledged that "it is possible" that it registered on his subconscious mind. (Steve Turner)

Morris Pryce Jones was the rector at St. Peter's throughout John's time as a Sunday school pupil, chorister, and Bible class student. His sermons provided a model for some of John's antichurch satires. (Courtesy of St. Peter's, Woolton)

Immediately to John's left in the Quarrymen is Pete Shotton, his childhood partner-in-crime. Shotton later felt that John's song "Help!" was directed at him. (Geoff Rhind/Universal Pictorial Press & Agency)

This never-before-seen photo was taken in John and Stuart's room at Gambier Terrace in July 1960 for a Sunday newspaper story exposing beatnik squalor. On the wall is a poster advertising a Silver Beetles concert. On the far left (with beard) is the Beatles' first manager, Allan Williams, talking either to John or his friend Rod Jones. Facing the camera in dark glasses is a character known as "Pete the Beat." (Harold Chapman/Topfoto)

John and Paul visited Paris for the first time in October 1961. It was the time that they first shed their rocker image for a more continental, bohemian look. (Sotheby's Picture Library)

John's blasphemous streak is shown in this cartoon added to a letter sent to a fan. He had a particular fascination with Jesus. (© 2006 Yoko Ono Lennon. Sotheby's Picture Library. All rights reserved.)

Stuart and Astrid Kirchherr photographed by fellow "Exi" Jurgen Vollmer. Astrid's fascination with French philosophers, writers, artists, and filmmakers rubbed off on the Beatles. (Jurgen Vollmer/Redferns)

Astrid's photos of the Beatles helped project them as artsy and bohemian rather than rough and greasy. They provided the template for their early image. This shot from 1962 was taken in the attic in Hamburg that Stuart had used as his studio. (Redferns)

February 9, 1964: Ringo, George, John, and Paul with Ed Sullivan on the show that would launch the Beatles in America. It had the largest viewing audience of any TV program up to that point. (Popperfoto)

The way that fans reacted to the Beatles in concert gave rise to the term "Beatlemania." Many observers at the time compared the ecstatic response to that of participants in primitive religious rituals. (TopFoto)

August 1963: Three years after their first meeting in Liverpool the Beatles get together with Royston Ellis after a concert in the Channel Islands. Ellis is convinced that he, the Beat poet, was influential in their changing their name from Silver Beetles to Beatles. (Steve Turner Collection)

The sight and sound that shook the world. Paul and George harmonize into a microphone while John stands back. (Mirrorpix)

February 22, 1964: Journalist Maureen Cleave (center) welcomes the Beatles back from their triumphant first visit to America. Two years later an interview she conducted with John produced the controversial "more popular than Jesus" quote. (Express/Hulton Archive/Getty Images)

August 12, 1966: Teenagers in Waycross, Georgia, burn their Beatles records as part of a protest against John's comment about Jesus. The bonfire was organized by a local radio station, WAYX. (© Bettman/CORBIS)

The September 1966 issue of *Datebook*, with part of John's controversial quote used on the cover. Paul's quote was ignored. (Steve Turner Collection)

August 18, 1965: Art Unger, publisher and editor of *Datebook*, talks to John backstage at the Atlanta Stadium. He was refused access to the 1966 tour because Beatles' manager Brian Epstein feared that observers might think the *Datebook* story was a publicity stunt. (Courtesy of Raul Nunez)

In an apartment on the ground floor of this building John and George, along with their partners Cynthia and Pattie, were given their first experience of LSD. They were so terrified of what was happening to them that they fled the premises with their hosts in hot pursuit. (Steve Turner)

John Riley, dentist to George Harrison, was responsible for turning the Beatles on to psychedelics. From this single experience would emerge their interest in Eastern religion and esoteric knowledge. (Courtesy of Moya Riley)

June 25, 1967: Live from Abbey Road performing "All You Need Is Love" for the first global satellite TV link-up. Prominent above the balloons and flowers is the yin/yang symbol derived from Buddhism. (Rex Features)

Yellow Submarine was a psychedelic odyssey that pushed the animation of its day to the limit. Although the voices of the Beatles weren't used, the group had considerable input and approved of the result. (United Artists/Retna)

August 7, 1967: George, pictured with Derek Taylor on the right, visited San Francisco's Haight Ashbury expecting to find love, peace, and beauty but instead found teenagers strung out on drugs who looked to him for leadership. This experience turned him off LSD and increased his desire for chemical-free enlightenment. (© Bettman/CORBIS)

It was through his fascination with the sitar, an instrument he first encountered on the set of the film *Help!* that George became interested in the religions of India. (Nancy Harrison)

March 18, 1968: Paul, his face smeared with red powder, participates in the Hindu festival of Holi, which celebrates the coming of spring and offers worship to Lord Krishna. (Popperfoto)

Maharishi Mahesh Yogi listens while Paul and John play their guitars on the grounds of the ashram in Rishikesh, India. Cynthia Lennon sits to John's left. (Nancy Harrison)

The Beatles' meeting with Maharishi led them to explore Transcendental Meditation, and while in India they wrote much of *The Beatles* (The White Album). Songs such as "Dear Prudence," "Sexy Sadie," "The Continuing Story of Bungalow Bill," and "Why Don't We Do It in the Road?" were written about specific incidents that took place at the ashram. (Rex Features)

In 1966 George went to study the sitar with master musician Ravi Shankar. This introduced him to the relationship between music and spirituality. On his tunic in this picture George wears the image of Paramahansa Yogananda, author of *Autobiography of a Yogi*. (Rex Features)

Apple was to be a driven by an ideal of "controlled weirdness" but ultimately there was too much weirdness and not enough control. In this picture John offers a mock blessing to Derek Taylor while being watched by (left to right) Denis O'Dell, Paul McCartney, "Magic" Alex Mardas, Brian Lewis, Ron Kass, and Neil Aspinall. (TopFoto)

March 5, 1970: George, surrounded by members of ISKCON (International Society for Krishna Consciousness). Directly behind George is Mukunda and at the top right is Syama-sundar. These two devotees played an important role in attracting George to the movement and were with him in Los Angeles when he died in 2001. (© Hulton-Deutsch/CORBIS)

March 12, 1969: Family life, vegetarianism, and the environment became Paul's passions after he married Linda Eastman. Here he is pictured at St. John's Wood Church with Linda's daughter, Heather, after a blessing given to the couple by Rev. Noel Perry-Gore. (Mirrorpix)

December 16, 1969: Yoko Ono discouraged John from looking for gurus. Under her influence he investigated Zen and the occult. At the time this picture was taken they were both addicted to heroin. (Mirrorpix)

July 19, 1971: During an interview with the author, John stares down at an open letter addressed to him and published in an underground newspaper published by Christian hippies. (Mike Putland/Retna)

The author interviews John while Yoko Ono looks on. (Mike Putland/Retna)

ings, music, art works, chanting, and special lighting so that their trips had "spiritual content" and weren't just "defiant antiauthoritarian gestures."

He set up the World Psychedelic Centre at a luxury apartment in Pont Street, Belgravia, a fashionable up-market location from which to contact movers and shakers. "I wanted to rid people of their inhibitions about mystical writings and demonstrate to them that *The Tibetan Book of the Dead*, the *Tao Te Ching*, and the *I Ching* were really basic manuals with fundamental instructions about taking LSD sessions," he wrote. "We felt we had supplemented this ancient knowledge by the exploitation of modern technological means of transmitting aesthetic phenomena."

Before leaving America he had sent ahead of him by ship a consignment of helpful books: three hundred copies of *The Psychedelic Experience: A Manual Based on the Tibetan Book of the Dead*, by Timothy Leary, Richard Alpert, and Ralph Metzner; two hundred issues of *The Psychedelic Review*; and two hundred copies of *The Psychedelic Reader*, edited by Gunther Weil. Copies of these books were placed in the hands of the Beatles by Peter Asher's friend Barry Miles, who was now managing the Indica Bookshop in Southampton Row. It was a time when Paul, the only Beatle still living in London, was excited by the city's burgeoning avant-garde art scene, and he would frequent Indica, which was one of the city's few independently owned "alternative" bookstores, and load up with books recommended to him.

To browse the shelves of Indica at the time was to glimpse the future. There was an experimental, liberal feel to the place, and most of the books and magazines it stocked weren't available anywhere else in England. There were underground newspapers from New York and Los Angeles, uncensored sex novels from France, Provo material from Holland, "Ban the Bomb" propaganda, small duplicated poetry journals, university magazines, and sections on drugs, Eastern religion, the occult, and revolutionary politics. Beat authors such as Allen Ginsberg and William Burroughs were featured, as were books by psychiatrist R. D. Laing, communications guru Marshall McLuhan, and black radical Eldridge Cleaver. There were albums by Albert Ayler, Ravi Shankar, and the Fugs.

"On the one hand Paul was living with Jane Asher's family where he was meeting people who were more intellectual than his music industry friends. Jane's father was a psychiatrist and her mother was a teacher at the Royal College of Music," says Miles. "On the other hand he was being exposed to all the underground stuff coming from America which he got through me. He saw underground newspapers like the *East Village Other* and the *L.A. Free Press*."

On John's first visit to Indica in late March 1966 Miles showed him a copy of *The Psychedelic Experience*, a manual specifically produced to guide LSD takers through their trips using, as a pattern, the stages of death and rebirth as understood by Tibetan Buddhism. Timothy Leary's paraphrase of the *Tibetan Book of the Dead*—scriptures meant to be read to people as they approached death—was part of the book. "Trust your divinity, trust your brain, trust your companions," wrote Leary in the introduction. "Whenever in doubt, turn off your mind, relax, float downstream."

Apparently John, who bought the book, recorded sections of this paraphrase to listen to on his headphones when tripping in his den. There were parts of the book where the tripper was encouraged to personalize the text. Experts stressed the need for "banisters," either musical or spoken, that trippers could hold on to when tripping in order to avoid getting "freaked out." If, as recommended, John had personalized the First Bardo Instructions in the section headed "Instructions for Use during a Psychedelic Session," he would have recorded:

O John,
The time has come for you to seek new levels of reality.
Your ego and the John game are about to cease.
You are about to be set face to face with the Clear Light.
You are about to experience it in its reality.
In the ego free state, wherein all things are like the void and cloudless sky,
And the naked spotless intellect is like a transparent vacuum;
At this moment, know yourself and abide in that state.

O John,
That which is called ego-death is coming to you.
Remember:
This is now the hour of death and rebirth;
Take advantage of this temporary death to obtain the perfect state—
Enlightenment.
Concentrate on the unity of all living beings.
Hold on to the Clear Light.
Use it to attain understanding and love.
If you cannot maintain the bliss of illumination and if you are slipping back
     into contact with the external world,
Remember:
The hallucinations which you may now experience,
The visions and insights,
Will teach you much about yourself and the world.
The veil of routine perception will be torn from your eyes.

The *Tibetan Book of the Dead* was designed to ready people for their final moments, Buddhist belief being that the state of mind at the point of the last breath determined the condition of the next incarnation. By reinterpreting these instructions for LSD use, Leary was equating the savage restructuring of the senses on a trip with actual physical death. He was implying that something in you died, or at least should die, when tripping out.

LSD seemed to answer the questions that had most perplexed the Beatles. The question of fame that bothered George—the "Who am I to deserve so much attention?" question—was answered by the dissolution of the ego. In the cosmic scheme of things, George Harrison was insignificant. "The LSD ecstasy is the joyful discovery that ego, with its pitiful shams and strivings is only a fraction of my identity," wrote Leary. Endorsing this view, George said in 1967: "Acid was the big psychological reaction. Acid pushes home to you that you're only little, really. There's all that infinity out there."

It answered the freedom question by revealing that the conventional life they'd always rebelled against was a fiction anyway. LSD vindicated all their feelings of antagonism toward conformity, class, convention, and competition. It was all pretense. Leary advised his followers to "drop out," meaning that those who were serious about discovering their part in the molecular dance should unhook themselves from the fantasy, "gracefully detach yourself from the social commitments to which you are addicted," as he put it.

Taken to its logical conclusion it meant that life, as we experience it through normal consciousness, is a charade. We are engaging in make-believe. As the pretty nurse suspected in "Penny Lane," we're in a play. In 1967 George praised Shakespeare's observation that all the world's a stage. "He was right because we're Beatles and it's a little scene and we're pretending to be Beatles, like Harold Wilson's pretending to be Prime Minister. . . . They're all playing. The Queen's the Queen. The idea that you wake up and it happens that you're Queen, it's amazing, but you could all be Queens if you imagined it."

LSD answered the transcendence question. It revealed to them ways of escaping from the mundane because the drug apparently opened up areas of unexplored consciousness that allowed them, like Blake, to see "heaven in a grain of sand" or, like Huxley, to see that "the folds of my grey flannel trousers were charged with 'is-ness'." George said of his early experience with LSD, "My brain and my consciousness and my awareness were pushed so far out that the only way I could begin to describe it is like an astronaut on the moon, or in his spaceship, looking back at the Earth. I was looking back to the Earth from my awareness."

The love question was answered because when they were on acid they felt as though they were bursting with love for everyone and everything. It seemed that love powered the universe. Effusive feelings of love were common among trippers. War and hate came as a result of the divisions we perceived with our normal, nonpsychedelic consciousness. If we could only realize that we were all one, strife, jealousy, and competition would end. Love would flow within us and without us.

This psychedelic vision of love became a powerful ingredient not only in the hippie movement most visible in San Francisco but in the antiwar movement. There was no need for debate on neighborliness, friendship, forgiveness, or reconciliation, because love was something you just felt and LSD short-circuited the need for having to work for it. This was why John could so confidently sing "All You Need Is Love" in June 1967 and make it seem that love for everyone was the most natural passion to have.

Although *Rubber Soul* had been affected by drugs, it was *Revolver* that most comprehensively displayed their altered perceptions. The whole ambience of the record was different from anything they'd done before. The ways in which long-playing records had become guide tracks for drug experiences introduced them to a greater range of music and made them aware of the potential for orchestrating trips. Hollingshead, for example, recommended the following music for a trip: Buddhist *Chakra* music, Japanese flute, bossa nova, John Cage, Ravi Shankar, Bach, Alexander Scriabin, Debussy, Indian flute music by Pandit Ghosh, and the Ali Brothers (Nazakat and Salamal), along with readings from *The Psychedelic Experience*.

Exposure to sequencing that mixed Western classical with Asian music, *musique concrete* with Brazilian pop, was tremendously liberating. It was rare at the time for the average British music lover to hear music from other traditions and cultures. Even though Paul had yet to take LSD, he had visited the World Psychedelic Centre and was used to smoking pot in the company of mind-stretching albums by Eric Dolphy, Miles Davis, and Karlheinz Stockhausen. *Revolver* was put together in the same spirit, switching from the *Batman* theme-tune–influenced "Taxman" to the string quartet of "Eleanor Rigby," from the backward guitars of "I'm Only Sleeping" to the nursery rhyme–like "Yellow Submarine."

Beatles records were becoming trip music. Lights would be dimmed, joss sticks lit to perfume the air, and headphones adjusted to get the maximum benefit from the relatively new stereophonic sound. Under such circumstances, album covers would explode with meaning. Klaus Voorman's collage on the cover of *Revolver* was particularly vibrant because the lines of the hair seemed to come alive and there were Beatles from each stage of Beatle history crawling out of ears and brains and hair. The more you looked, the more you saw, and the whole picture appeared to be a visual analogue of hallucinogenic regression.

The Beatles appeared to be aware that their records were being used in this way. They started dropping sounds into the mix that would be picked up by the psychedelically distorted mind. Instructions such as "Turn off your mind" and "Let me tell you" emphasized their position as friendly but experienced guides. Whether intentional or not, *Revolver* started with the drab reality of death and taxes ("Taxman," "Eleanor Rigby"), progressed through a dream state ("I'm Only Sleeping," "Yellow Submarine"), and ended in drug reverie ("She Said She Said," "Doctor Robert," "Tomorrow Never Knows"). The last piece of advice on the record was to listen to the color of your dreams. (Synesthesia—a condition of concomitant sensation, for example, where colors can be heard or sounds seen—is common while on LSD.)

In most of the songs messages about psychedelic change were implicit rather than explicit. Even though the drug was still legal in Britain, the Beatles hadn't yet publicized their newly acquired habits. "I'm Only Sleeping" might have been about John's legendary laziness or his increasing tendency to lounge around stoned. The music suggested something more surreal than afternoon naps. "Yellow Submarine" was an exercise in writing a song for children, but it was psychedelia that had been responsible for making childhood innocence hip. (The image of the submarine may have been suggested by John's experience at George's bungalow during his first trip.)

There were references in George's songs that made sense to those who were already turned on. They knew that when he sang about the "games" that had begun to drag him down in "I Want to Tell You" he was referring to the unreality of the "real world," where people adopted illusory identities. It was fashionable to talk about "games," and Eric Berne's recently published *Games People Play* had become a best seller. "To me it's very obvious that life is just a big game," George told Art Unger in 1966. "From when they're born until they die it's up to people to try to work out what it's all about." After the Jesus incident John told Leroy Aarons of the *Washington Post*, "That's the trouble with being truthful. You try to apply truth talk, although you have to be false sometimes because the whole thing is false in a way, like a game. But you hope sometime that if you're truthful with somebody they'll stop all the plastic reaction and be truthful back and it'll be worth it." "I Want to Tell You" expressed George's difficulty in articulating sublime experiences, the "avalanche of thoughts that are so hard to write down or say or transmit," as he later explained. The hip audience also knew that when he referred to the people who would "fill you in with all their sins" he was talking about the straight world or maybe, more specifically, the church. (John would later write about teachers "filling" him up with rules, so possibly George also meant that the laws against sin had themselves become sins because they inhibited our development.)

"Doctor Robert" was about a notorious "speed doctor" in New York (Dr. Robert Freymann) who supplied socialites and celebrities with "vitamin shots" to keep them almost permanently wired. He had been Charlie Parker's physician when the great jazz saxophonist died of heroin addiction. In John's song the doctor became the archetypal drug dealer, the man with the magic potion who was able to transform him into something new and better. This was an indication of the world the Beatles now inhabited. As John said of himself, he had been on one drug or other since Hamburg. He had rarely faced the world straight.

When Dylan's road manager Victor Maymudes first met John in August 1964 he had been surprised to find how dependent he was on pharmaceuticals. "He met the doctors with the shots and the pills," Maymudes wrote in his unpublished manuscript. "They [the Beatles] had handfuls of pills—uppers and downers. They'd been downloaded on them by the doctors. I put the doctors down and John said that was the first time he'd ever heard anyone talk about the doctors and their drugs. To me they were the enemy. They were the enemy then and they're the enemy now."

"Tomorrow Never Knows," the first track recorded for the album, was the most obviously connected to LSD. It consisted of John intoning words adapted from Leary's *The Psychedelic Experience* over a collection of randomly spliced tapes, most of them music played backward. John told George Martin that he wanted to sound like "a Dalai Lama singing from the top of a mountain." The words encouraged the listener to abandon ego ("lay down all thought") but not to fear the loss because once ego is surrendered to the void, the nothingness is discovered to be the White Light and then the answer arrives ("the meaning of within"), which is simply "being." If you fail to follow this path you will remain caught up in the world of ego and will be condemned to play games.

John and George interpreted their experience of LSD differently. Although both felt themselves absorbed into a powerful force of energy, George took this as confirmation that we were all divine whereas for John it proved that divinity didn't exist, that all we can know for sure is that we are here. Although certain that there was more than meets the eye, he wasn't convinced that this meant that there was an ultimate purpose to the universe and, by implication, for our lives.

It was during the time when he was regularly using hallucinogenic drugs—almost a year after his first trip—that John made his comment about the weakness of Christianity in comparison to the increasing strength of rock 'n' roll.

Off the record he told Maureen Cleave about his experience at John Riley's apartment. It was LSD that led him to wonder whether Christ might have had similar transcendent experiences that had since been reduced to dry dogma by the church. There were times when he thought he understood the Bible afresh. He wondered whether when Jesus said, "The Kingdom of God is within you," he meant that we should be exploring the "within" rather than living obedient lives in return for "pie in the sky." Had Christ been thinking of mystical experience when he said, "the truth shall make you free"? Was he talking about the dissolution of ego barriers when he said, "I am in my Father, and ye in me, and I in you"?

To John the new "drug-based religion" was more dynamic than formal Christianity. All he could remember about his days at St. Peter's, Woolton, was the tedium of the services, during which he would count the panes in the church windows to help pass the time. Psychedelia, on the other hand, "blew your mind" as the new expression had it. LSD might be dangerous and had the potential to be terrifying, but it was never boring. The passion of people like Hollingshead, Leary, and Ginsberg was infectious. They really believed that the world could be made a better place if more people turned on. "Drugs are the religion of the twenty-first century," Leary predicted in 1963. "Pursuing the religious life today without using psychedelic drugs is like studying astronomy with the naked eye because that's how they did it in the first century A.D."

Paul didn't take LSD until late 1966, after the release of *Revolver*. He took it at the Eaton Row, London, home of Tara Browne, the socialite and heir to Guinness money, who was soon to die and be immortalized in the Beatles' "A Day in the Life" (he was the man who "blew his mind out in a car"). John had warned Paul that he would never be the same again after it, and he has since said that this proved to be true, although it didn't have the same deep and long-lasting effect it had on John and George. This may have been so because he was not trying to resolve unanswered questions. He was content with his fame, had no deep anxieties about his identity, and wasn't looking for profound insights to incorporate into his songs. The main reason he indulged was because he felt under pressure from the rest of the group and didn't want to be the odd one out.

Having taken it, he then became the first rock star to publicize it, admitting to a journalist from *Life* magazine that he had tripped three or four times. This became a major international news story and annoyed the psychedelic veterans John and George because it made Paul seem the most adventurous, experimental, and law-defying Beatle (it had recently become an illegal substance in Britain under the 1966 Dangerous Drugs Act). As John and George would later do, Paul used religious terms to explain what had happened to him.

He told *The People*, a British Sunday newspaper, that LSD had made him "a better, more honest, more tolerant member of society—brought closer to God." He went on:

> It [his first LSD trip] lasted about six hours. In that time you realise things as if you were having a lesson. This opened my eyes to the fact that there is a God. A similar experience would probably do some of our clergy some good. It is obvious that God isn't in a pill but it explained the mystery of life. It was truly a religious experience. I had never realised what people were talking about when they said God is within you, that He is love and truth. The only image I had was of an old man in the sky with a long beard. I'm not saying that I intend devoting myself to the Church or anything like that. To me it is much more personal than that. God is a force we are all part of. But it means that I now believe the answer to everything is love.

Peter Asher's friend John Dunbar was seeing a lot of Paul at the time. He says, "Acid made a big difference to the Beatles. They stopped being so straight. I don't think I've known anybody that it hasn't made a big difference to. Paul was a bit of a latecomer, but I think eventually he just didn't want to be left out."

Appropriately, the Beatles' next single, presented to the world on the first live international satellite TV link-up exactly a week after the newspaper revelation, was "All You Need Is Love," written by John for the historic media event. Along with Scott McKenzie's "San Francisco (Be Sure to Wear Some Flowers in Your Hair)," written by John Phillips of the Mamas and Papas, it was the song that best captured the spirit of what would later be known as "the Summer of Love." For a few months the psychedelic vision of advocates like Leary appeared to have led to a bloodless revolution. Young people were dropping out of university; fashions featured hallucinatory patterns; through the use of increased volume and synchronized light shows, rock concerts were becoming rituals for electronic shamans; and huge outdoor festivals saw Beat poets mingling with psychedelic prophets, Indian gurus, and heavy rock bands.

John's lyric to "All You Need Is Love" didn't make a lot of literal sense. It was struggling to express something beyond words and reflected the hesitant, disjointed thoughts of a tripper. Yet it communicated a sense of infinite possibility. The Beatles had always promoted the belief that if something could be imagined, it could be done, and here they were saying it again. There was nothing you could know that wasn't known. There was nowhere you could be that wasn't where you were meant to be. The chorus was as simple as a Sunday school sing-along and as memorable. John was back in the pulpit, and the Beatles were leading a generation. "Close your eyes and listen to the sermon from Liverpool," Leary advised the parental generation. "Learn that it's the oldest message of love and peace and laughter, and trust in God and don't worry."

Essential to the experience of the Summer of Love was *Sgt. Pepper's Lonely Hearts Club Band*. By now the group couldn't avoid knowing that they were being looked to for answers. John's hunch eighteen months earlier that rock 'n' roll would battle with Christianity for hearts and souls was coming true. "We've got our own subtle way of getting our beliefs over," he told *Disc* in May 1967. "The message is there alright, man." George told the same paper that pop music was "the nearest thing to salvation we're going to get. It should be a balance for all the other rubbish going on in the world." Only two years previously interviews with the group had remained on the level of "To what do you attribute your success?" Now they were being asked, "How important do you think positive music is in this huge evolutionary cycle?" (*Melody Maker*) or "If you are able to see everything in its own terms, do you find that this has eliminated the western concept of finding some things beautiful and others repulsive?" (*International Times*).

Those who had spent years on the fringes trying to spread the drug-based religion saw themselves as having been John the Baptists crying in the wilderness whereas the Beatles were messianic figures entering Jerusalem to cheering crowds. A few thousand might hear a lecture by Leary, but millions would listen to a Beatles album or read their interviews. Leary, who spent the summer of 1967 tripping to Beatles music, raved about them. "How clever and unexpected and yet typical of God to send his message this time through the electric instruments of four men from Liverpool," he wrote. In his essay "Drop Out or Cop Out" he referred to them as "holy men," declaring: "The rock 'n' roll bands are the philosopher-poets of the new religion. Their beat is the pulse of the future. The message from Liverpool is the Newest Testament, chanted by four Evangelists—saints John, Paul, George and Ringo. Pure Vedanta, divine revelation, gentle, tender irony at the insanities of war and politics, sorrowful lament for the bourgeois loneliness, delicate hymns of glory to God."

The Beatles had risen to the occasion by making *Sgt. Pepper* an artifact of the era rather than just another release. Although it wasn't a concept album of songs linked either by narrative progression or theme, it was conceptual in that every element was designed to produce a harmonious whole. There had been thematic albums before, such as Merle Travis's *Folk Songs of the Hills* (1948), Frank Sinatra's *In the Wee Small Hours* (1955), Marty Robbins's *Gunfighter Ballads and Trail Songs* (1959), Johnny Cash's *Bitter Tears* (1965), and *Freak Out!* (1966) by the Mothers of Invention, but the unity of *Sgt. Pepper* was in the conceit of the concert by a fictional band; the reprise of the opening song, the segueing of tracks, the way in which everything seemed to build toward the explosion of sound at the end of "A Day in the Life."

Sgt. Pepper seemed to be a work of art to be consumed in its entirety rather than a collection of Beatles songs from which to pick and choose. The opening song was a request to sit back and enjoy the entertainment, and the last song ended with the wish to turn the audience on. Were we being invited to a show or a form of ritual where we would be taken on a spiritual journey? Was this an invitation or an initiation?

Although the songs were not linked by an obvious theme, they shared the same outlook. In the context of LSD, "When I'm Sixty-four," written by Paul as a teenager in a 1920s style, fit in with the experience of time shifts, as did John's "Being for the Benefit of Mr. Kite!" which was based almost word-for-word on a circus poster from 1843. On psychedelic trips it was common to feel transported to different periods of history or different cultures. Psychedelic culture expressed this by mixing Native American beads with Victorian jackets, Afghan coats with crushed velvet trousers. (The cover of *Sgt. Pepper* reflected this—the Beatles dressed in Edwardian military jackets, Aubrey Beardsley and Karl Marx lining up with Marlon Brando and Marilyn Monroe.)

Similarly, "She's Leaving Home," although not about drugs, was based on a true story about a teenage runaway whose perplexed father had been quoted in a newspaper saying that he'd given her all she'd ever wanted. She seemed to have followed Leary's advice to "drop out," realizing that there was more to life than the material. The father's comment that he had given his daughter everything money could buy resonated with hippies, who saw it as symptomatic of the older generation's belief that all human needs could be satisfied materially.

"Fixing a Hole" referred to Paul's newfound freedom to organize his own life now that the Beatles had stopped touring. He'd bought a dilapidated hill farm in a remote part of Scotland and had recently acquired a London home close to the Abbey Road studios in St. John's Wood. No longer bound by such hectic schedules, he felt able to let his mind "wander." He now had the time to pay attention to things "that weren't important yesterday." Some interpreted "Fixing a Hole" as a needle junkie's confession, just as they assumed John's "Mr. H." in "Being for the Benefit of Mr. Kite!" was a code for heroin when it was actually a reference to a circus performer, Mr. Henderson.

Personal transformation was more obviously the subject of "Getting Better." The narrator had once been frustrated, angry, cruel, violent, and mean but now, since getting "the word" (an allusion to John's song of 1965?), he'd changed his "scene" and everything was getting better. It was the only time the Beatles referred explicitly to school experience. They blame their teachers for not being "cool," saying that they held them down and filled them up with their rules. John adds that in those days he was an "angry young man," a reference to John Osborne's play *Look Back in Anger* and writers like Colin Wilson and Kingsley Amis.

The Beatles had some fun with the public's eagerness to find drug references, speaking of taking "some tea" in "Lovely Rita," getting "high" in "A Little Help from My Friends" and having "a smoke" in "A Day in the Life." "Lucy in the Sky with Diamonds," which John always said was written about a painting that his son Julian brought back from school of a friend, Lucy O'Donnell, "in the sky with diamonds," without knowing that it was an acronym for LSD, was a fantasy inspired by the writing of his favorite childhood author, Lewis Carroll. Even though the images may have been suggested by *Alice's Adventures in Wonderland*, it's unlikely that he would have conceived of the song if he hadn't been regularly using psychedelics. Paul said at the time: "This Lucy was God, the big figure, the white rabbit."

Film director Joel Schumacher, who was part of the New York underground arts scene in the 1960s, recalls the impact on his circle of friends. "If you were young and on drugs, which almost everyone I knew was, it seemed that everything the Beatles did and sang about was a reflection of what we were going through. I remember being with tons of other stoned people out at Fire Island when I heard *Sgt. Pepper* for the first time, and it seemed that they were experiencing exactly what we were experiencing. 'A Day in the Life' seemed to have been made by someone who had done a lot of acid."

George's "Within You without You" linked the drug experience with the language of Eastern religion. (Among the faces on the album cover were three Indian gurus—Sri Yukteswar, Sri Lahiri Mahasaya, and Sri Paramahansa Yogananda—and *Doors of Perception* author Aldous Huxley.) As with John's "The Word" and "Nowhere Man," it called for awareness and stated in song for the first time his belief in the urgency of asking the big questions: who am I? where do I come from? where am I going?

The life that flows on "within you and without you" is *prana*, the universal energy, and those who can't "glimpse the truth" are the victims of illusion. He mentions those who "gain the world and lose their soul," a reference to the saying of Christ: "For whosoever will save his life shall lose it; but whosoever shall lose his life for my sake and the gospel's, the same shall save it. For what shall it profit a man, if he shall gain the whole world, and lose his own soul? Or what shall a man give in exchange for his soul?" (Mark 8:35–37). The way to preserve the soul, he says, is self-realization. Once you've "seen beyond yourself," beyond the restriction of normal waking consciousness, the result is "peace of mind" and feelings of "love." (The "Are you one of them?" echoes John's "Isn't he a bit like you and me?" in "Nowhere Man.")

More phrases that summed up the hippie ethos of 1967 were in "Within You without You" than on the rest of the album—"the space between us all," "a wall of illusion," "it's all within yourself," "we're all one," "with our love we could save the world." George was consolidating his position in the Beatles by helping formulate the group's doctrine, at a time when John was playing a less pivotal role. Only three songs on *Sgt. Pepper* had been originated and completed by John—"Lucy in the Sky with Diamonds," "Being for the Benefit of Mr. Kite!" and "Good Morning, Good Morning." He'd written a large part of "A Day in the Life," but his approach to writing was increasingly a lazy one. "Good Morning, Good Morning" was about being at home doing nothing and having nothing to say.

By 1967 John had taken so much LSD—between 1965 and 1970 he claimed to have taken literally "a thousand trips," although this must have been an exaggeration—that his already fragile sense of self had been dealt a severe blow. Prone to feeling unworthy, misunderstood, and unloved, he eventually had a mental breakdown. He lost his sense of purpose and became reclusive. "I got a message on acid that you should destroy your ego, and I did, you know," he told *Rolling Stone.* "I was reading that stupid book of Leary's (*The Psychedelic Experience*). . . . We were going through a whole game that everybody went through, and I destroyed myself. I destroyed my ego, and I didn't believe I could do anything. I let people do what they wanted . . . and I just was nothing."

George stopped taking LSD after his first visit to San Francisco in August 1967. While in Los Angeles for business meetings, he and Pattie, along with Derek Taylor, Neil Aspinall, and newly arrived electronics expert Alex Mardas, chartered a plane to the Bay Area to visit Pattie's sister Jenny. While he was there he visited Haight Ashbury, the district of San Francisco that had become the center of the psychedelic counterculture. On Haight Street "head shops" openly sold drug paraphernalia (despite LSD having become illegal in the state of California in October 1966), bands such as the Grateful Dead and Jefferson Airplane lived in old Victorian houses on neighboring streets, and hippies from all over America headed for the area in search of the new way of life that Timothy Leary spoke about and Scott McKenzie praised in song.

Wearing sunglasses with heart-shaped lenses, a denim jacket, and paisley-patterned trousers, George walked along Masonic Avenue toward Golden Gate Park and was almost immediately surrounded by street people. "There was a sense that they thought George had come to show them the path, that he'd come to show them the way forward," says Pattie. "It was as though they'd been scrutinizing every track on every album and trying to work out where they should go. They thought he was coming like a savior to give them new information."

One hippie came up to him and said, "You are our leader, George." George insisted that he wasn't. The man persisted. "Yes you are, man," he continued. "You know where it's at, man." Embarrassed by the attention, George answered, "It's you who should be leading yourself. You don't want to be following leaders—me or anyone else." Someone else tried to hand George some STP, a powerful hallucinogen, and there was a scramble by others to be in on what could be a psychedelic Last Supper. "Give us some, man. Us too. Lay it on us. Let's do our thing all together with George."

George felt inadequate for the task and was profoundly disturbed by what the drug culture had become. His expectation of Haight Ashbury had been of somewhere like the King's Road in London's Chelsea where dandified men escorted pretty young women on shopping sprees for expensive boutique clothing, but the reality was junkies with bad complexions who slept out on the streets. He told the STP man to take his drug away. "It isn't the answer," he told him. "The answer's in your own head, isn't it? I don't want that. Get it away." That day he vowed never to take a hallucinogen again.

"LSD isn't a real answer," he told *Melody Maker* on his return to England. "It doesn't give you anything. It enables you to see a lot of possibilities that you may never have noticed before, but it isn't the answer. . . . If you're really hip . . . you see the potential that it had and the good that can come from it, but you also see that you don't really need it."

The position the Beatles now took was that LSD was a step on the pilgrimage rather than the destination. It had allowed them a glimpse of the way things really were, but it didn't offer the final solution. The question posed in "Baby You're a Rich Man," the flip side of the single "All You Need Is Love" was: "Now that you know who you are, what do you want to be?" The new task was to go from knowing to doing and being. It wasn't possible to live on a permanent drug high, and a vision was useless if it couldn't be implemented. "LSD can help you get from A to B," said George, "but when you get to B, you see C. You see that to get really high you have to do it straight. There are special ways of getting high without drugs—with yoga, meditation, and all those things."

In an interview with *Datebook* editor Art Unger, which couldn't be published for a teenage audience at the time, George said that the shortcoming of LSD was that it didn't develop a pure state of mind. "Although it's good in some respects, LSD isn't good because your mind isn't pure. My experience with LSD led me to look for something higher. I want whatever it is that's the highest high of all time. Something that surpasses LSD. And I found out that that is what God is. God is the biggest buzz of all time. You don't need any acid, and also acid is not good for you. It's not good for your mind. It makes your mind rot after a while."

Magical Mystery Tour was a fifty-minute TV film conceived by Paul during a visit to America in April 1967. In order to capture the free-form nature of a drug trip, Paul relied on spontaneity and improvisation rather than conventional structure. His "script" was no more than a circle drawn on a sheet of paper with the action divided into eight sections and a few ideas for characters: courier, driver, busty hostess, fat woman, small man. In the spirit of the times he thought that genuine creativity would be hampered by too much prior organization.

Although it was based on the British convention of coach trips where passengers pay to go on a day's outing without knowing the final destination until they arrive, its style was also informed by a tour of America taken by the turned-on novelist Ken Kesey (*One Flew over the Cuckoo's Nest*) and his Merry Pranksters, who traveled in a psychedelically painted school bus with rock music pouring from speakers, filming their drug-crazed antics while bemusing the unsuspecting straight public. Kesey's main driver was Neal Cassady, Jack Kerouac's model for the character of Dean Moriarty in his 1957 novel *On the Road*. Tom Wolfe chronicled the adventures of Kesey and the Pranksters in the 1968 book *The Electric Kool-Aid Acid Test*.

Paul wanted *Magical Mystery Tour* to operate on two levels. For the general public it would be another Beatles caper—the four lads let loose with a cross-section of good down-to-earth British folk—but the hip young would be aware of the drug metaphor. To parents the command to "Roll up" was the language of the fairground barker. To the kids it was an invitation to roll a joint. Similarly, the reference to "dying" to take the audience away with them was intended as a reference to the *Tibetan Book of the Dead* that would not be recognized by the older generation. "It was the equivalent of a drug trip, and we made the film on the basis of that," said Paul.

The result was messy. The formlessness, undeveloped characters, and improvised dialogue failed to either stimulate or entertain. The only real connection between it and a drug trip was the randomness of events and the use of dream sequences. The Beatles tracks—"Magical Mystery Tour," "Fool on the Hill," "Flying," "Blue Jay Way," and "Your Mother Should Know"—stood out like diamonds in a cow pat. When the film was conceived, *Sgt. Pepper* hadn't been released and the Summer of Love hadn't yet started. It was shown on television on December 26, 1967, and was trounced by critics, who were sure that the Beatles were now floundering.

The animated film *Yellow Submarine* wasn't released until later, but the new songs for its soundtrack were recorded immediately after completing *Sgt. Pepper*. Although the Beatles didn't write the screenplay, they gave it their approval and were pleasantly surprised by the result. The story is a psychedelic version of a creation, fall, and redemption story with the Beatles cast as savior figures. Pepperland is a colorful earthly paradise full of love, music, rainbows, birds, flowers, and butterflies. It gets spoiled by the demonic force of the Blue Meanies, meant to represent the repressive straight world; they are the kind of people whom John had lambasted for not being cool and for filling him up with their rules. The Blue Meanies want to destroy Pepperland because they hate music, love, and friendship. When they attack, the citizens are fossilized and turned gray. The huge sculptures NOW and YES are crushed. Everything pleasurable is forbidden. "We Meanies only take no for an answer," says the chief Blue Meanie.

Old Fred, assistant to the mayor, sails to Liverpool in a yellow submarine and collects John, Paul, George, and Ringo. The return journey is constructed like a trip that appropriately starts with the crescendo that ends *Sgt. Pepper*. The Beatles are the shamans capable of bringing the love and music back to Pepperland, but they can only do so after descending to the underworld where they battle with monsters, are confronted with optical illusions, get caught in a time warp, and are blitzed by a kaleidoscope of colors. The dialogue links their Goon-show–style humor with stoned wordplay.

The Beatles defeat the Blue Meanies simply by playing music and spreading the gospel of love, and as a consequence all the fun is restored. Eventually (in the American version, at least) even the chief Blue Meanie is converted. The huge NO erected by the Meanies is altered to NOW and then to KNOW. This was one way of viewing the journey of the Beatles thus far. They started in the days of No, when many things were forbidden. Then came the time of Now, when they seized the day. Currently they were in a period of Know, where all that counted was the changes in your head. (George's catchphrase in the film is "It's all in the mind.")

Yellow Submarine was an artistic triumph that soon erased the memories of *Magical Mystery Tour*. It illustrated the power the Beatles had to energize other artists. It expertly captured the ethos of the Beatles during the period when most of the songs were recorded—the summer of 1967. But by the time it came out, in July 1968, the group was into something new. By the time the world woke up to the idea of chemical salvation, the Beatles were advocating getting high the natural way.

Chapter Eight

The Inner Light

The youth of today are really looking for some answers, for proper answers the established church can't give them, their parents can't give them, material things can't give them.
—John Lennon, 1967

Religion is here and now. Not just something you do on Sundays.
—George Harrison, 1967

If we had met the Maharishi before we had taken LSD, we wouldn't have needed to take it.
—Paul McCartney, 1967

We have found something now which fills the gap. Since meeting His Holiness, I feel great.
—Ringo Starr, 1968

*I*n August 1967 the Beatles boarded a train at Euston Station, London, bound for Bangor in North Wales. They were going to a weekend retreat for spiritual guides led by a fifty-year-old teacher from India, Maharishi Mahesh Yogi, who had shoulder-length hair, a graying beard, and wore a string of beads over his long white dhoti. By taking public transport the Beatles made it clear that they wanted their journey, and the goal of their journey, to be publicized. Journalists swarmed over the train, and the next day the world woke up to stories and photos of the Beatles and their guru.

To the public it seemed like one more zany adventure for the Fab Four. What would they do next? In the days before mass immigration and widespread talk of multiculturalism, most British people didn't know what a guru was and only had an inkling of Hindu philosophy. Maharishi Mahesh Yogi, founder of the Spiritual Regeneration Movement Foundation, instructed his followers in Transcendental Meditation (TM), something else few had heard of.

The Beatles' interest in Eastern religions originated with George. His introduction had come on February 25, 1965, six months after his first experience with pot and two months before taking LSD. While George was in the Bahamas filming *Help!* with the rest of the Beatles, Swami Vishnu-devananda spotted him and handed him a copy of a book he'd written in 1960, *The Complete Illustrated Book of Yoga.* Besides being a guide to yogic exercises, it gave an introduction to Hindu religion, explaining that truth can't be comprehended by the mind, and therefore to achieve enlightenment it is necessary to develop techniques that bypass the intellect. "Yoga has its own method and declares that the truth can be experienced," Vishnu-devananda had written in the book's introduction. "The truth can be experienced only when one transcends the senses and when the mind and intellect cease to function."

Devananda was a thirty-seven-year-old spiritual teacher and expert in Hatha and Raja Yoga who in 1957 had been sent to establish ashrams and yoga centers in the West by his guru Swami Sivananda. One of the centers he established was the Sivananda Ashram Yoga Retreat on Paradise Island in the Bahamas, and it was from here that he heard of the Beatles' impending visit. While meditating on the morning of February 25, he had a strong feeling that he should approach the group. He found them filming a cycling scene on Interfield Road. "I didn't look at [the book] in detail for some time," said George, "but at a later date I found it and I opened the cover, and it had a big OM written on it." (OM is Hinduism's sacred symbol that represents the Absolute.)

Yoga was the first step in George's journey East. The second step was the music of India. In *Help!* Ringo was pursued by the members of a fictitious Indian religious cult because he had come into possession of a sacred ring required by the next sacrificial victim of the goddess Kaili. In one scene, the Beatles are pursued by the gang, who discover them eating in an Indian restaurant where musicians are playing. After the filming, on April 5, 1965, George picked up one of the sitars on the set and began strumming it. It was to be the start of a lifelong passion.

The interest developed when he befriended David Crosby and Roger McGuinn of the Byrds while in Los Angeles during August 1965. Crosby had been introduced to the music of Ravi Shankar and John Coltrane by his manager, Jim Dickson, and that summer had become a passionate advocate of their music. For anyone who cared to listen he would play a tape of Coltrane's *Africa Brass* (Coltrane had briefly studied under Shankar) and a selection of Shankar's ragas. In order to avoid being seen by fans who were besieging the Beatles' rented Bel Air property, the four musicians held an informal jam session in the bathroom. Here Crosby raved to John and George about

Shankar's melodic brilliance. He thought the Indian master surpassed the greatest rock guitarists of the period. "Crosby and I had our twelve-strings [guitar] with us, and John and George were there listening to David tell them about Ravi Shankar," recalled McGuinn. "We showed them the licks, and they were blown away. They loved it." The impression stuck. Seven weeks later George used the sitar on "Norwegian Wood" during the recording of *Rubber Soul*.

Over the next three months George began attending meetings of the Asian Music Circle at the Hampstead home of Ayana Deva Angadi, an Indian musician married to an English painter. Founded by the internationally recognized violinist and conductor Yehudi Menuhin in 1953, the Asian Music Circle existed to promote the region's music in the West. Angadi ran the group and promoted the earliest Ravi Shankar concerts in London. In John's March 1966 interview with Maureen Cleave he mentioned that George had introduced him to Indian music, and in an April 1966 interview with disc jockey Alan Freeman for the British teenage magazine *Rave,* Paul said, "The really big change is in our tastes, in finding out about things we didn't know before. For instance, George spends all his time now listening to Indian music. He's joined the Asian Music Circle. He's really serious about it too."

On April 11, 1966, George played sitar on the *Revolver* track, "Love You To," supplementing it with tabla by Anil Bhagwat, a musician recommended to him by Ayana Angadi. For "Norwegian Wood" the sitar had been an afterthought, but "Love You To" was the first song George had written with the sitar specifically in mind.

In June while Shankar was in London to play at the Royal Festival Hall, he and George were introduced. It was no big deal for Shankar, who'd long been a world traveler and was used to meeting the top people in every profession. He'd been lionized by artists connected with the Beat movement in San Francisco in the early 1960s and later by London's folk revivalists. He'd seen fashions come and go, and yet he was always gracious enough to share his experience and insight with new generations. "I had just vaguely heard the name of Beatles, but I didn't know what it stood for or what was their popularity," he says. "I knew that they were very popular, but I had not heard a single record or song. But it was nice to see his humility and that he wanted to learn."

According to what both of them subsequently said, they clicked—the twenty-three-year-old pop guitarist from Speke and the forty-six-year-old classical musician from Benares had much in common. Shankar explained that, unlike guitar playing in rock music, playing the sitar required devotion and continuous practice. It couldn't be mastered by learning basic chords and then developed in isolation. For the first seven and a half years of his playing life he had practiced for fourteen hours a day. Even the improvisations in ragas, which to Western ears can sound like freak-outs, are carefully controlled by disciplines.

Although it's possible for a Westerner to gain a rudimentary knowledge of the sitar at home, a serious student has to travel to India to learn about the culture and religion that gave rise to the music which grew out of the chanting of the Vedas. "It's like someone in India learning opera, not knowing Italian, not knowing Western culture, not knowing the Renaissance period," he says. "You can mimic it, but you can never get deep into it."

He agreed to visit George at home for a two-hour lesson—teaching him how to hold a sitar and the fingering positions for both hands, as well as writing out the notes in the *sargam* and leaving him with some elementary exercises. A few days later he returned with his tabla player, Alla Rakha, and gave an intimate ninety-minute recital for George, John, and Ringo. At the end, George committed himself to spending at least a month in India as Shankar's private student.

"He was the first person who impressed me in a way that was just beyond being a celebrity," said George. "Ravi was my link to the Vedic world. Ravi plugged me in to the whole of reality. I mean, I met Elvis—Elvis impressed me when I was a kid, and impressed me when I met him because of the buzz of meeting Elvis—but you couldn't later on go round to him and say, 'Elvis. What's happening in the universe?'"

In July 1966, en route to London from Manila, the Beatles made an overnight stop in Delhi, their first visit to India. They asked to see the best musical instrument store and were sent to Rihki Ram and Sons, a Connaught Circle fixture since 1947. In a forty-five-minute spending spree they bought a sitar, tabla, sarod, and tempura, posing for photographs with the staff while fans gathered on the street outside. "The crowd started to be annoying," says Ajay Sharma. "So, they asked my father, Bishan das Sharma, to take the instruments over to their room at the Oberoi Sheraton. When he was there he taught Mr. George Harrison to tune his sitar and Mr. Paul McCartney to tune his tempura. My father made the sitar that Mr. George Harrison bought, and this was the one he would later play on Beatles' records."

On September 14, two weeks after the Beatles' final concert at Candlestick Park in San Francisco, George and Pattie flew to Bombay and checked into the Taj Mahal Hotel as Mr. and Mrs. Sam Wells. It was the first time since he had joined the Beatles that he'd been able to pursue his own philosophical and artistic interests without worrying about keeping to a schedule. Shankar came to their suite every day to give George lessons and then left Shambu Das, one of his star students, to oversee his progress.

George assumed that he could enjoy anonymity in India, especially as he'd just had his hair cut short. But as he visited the shops, he was noticed and his peaceful idyll was over. Shankar advised him to grow a moustache as a disguise and retreat with him to a houseboat on Dal Lake in Kashmir. George brought books on Eastern philosophy with him to study: *Autobiography of a Yogi*, by Paramhansa Yogananda (a gift from Shankar), Vivekananda's *Raja Yoga*, and the *I Ching*. "All the time we were there he was reading and studying and asking me questions," said Shankar. "I had brought many Indian classical LPs, so we were playing plenty of music, vocal as well as instrumental, and I was of course teaching him. He was also particularly interested in the whole area of yoga—and not only of hatha yoga, the physical exercise which trains you up to concentrate and have control of the body, but also the mental yoga, or meditation, which hatha yoga prepares you for."

Totally enchanted by the people, culture, music, and religion of India, George later surmised that he must have been an Indian in a previous incarnation. It impressed him that the Hindu religion pervaded the country's life in a way that Christianity didn't in the West. For the Christians that he knew, religion was something practiced between certain hours on a Sunday, something that didn't impinge on the rest of the week. Their lives weren't characterized by devotion and discipleship. He was fond of Swami Vivekananda's comment in *Raja Yoga*: "Each soul is potentially divine. The goal is to manifest that divinity. Do this through work and yoga and prayer, one or all of these means, and be free. Churches, temples, rituals and dogmas are but secondary rituals."

He was interviewed in Bombay for a BBC radio program, *The Lively Arts*, giving his first impressions of the country. Coming so shortly after the "Jesus" controversy that had given the world the impression that the Beatles were irreligious, his comments were widely reported. "The difference over here is that their religion is every second and every minute of their lives," he told the interviewer. "Their religion *is* them. It is how they act and how they conduct themselves and how they think."

His time with Shankar opened him up to a conception of music far deeper than anything he'd known before. This was music making as an act of devotion and an act of self-realization that had a lot in common with yogic discipline. "It's supposed to be one of the best methods to reach God," says Shankar. "That's what we have been told from the very beginning. When I play I go deep down and I have visions. I have so many things I can't explain. It's not like taking LSD and thinking. It's something where you feel very humble. You feel the godliness. It's almost a state of *samadhi*. They are the effects that are possible and what we aim for. But it's not only for me, but I can also make hundreds or thousands of people who are listening to it also feel it. At least at that time they feel a very divine feeling."

The time in India excited George about religion but also forced him to recognize that with all the will in the world he would never master the sitar. He was not only too busy to devote the time but too old to start. "You have to start from childhood," says Shankar. "You have to surrender to the guru. Forget everything else. You just have to be in that atmosphere for years and years and memorize and work for ten or twelve hours a day. It's like becoming a hermit. You can have all the talent in the world and do great things by yourself, but there is a limit to that. George really understood this after a few weeks and admitted it was too late for him to start. Being so popular and being one of the Beatles he had too many commitments and couldn't give it that much time. So he himself left it. I praise him for that. He left with good grace and had a genuine love and understanding for it. Using a sitar on a song or a little tabla on a song, that he did, but that has nothing to do with the music itself."

In George's case it was LSD that initially opened him up to the East. Concepts in Swami Vishnu-devananda's book such as "the world is unreal from an absolute point of view," "every human has an astral body," and "the whole universe is made up of one infinite ocean of love" that were impenetrable to him in the Bahamas in February 1965 now made sense. The sculptor David Wynne, an early convert to the teachings of Maharishi Mahesh Yogi, had spoken to George about TM when he visited them at the Hotel George V in Paris in January 1964 to do some preliminary sketches of the group, but found him uninterested.

India, which had gained its independence from Britain only in 1948, had the added allure of not being part of the modernist world that the counterculture was rebelling against. It wasn't involved in Vietnam, ecological destruction, or economic oppression. Its religion wasn't grim and puritanical. To young Western eyes, the gurus in their simple clothing and long hair, with garlands of flowers around their necks, were far hipper than the average Protestant evangelist in his polyester suit. As James W. Sire observed in his 1976 book *The Universe Next Door*, "The swing to Eastern thought is . . . primarily a retreat from Western thought. The West ends in a maze of contradictions, acts of intellectual suicide and a spectre of nihilism that haunts the dark edges of all our thoughts. Is there not another way?"

George deduced from his reading and experience of Hinduism that God is present within each person. God is not "out there" waiting to be contacted, God is "in here" waiting to be discovered. LSD had hinted at this, but the higher level of understanding came from maintaining the realization through spiritual exercises such as yoga, meditation, sensory deprivation, and music. These techniques were all designed to loosen the grip of the rational mind, in line with the belief that the mind draws a veil over the true nature of reality. Jesus, in his view, was not the son of God in a unique way but an example of a fully realized person. His achievement was that he knew he was God. He could confidently say, "I and the Father are one." As George explained to *Melody Maker*, "Everyone is a potential Jesus Christ, really. We are all trying to get to where Jesus Christ got. And we're going to be on this world until we get there."

Most of what he explored in India during his first visit was connected to yoga, but early in 1967 he was introduced to another tradition. In December 1966 a teacher named Srila Prabhupada had recorded a selection of chants devoted to the Hindu God Krishna for an album called *Krishna Consciousness*. Prabhupada had been sent to the West in 1965 to make converts and had soon realized that the people apparently most prepared to listen to what he had to say were the hippies and dropouts of America, particularly those who'd experimented with LSD and marijuana. He leafleted New York's East Village with flyers that said: "STAY HIGH FOREVER! No more coming down. Practice Krishna Consciousness. Expand your consciousness by practicing TRANSCENDENTAL SOUND VIBRATION." One of his approaches when confronting acid heads was to ask, "Do you think that LSD can produce ecstasy and higher consciousness?" If the person said yes, he would respond, "Then just imagine a room full of LSD. Krishna Consciousness is like that."

Prabhupada, like Alan Watts, Aldous Huxley, Timothy Leary, and Allen Ginsberg, knew that an LSD experience was closer to the moments of realization experienced in Hindu or Buddhist meditation than to Christian rapture. In Christian theology the will and the intellect are not seen as enemies of salvation but as God-given attributes reflecting the fact that God, like us, is personal and has a will and an intellect. The god encountered on LSD, by contrast, was impersonal. It was a force or energy with no definable character, morality, or plan for the world. John once described this god as being like electricity. You could tap into it and use the power to light a room or electrocute someone.

Leary argued that LSD was "Western yoga." He once said, "Our religious philosophy, or our philosophy about the meaning of LSD, comes closer to Hinduism than any other religion." He thought that the "spiritual cord that holds our civilization from suicide" stretched from the Himalayas of the Vedic philosophers to modern-day Liverpool and said that it was "as inevitable that George Harrison would go to India as it was that Elvis Presley would go to Hollywood."

Yet despite Leary's knowledge of Buddhism and Hinduism, he continued to trip, and this was something that disturbed George. "LSD does have its shock value," he said to Art Unger in an unpublished interview.

> Once you've taken it you do have some sort of realization. I realized that— yeh, that's it—but it's even more than that, and it's without the acid. I think Leary's just promoting it, trying to get more and more people to turn on. In actual fact it's going bad because all the people who are on it are thinking, well, from what he's said, this must be it. So they're staying on it. They're trapped.
>
> I don't doubt that he's doing it for the good and that he's basically good, but I can't really believe that he believes that this is it. If he does believe that this is IT, then he's wrong. I'll be outspoken enough to say that he's wrong. But if he believes that it is a stepping stone to IT, then he's right.

Srila Prabhupada's teaching was different from Swami Vishnu-devananda's in one crucial respect. Instead of presenting God as amorphous, he spoke of Lord Krishna as a personal deity in much the same way that Christians spoke of Christ. The goal of life was unity with Krishna, and this could be achieved by repeating his name as a mantra. The similarity with Vishnu-devananda's teaching was the shared belief that the mind had to be defeated before God consciousness was possible. Prabhupada taught that Krishna was identical to the sound of his name, so by chanting Hare Krishna, Hare Krishna, Hare Rama, Hare Rama, Hare Hare, the devotee became absorbed into Krishna.

John and George discovered the *Krishna Consciousness* album in January 1967, and it became one of their favorite records of the year. In the summer when all four Beatles and their families sailed around the Greek islands on the *MV Arvi*, they chanted together as George played ukulele and Paul and John joined in on banjos.

George encountered a third variety of Indian spirituality when Pattie and a model friend of hers, Marie-Lise Volpeliere-Pierrot, became interested in meditation. In was February 1967, at the time the Beatles were recording *Sgt. Pepper.* "We hung out a lot together, and we'd got to the point where we realized that there had to be a lot more to life," she says. "She saw an advert in the *Sunday Times* for some meditation classes. So we went to the classes and were eventually initiated into Transcendental Meditation. Then the Maharishi came to London. I'd told George about the meditation, and, at that time, they seemed to do everything as a group. If one of them did something, they would all want to do it. So we all went to this lecture at the Hilton Hotel in Park Lane."

After this lecture the Beatles were invited to Bangor for the weekend course for more advanced initiates. Being new to TM, the Beatles hardly fit the category, but Maharishi, who'd been selling his brand of meditation in the West for eight years, knew what a publicity coup they presented. He had something they wanted—a technique that promised enlightenment. They had something he wanted—the power to make TM known the world over in a matter of days. An unspoken deal was done.

While they were in Bangor being initiated into TM, news came through to the Beatles of Brian Epstein's death from a drug overdose. He had been due to join them. Epstein had many personal problems and felt threatened by Maharishi's growing influence over them. Their plans for the next twelve months had been reorganized after meeting Maharishi to include at least two months of intense meditation in India. Their spiritual well-being was now at the top of their agendas. Music making, and money making, came second. Epstein, understandably, felt that his role was being diminished.

As befitted a group in the middle of a course designed to produce understanding and tranquility, they reacted to the news of Epstein's death philosophically. "We all feel very sad, but it's controlled grief and controlled emotion," said John. "These talks on Transcendental Meditation have helped us to stand up to it so much better. You don't get upset when a young kid becomes a teenager or a teenager becomes an adult. Well, Brian is just passing into the next phase. His spirit is still round, and always will be."

After refusing for so long to attach their name to any specific cause or religion, the Beatles now spoke openly about using their influence to change people. In September 1967, John said, "We want to learn the meditation thing properly, so that we can propagate it and sell the whole idea to everyone. This is how we plan to use our power now. They've always called us leaders of youth, and we believe this is a good way to give a lead." Specifically, they talked about setting up a meditation academy in London to prove that for them meditation wasn't just a fad or a gimmick.

In an interview with a short-lived British teen magazine, *Intro*, John and George discussed how their newfound beliefs could affect their records. "We don't know how this will come out in the music," said George. "Don't expect to hear Transcendental Meditation all the time." John added, "I don't honestly know how anything I've felt has come out in my music. It's usually in retrospect I've seen what I've been saying." George didn't want the Beatles' relationship with Maharishi to appear to be like that between "Cliff and Billy Graham." The previous year Cliff Richard, who until 1964 was the Beatles' main opponent in the U.K. charts, had announced his Christian conversion during an appearance on stage with the American evangelist at one of Graham's mass meetings at the Earls Court Arena in London.

"I'd rather not use any obvious things until you can see how it's naturally affected the music," said George. "The same as we didn't really shove our LP full of pot and drugs, but there was an effect," said John. "We were more consciously trying to keep it out. We wouldn't say, 'I had some acid, baby. So groovy!' but there was a sort of feeling that something happened between *Revolver* and *Sgt. Pepper*."

The songs recorded between their meeting Maharishi and studying under him in India exemplify this approach. Unlike the Beach Boys, who wrote "TM Song," the Beatles avoided any hot gospel for Maharishi, allowing their beliefs to implicitly affect their music. Their familiarity with mantras led to an increased use of repetition, noticeably on "I Am the Walrus" ("jooba, jooba") and "Hello Goodbye" ("hela, heloa"). This reached its high point in "Hey Jude" (with over four minutes of the sound "la" repeated 220 times), "You Know My Name (Look Up the Number)" ('You know my name" repeated 28 times), "All Together Now" (title repeated 49 times), and "Let It Be." "All music is mantra," John said in 1969. "Everything is mantra. . . . Pop music is like the people's mantra, and the offbeat keeps it steady."

It affected the stories they told as new concerns began to hold their attention. In "Fool on the Hill" Paul wrote about an enlightened individual mocked for being different. The image of him seeing the world turning on its axis implied divine insight. He saw things as if from outside. The conclusion was that the mockers were the real fools. "I think I was writing about someone like Maharishi," said Paul. "His detractors called him a fool. Because of his giggle he wasn't taken too seriously. It was this idea of a fool on the hill, a guru in a cave, I was attracted to. . . . Saviours and gurus are generally spat upon, so I thought for my generation I'd suggest that they weren't as stupid as they looked."

"Across the Universe," a beautiful evocation of a mind trying to empty itself in the search for realization, came to John when he was half asleep. The narrator negotiates slithering words and waves of joy in a search for "limitless undying love." His reference to "Jai Guru Dev" frames the quest in the context of Transcendental Meditation, Dev being the teacher who schooled Maharishi in the Vedanta tradition.

After letting their beliefs seep naturally into the songs it was time to try something more "obvious." At the end of September John and George had appeared live in an edition of the British TV show *The Frost Report* devoted to Transcendental Meditation. In the invited audience was a Sanskrit scholar from Cambridge University, Juan Mascaró. In 1962 Mascaró had published a translation of the Hindu holy book the *Bhagavad Gita* and in 1965 had translated the *Upanishads*. A few weeks after the show, having now listened to "Within You without You," Mascaró mailed George a copy of *Lamps of Fire*, an anthology of spiritual wisdom that he had published in 1958. As a postscript to the letter he enclosed he wrote, "Might it not be interesting to put into your music a few words of TAO, for example No. 48, page 66 of LAMPS?"

On page 66 was a ten-line rendition of the forty-seventh chapter of the *Tao Te Ching* that Mascaró had titled "The Inner Light":

> Without going out of my door
> I can know all things on earth.
> Without looking out of my window
> I can know the ways of heaven.
>
> For the farther one travels
> The less one knows.
>
> The sage therefore
> Arrives without travelling,
> Sees all without looking,
> Does all without doing.

These verses struck a chord with George. Although Taoist rather than Hindu, they chimed with his view that all spiritual riches were within, and there was no need to search to find them. George told *Melody Maker* in December 1967: "Yes, that's the whole thing why people have missed God. They haven't been able to see God because he is hidden in them. All the time people concentrate their energies and activities outwards on this surface level that we live on. But it's only by turning your concentration and directing it inwardly, in a form of meditation, that you can see your own god in there. When you realise that, then you can realise a lot more things about the surface level, because you're now looking at it from a more subtle point of view."

The *Tao Te Ching*, reckoned to have been composed by Lao Tse, was over two and a half thousand years old but seemed contemporary to the Beatles. Observations in songs like "All You Need Is Love," "Baby You're a Rich Man," and "Within You without You" were remarkably similar to those of the Chinese sage. George composed music for "The Inner Light," and in January 1968, when in Bombay putting together the soundtrack to the movie *Wonderwall*, he recorded the backing track with local musicians, adding his vocals at Abbey Road on his return to London. Next to "Within You without You" it was the most explicitly religious track the Beatles would ever put their name to. It became the B side of "Lady Madonna."

On February 15, 1968, all four Beatles and their partners flew to India for what was intended to be a two-month course at Maharishi's ashram at Rishikesh, in the foothills of the Himalayas close to the sacred Ganges River. They were to be among seventy international students wanting intensive study to be TM teachers. By the end of their stay it was promised that they would be able to meditate for increasingly long periods and reach higher levels of consciousness than ever before.

For John, Paul, George, and Ringo it was the first prolonged non-Beatle activity they'd ever engaged in together. Leaving behind the only culture they'd ever known, they found themselves living in sparsely furnished bungalows with no air-conditioning, attending two ninety-minute lectures a day, spending hours alone learning to meditate, and studying books like the Maharishi's *Commentary on the Bhagavad Gita* or *The Science of Being and Art of Living*. Because the Beatles had missed two weeks of the course, the Maharishi gave them additional private instruction in the afternoons at his bungalow.

"We were all ready for it," says Cynthia Lennon. "We were ready to step off the merry-go-round of lunacy. I think they were all overdoing it on every level. They'd lost Brian. It was an escape route. It was a very good escape route because it was something that was totally opposite that would hopefully replenish and revitalize them and give them more spiritual awareness."

Although Maharishi liked to promote his teaching as a science, there was no disguising the fact that his ideas came from the Vedic tradition of Hinduism. Asked if TM could become a substitute for religion in his life, George responded, "It's not a substitute for religion. It is religion. The problem is that if you talk about it as a religion it puts people off because they have a concept of religion that has made religion unsuccessful." Maharishi said that life is composed of Being (absolute existence) and karma (relative experience). The goal of the meditation is to escape the karmic wheel, the cycle of birth and death, and be brought into the realm of Being. "Since karma is opposed to the state of Being," he wrote, "any process which brings karma to an end will result in the state of Being."

The scientific bit (he studied physics and math at Allahabad University in the 1930s) came in Maharishi's contemporary explanation of why meditation produced such satisfying results. His theory was that the mind is like an ocean, and thoughts are bubbles rising from the sea bed that are only spotted by the conscious mind when they break on the surface. In meditation the bubbles are traced back down to the sea bed, the source of thinking, where pure consciousness can be found. Frequent meditation supposedly assures access to this purity and therefore makes it easier to escape the "gross level" of existence. "The continued practice of transcendental meditation results in such a strong infusion of Being into the nature of the mind that the mind, while continuing to behave and experience in the field of relative existence, begins to live the nature of eternal Being," Maharishi wrote. "This has tremendous practical value for the mind engaged in day-to-day existence."

Those initiated into TM received a secret mantra supposedly chosen to fit the specific bodily impulses of each individual. "Your body is full of little pulses," George explained.

> These pulses act together to form a whole impulse. It depends what type of life you lead and what sort of things you do. The instructor gives a mantra, the sound of which goes with this impulse and by thinking of it, or by turning it over and over in your mind, your thoughts become finer and finer until you arrive at a transcendental state.
>
> You say it out loud at first and then you turn it down and keep repeating it until it's just in your mind. Then you find you're not thinking of it as a word or a syllable, and the rhythm becomes fainter and fainter until you can hardly recognise it at all. Then it just fades out, but when it does that, you have reached the subtle state of thought. You're still conscious, but it's just as if you're in a nice warm experience.

According to Nancy Cooke de Herrera, a wealthy American socialite assigned by the Maharishi to look after the Beatles' needs in Rishikesh, the lectures took the form of storytelling, wise sayings, and question-and-answer sessions. The evening gatherings, for example, were devoted to picking apart the conventional wisdom of the West, especially the claims of Christianity, the religious background of most of the students. "Let the knowledge flow from me to you," Maharishi said, advising students not to take notes but rather to "comprehend the course as a whole."

He dismissed Christ's divinity, saying that no one who was divine would have suffered in this world. He said the suffering Christ was a "humiliating teaching." If a man in communion with God can suffer, then what is the use of self-realization and God-realization? He believed that the West had been infected by the teaching that grace came through suffering. He said this was a misunderstanding. "If you want to pray, meditate first," he said. "That is systematic communion. And then pray. When man has the sympathy of nature, creation will support his desires. A loving son eventually will not even have to desire; the father will know his needs and simultaneously fulfill them. This is the role nature will begin to play in your lives." Paul wrote "Mother Nature's Son," which was inspired not only by a particular lecture given by Maharishi but by the trees and streams of the Himalayas, the smell of the flowers, and the feel of the breeze. Separately, John wrote a song called "Child of Nature," which was recorded as a demo but never used.

Songwriting flourished under these unusual but stimulating conditions. They would trade music in the afternoons on the flat roofs of the bungalows or in the cool of the dining area with other musicians including Donovan, Beach Boy Mike Love, and flautist Paul Horn. Love inspired Paul to write the

Beach Boys' pastiche "Back in the USSR," and Donovan taught John the finger-picking style of guitar he used on "Julia," a song about his mother that started with two lines from a poem by the Lebanese poet Kahlil Gibran.

Composing on acoustic instruments in the open air while dressed in basic white cotton clothes, their music was informed by the simplicity of their surroundings. The long periods spent alone trying to reach pure consciousness put them in touch with previously neglected areas of their minds—long-buried memories of childhood, unresolved problems, lost love, comic books, movies. Paul invented characters such as Desmond and Molly Jones, Martha, Rocky Raccoon, Nancy McGill, and the working girl from the north of England who went to Hollywood. George wrote *Animal Farm*–style social comments about the bourgeois in "Piggies" and about the need for illumination in "Sour Milk Sea," a song based on a tantric picture, *Kalladadi Samudra*, and later recorded by Jackie Lomax.

Birds, flowers, clouds, the sun, and the wind appeared in more lyrics than ever before, and events in the ashram inspired several songs. "Dear Prudence" was written for Prudence Farrow, sister of the actress Mia Farrow, who meditated for too long, too soon, locked herself in her bungalow, and went into a catatonic state. John's song was a plea for her to come out and join the rest of them. The idea for "Why Don't We Do It in the Road," Paul's most minimalist song, came to him when he saw the mating habits of the local monkeys. He envied their freedom to have sex whenever and wherever they wanted, unhindered by human concerns for decorum or guilt. This was Paul at his most existential. Some students had been concerned about the unmarried Paul sharing a bungalow with Jane Asher, wondering if it was consistent with the search for spiritual transcendence. Maharishi told them it was OK because actions had to be "life destructive" to be sins.

"The Continuing Story of Bungalow Bill" was John's report of a tiger shoot that Nancy Cooke de Herrera went on with her son Rik. When the group returned to the ashram, Rik having scored his first kill, John wanted to know if game hunting squared with the nature-loving principles behind the Maharishi's teaching. Along with Paul and George, he was contemplating vegetarianism. If all life was sacred, how could one life justify taking another? "The whole point of life is to harmonise with everything, every aspect of creation," George told *Melody Maker*. "That means down to not killing flies, eating meat, killing people or chopping the trees down."

For John the times of contemplation seemed to stir dark sediment in the depths of his mind. Some of the images in the songs he wrote in India are more disturbing than anything he had written before. "Yer Blues" with its wish for death and its images of an eagle picking at an eyeball and a worm licking a bone was startling in both its despair and the graphic horror of the images. It was as though he had been put in touch with a new and unpleasant realm, something that would reappear in his songs from then on.

Paul Horn believes that Rishikesh opened the Beatles up and reconnected them with their feelings. "You find out more about yourself on deeper levels, and it stimulates your creativity," he says. "Look how prolific they were during that time. Whenever you have time away from the hustle and bustle it helps. Here they were in India, away from all the pressures. They were away from the telephone and staying in the Himalayas with a wise man. It's a rare time. When you're able to be quiet inside, that's when the creativity starts coming up. They were very creative, and so was Donovan."

The Beatles' visit ended abruptly and unsatisfactorily. Ringo, who had always intended only to drop in for a short time, left after a fortnight. "Really his meditation camp is a bit like a Butlin's holiday camp," he said, referring to a chain of chalet-style holiday camps that were popular with the British working class in the 1950s and 1960s. "Of course, there were lectures and things all the time, but it was very much like a holiday." Paul and Jane stayed for five weeks and left John and George and their partners to complete the final two weeks. In the end there was a falling out, and George and John left in disgust after having been told by one of the girls taking the course that Maharishi had made a sexual advance. Paul Horn explains: "One of the American students, a teacher from New York, became more interested in the Beatles than in meditation, and she started all this crap about Maharishi having made a pass at her and chasing her. She told the Beatles and, for whatever reason, they bought it. They got very upset about it and left. I wasn't in the room when it happened, but I know that there were a lot of rumors, triangles, and jealousies, and she got at the Beatles through saying this about Maharishi."

This event coincided with dissatisfaction over a TV film apparently financed on the promise that the Beatles would be featured. "[Maharishi's] main trouble," said George, "was his tendency to spread something subtle in a gross way. I don't agree that mass media—like TV—was a suitable way to spread Maharishi's teachings." Paul Horn sees these objections as mere surface reaction. "The bottom line was that it was time for them to go home," he says. "This was just the catalyst."

Whatever the truth, John was disenchanted, not only with Maharishi but with spiritual leaders in general. Paul's attitude, appropriately enough for someone who had just written "Why Don't We Do It in the Road," was that it didn't matter. Even if the claim was true, Maharishi was unmarried and hadn't taken a vow of chastity. Feeling that he'd made himself vulnerable only to be let down again, John was eager to believe that the guru was a fraud who was primarily interested in the Beatles for money and publicity. At a press conference in New York, Paul said, "We made a mistake. We thought there was more to him than there was. He's human. We thought at first he wasn't." John wrote a blistering song called "Maharishi" that tore into the guru for having "made a fool of everyone"; it was so bitter it had to be renamed "Sexy Sadie" to avoid being libelous.

At least half the tracks on their new album, recorded between May and October of 1968, were written in Rishikesh. After *Revolver*, *Sgt. Pepper*, and the tracks for *Magical Mystery Tour* some expected that they would now carry their experimentation to a point where their music was barely recognizable as pop. The surprise was that instead of going further out, they ventured further in. Instead of a mind-boggling full-color cover, they went for plain white. Instead of complex mixes and sound effects, they went for a more acoustic sound on a lot of tracks. Instead of puns and psychedelic-sounding names, they called the album simply *The Beatles*.

The white cover design, conceived by the painter and collage artist Richard Hamilton, served two purposes. It confounded all the expectations that had built up since *Rubber Soul* that the Beatles' artwork would get more complicated, and it was a visual analogue to the meditative state. During meditation—George had managed to achieve fourteen-hour stretches and John eight-hour meditations—the object was to release the conscious mind and descend to the deep level of pure consciousness.

During the recording, as the Beatles came down from their Himalayan high, it was obvious that their paths would soon diverge. Ringo had never had more than a loose interest in the group's philosophical meandering. He'd taken pills, smoked dope, dropped acid, and meditated along with John, Paul, and George, but he was never as dedicated a pilgrim. Keeping up mattered less to him because he wasn't a songwriter and wasn't in search of material or a message.

Paul didn't want to be left behind by John and George, and he only took LSD to find out what it was like. His approach to meditation was more businesslike than religious. He saw it primarily as an effective stress-buster, not a path to godhood, and he had a glass-paneled geodesic meditation dome built in the garden of his London home as a place where he could unwind beneath the stars. He remained the "post-Christian pragmatic realist" identified by *Newsweek*. "If I was working ten hours a day, it would be an incredible help because meditation really sets you up," he told the *Daily Sketch* in March 1968. "You are ready for what the next day might bring. And you have a good day."

Although John seemed won over to the Hindu worldview when he was in Bangor, he never again showed such unwavering conviction. He didn't disagree with the idea that he was part of a cosmic whole, but he didn't see the need to deify it. He had returned to the existentialist outlook of his early days: if everything that existed was part of God, we were still alone and without guidance. He was suspicious of anyone claiming to understand the mysteries of existence. His approach was to pick whatever wisdom seemed useful but not to subscribe to a single coherent philosophy or religion. He summed this up in 1969: "I found that the best thing for me is to take a little bit from here and a little bit from there."

George was the only Beatle to remain convinced by Eastern religion, although his view was syncretistic, combining elements of Hinduism with Taoism, Buddhism, and even a dash of Christianity. His two contributions to *The Beatles*, both written on his return to Britain, were informed by his faith. "Long Long Long" was a love song to God. "While My Guitar Gently Weeps" grew out of an experiment with chance principles learned from the *I Ching*. Picking a random book off the shelf at his parents' home in Lancashire, he flicked it open and wrote a song based on the first words his eyes focused on. The words happened to be "gently weeps." The method, he said, was based "on the Eastern concept that everything is relative to everything else, as opposed to the Western view that things are merely coincidental." It was a method of composing that John Cage had taken to extremes in his *Music of Changes* (1951). Believing that purity is achieved when personal choice is eliminated, every note in the piece was decided by the toss of the yarrow sticks.

During sessions for *The Beatles* George was contacted by the International Society for Krishna Consciousness, the group that had made the Krishna chant record he'd been so enamored of in 1967. Perhaps encouraged by John's mention of Krishna in "I Am the Walrus," its devotees had targeted Apple Records to suggest that the Beatles record the Hare Krishna mantra. When a demo tape of the chants was formally rejected, and suspecting that the Beatles themselves hadn't heard it, they resorted to a number of gimmicks to attract attention. Once they had an apple pie with "Hare Krishna" lettered on it delivered to the office. Another time they sent a clockwork apple with the words of the mantra painted on it.

A devotee known as Syamasundara continued the campaign to attract a Beatle, and his persistence paid off. He hung around the Apple office, and George spotted his shaven head and orange dhoti. According to Syamasundara George came over and said, "Where have you been? I've been trying to meet the Hare Krishna people for the last couple of years. Why don't you come to my place tomorrow?"

Thus began the connection between the Beatles and ISKCON (International Society for Krishna Consciousness). George, in particular, wanted to learn more about bhakti yoga and the Vedic philosophy, and he socialized with a vanguard of devotees who'd been sent to London to establish ISKCON in Britain. Just as Maharishi had seen the Beatles as a spearhead for his Spiritual Regeneration Movement Foundation, so now Srila Prabhupada saw the potential for the Beatles to publicize ISKCON. In one letter he speculated that if the Beatles combined forces with ISKCON, "surely we shall change the face of the world so much politically harassed by the manoeuvres of the politicians." On January 11, 1969, after being told that George was composing songs in praise of Krishna, he wrote to the London group: "He [George] is very thoughtful. When we actually meet, I shall be able to give him thoughts about separation from Krishna, and they will be able to compose very attractive songs for public reception. The public is in need of such songs, and if they are administered through nice agents like the Beatles, it will surely be a great success."

John vacillated in his opinions about Krishna Consciousness. In May 1969 he invited devotees to his hotel room in Montreal to sing on his recording of "Give Peace a Chance," and at the close of the song he repeated the Hare Krishna mantra. He told the *Montreal Star* that he now got his strength "from Hare Krishna." He then added the confusing statement, "We don't mind arguing with a few disciples, but Hare Krishna's where it's at. And whether we get round to chanting; only time will tell. It's not where we're at right now, but we fully believe it." If Krishna was "where it's at," why not chant? If he "fully believed" it, why not commit?

Resisting the idea of the Beatles recording the Hare Krishna mantra, George asked the London devotees to record it themselves as an Apple Records single. They sang and played Indian instruments at Abbey Road while George added organ and then overdubbed bass guitar and additional vocals. Released in the summer of 1969, it became a Top 20 hit in Britain, and the Krishna devotees ended up performing it on *Top of the Pops*, Britain's weekly half-hour TV chart show.

While the single was still on the charts, the British followers moved into a building on John's seventy-six-acre estate at Tittenhurst Park, Ascot. A musical recital room in the main house was turned into a makeshift temple to Krishna, while the movement's central London building at Bury Place in Central London was being refurbished. When Srila Prabhupada made his first visit to England, he went straight from Heathrow to Tittenhurst Park, where an apartment for him and his servant was made ready.

When Prabhupada was settled in, he and some of his disciples debated with George and John. George was still practicing meditation, using the mantra given to him by Maharishi, but John had already stopped. His big question was, how was it possible to tell a true spiritual teacher from a false one, and how could he be expected to know which mantra would revive the "original, pure consciousness" as Prabhupada described it?

A tape recording of the meeting shows that Prabhupada found it difficult to satisfy John's insistent probing.

Prabhupada: If you don't receive the mantra through the proper channel, it may not really be spiritual.

John: How would you know, anyway? How are you able to tell? I mean, for any of your disciples or us or anybody else who goes to a spiritual master—how are we to tell if he's for real or not?

Prabhupada: You shouldn't go to just *any* spiritual master.

John: Yes, we should go to a true master. But how are we to tell one from the other?

Prabhupada: It is not that you can go to just any spiritual master. He must be a member of a recognized *sampradaya*, a particular line of disciplic succession.

John: But what if one of these masters who's not in the line says exactly the same thing as one who is? What if he says his mantra is coming from the Vedas and he seems to speak with as much authority as you? He could probably be right. It's confusing. [It's] like having too many fruits on a plate.

Ultimately John didn't follow Krishna, and neither did Paul. On two of his early solo songs, "God" and "I Found Out," John made a point of announcing his rejection of Krishna, saying that the belief was "pie in the sky." George remained faithful, particularly up to the time of Prabhupada's death in 1977, writing an introduction to his book *Krishna* (1970) and supporting the movement financially.

However, in key respects the Eastern view of life had now taken over from the rudimentary Christian outlook they'd inherited from their Liverpool childhoods. The god they would talk about from now on was an impersonal force rather than a personal being; they meditated rather than prayed; believed in the karmic wheel rather than heaven and hell; favored the *I Ching* over the Holy Spirit; would visit an astrologer for guidance rather than a priest.

Chapter Nine

Let It Be

I suppose now what I'm interested in is Nirvana, the Buddhist heaven. I don't know much about it, or really understand it enough to explain it.

—John Lennon, 1968

Religion and God are the only things that exist. I know that some people think I must be a nutcase. I find it hard not to myself sometimes, because I still see things in an ordinary way. But I know that when you believe, it's real and nice. Not believing, it's all confusion and emptiness.

—George Harrison, 1968

I'm quite happy to sit back and wait for whatever's coming next. I haven't found the answer to the question "What's life all about?" and I don't suppose I ever will. It would take millions of philosophers millions of years to sort that out.

—Ringo Starr, 1968

We're learning to be. That's all.

—Paul McCartney, 1968

*A*ware of their power and conscious of their key role in the cultural revolution of the 1960s, the Beatles developed utopian dreams. On a whim John bought Dorinish, an uninhabited ninety-two-acre island off the west coast of Ireland, and had his psychedelically painted gypsy caravan taken over by boat. In 1970, not having spent a single night there, he allowed it to be used by the Diggers, a hippie tribe dedicated to living outside the system who camped there for two years. In a private conversation George told *Datebook*'s Art Unger that they also planned to buy four Greek islands, one for each Beatle, so that they could live together in peace and harmony, protected from the outside world.

This plan never came to anything. The only utopian dream that got off the ground was Apple, the multifaceted company that was developed after Brian Epstein's death to embody their ideals. This was to be their Pepperland, built on a foundation of love, fairness, and beauty, with not a Blue Meanie on the payroll. The employees, like the Beatles, were almost all under thirty years old, there was no dress code or restriction on hair length, drugs were allowed on the premises, and no supervisors checked on progress. Apple was going to be the ultimate Yes and Now company. It would take seriously the ideas that the straight world dismissed. It would nurture the careers of neglected artists. There would be no red tape, no bureaucracy, no hype, and no suspicion of motives.

Apple Corps Ltd. had been formed in April 1967 to replace Beatles Ltd., and later that year the Apple Boutique opened at 94 Baker Street with clothes designed by a Dutch collective known as the Fool. Then, in 1968, largely at Paul's instigation, plans to expand into television, film, music publishing, recording, and electronics were unveiled. There was even serious discussion about opening a school on libertarian lines where astrology and electronics would be taught alongside math and science. There would be no obligation for Apple to make a huge profit. The real achievement would be to offer an alternative way of doing business that worked and would consequently challenge the principles of the straight world.

The assumption behind Apple was one that had been implicit in the Beatles' outlook. It was the belief that people are essentially good and if allowed complete freedom of behavior and imagination will behave honorably and flourish creatively. Prohibitions and censorship were the enemies of fulfillment. John even went so far as to say that he thought governments should be abolished, leaving each community to look after its own affairs. "To my mind there's no such thing as good or bad," he told a university magazine in 1969. "There's only comfortable or not so comfortable."

This new business provided a chance to return to the garden of Eden, to get back to where they once belonged. Significantly the company logo was an unbitten apple, and one of the first albums released on the Apple label was John and Yoko's experimental *Two Virgins* with its controversial cover photographs of the couple facing the camera completely naked, which had to be sold in a paper bag to avoid prosecution for obscenity. "There's no shame in appearing as you were born," said John. "Other people's minds were wrong, not ours." A headline in *Record Mirror* called them "Adam and Eve—Twentieth Century Style." Derek Taylor tried to stoke the controversy by including a quotation from Genesis 2 in the advance publicity: "And they were both naked, the man and his wife, and were not ashamed." John thought this was hilarious. "You see," he said to one journalist. "They were not ashamed! Get it? See, it's from the Bible."

The vision was that Apple would be an enterprise free of greed, corruption, and cynicism, and therefore it wouldn't need the normal company rules. Creative people would be treated respectfully, and no one would be brushed off or ripped off. The Statue of Liberty declared, "Bring me your huddled masses." Apple more or less said, "Bring me your weird, noncommercial, and previously rejected ideas." At the press conference launch in May 1968 Paul said, "If you come to me and say, 'I've had such-and-such a dream,' I will say, 'Here's so much money. Go away and do it.' We've already bought all our dreams, so now we want to share that possibility with others. There's no desire in any of our heads to take over the world. That was Hitler. There is, however, a desire to get power in order to use it for the good." On the *Johnny Carson Show* he explained it as an experiment in "controlled weirdness" or "Western communism."

The first thing that went wrong was that Apple was deluged with more manuscripts, demo tapes, and movie proposals than it could cope with. The second was that the nonjudgmental, no-pressure way of conducting business, which assumed the innate goodness of everyone, encouraged laziness, carelessness, and self-indulgence. The third was that rather than employing sound economic principles, the Beatles, still believing that the irrational was more desirable than the rational, began to trust in whim, coincidence, and even astrological charts when making decisions. This was the period when John, in all seriousness (May 1968), announced that he was the messiah. They even paid for a company fortune-teller, a former Apple Boutique employee named Caleb, to read tarot cards and consult the *I Ching*. According to Denis O'Dell, one of the original directors of the company, Caleb rapidly became a key figure in Apple. "In fact, such was his status during the first months of the organization that there were times when hugely important business decisions would be determined not by reasoned arguments thrashed out during board meetings but on the strength of Caleb's predictions. And a number of key posts and positions within Apple were determined in a similar way."

"Controlled weirdness" may have helped produce good art, but it didn't create good business. This was mainly because the weirdness became impossible to control. The Beatles were rarely on site to monitor it (they spent most of 1968 and 1969 recording) and, anyway, in this new garden of Eden, who would dare to make judgments about acceptable and nonacceptable weirdness? Only Blue Meanies stamped their feet and said no. The Beatles had succeeded in making the previously weird seem normal through changing people's perception of weirdness from "absolutely forbidden" to "unexplored and worth a try." To be labeled a "freak," in 1968, was a compliment. No one in the counterculture wanted to be accused of being normal, sensible, straight, or levelheaded.

In a world where there was "no such thing as good or bad," it was hard to rap knuckles when property went missing or expense accounts bulged unnaturally. Apple's Savile Row headquarters became a target for freeloaders, con men, and all types of social misfits. At the launch of the company, John and Paul's claim not to know "anything at all about business" was applauded because it sounded similar to their claim not to be able to read a note of music—a confession of an admirable primitivism. They had proved that you didn't need to be filled up with rules to write memorable songs, so maybe the same premise applied to other areas of life.

However, the untrained minds that could spot a good melody weren't so finely tuned to the world of employment, accountants, pension funds, mortgages, market shares, and profit margins. Apple Electronics, the division presided over by John's friend Alex Mardas, didn't produce a single invention. None of "Magic" Alex's ideas—the wallpaper that could act as a loudspeaker, the invisible force field to protect property, the paint that could change color at the flick of a switch, the phone that would dial up on hearing the name of the person to be called, or the flying saucer made from car engine components—resulted in a prototype being created. The school that was to have featured John's childhood friend Ivan Vaughan as head teacher never opened. The Apple Boutique had to close after six months with unsustainable losses, much of it caused by staff pilfering the stock. By the end of the year John admitted, "It's a bit messy and it needs tightening up. We haven't got half the money that people think we have. We have enough to live on, but we can't let Apple go on like this."

The study period in India was the last time that the four Beatles were ideologically united. Since the group's formation they had shared a communal mind, and one member could confidently answer questions on behalf of the others. There had been times when George was more deeply involved in meditation, Paul in art, or John in politics, but inevitably the gap would close. Roger McGuinn of the Byrds remembered asking George in August 1965 whether he believed in God. George had replied, "We're not sure about that one yet." The answer had struck McGuinn as unusual because it suggested that their opinions on the crucial issues of life were decided jointly rather than individually.

By the end of 1968 the sense of a single Beatles' point of view had gone. As they went on their explorations, they were no longer linked by the same rope. Paul had started a new life with Linda Eastman and found his contentment in hearth and home. John was living with the avant-garde artist Yoko Ono after having divorced from Cynthia and was taking part in performance art and political protest outside of the group. Ringo was still searching. *The Beatles* (White Album) had confirmed this division. More than any previous Beatles album it was a collection of solo tracks, a fact underlined by the absence of any group photo on the sleeve. When they started to record the album that would eventually be titled *Let It Be*, they each had different ambitions, priorities, and outlooks. "When we make it we're one," muttered a frustrated John between takes on one track. "When we don't, we're one person in turmoil."

Only George would doggedly pursue the religious path. He continued to meditate, practice the sitar, and read books of Eastern philosophy. When he spoke of his view of life his conversation was always peppered with references to *samsara*, *karma*, and *maya*. On the question of Maharishi he was most careful not to denigrate him even though he had since shifted his allegiance to the Krishna leader Srila Prabhupada. "Life is a process of finding stepping stones and treading on them," he said. "The Maharishi was one of the stepping stones in our life."

George became so devout that it affected his commitment to the Beatles. His uncertainty about fame, which had started very early in his career, found support in the theory that our purpose is discovered through being cosmically conscious and not in living on the "gross" level. He was aware that the music industry survived by glorifying the very things that his religion encouraged him not to get tangled up in. "This actual world is an illusion," he said. "It's been created by worldliness and identification with objects."

This conclusion created tensions over what was expected of a Beatle. As Hunter Davies noted in his official biography of the group, published in 1968, George was "the one who has an absolute mania about any publicity of any sort. Anything getting into the papers about him personally makes him furious." He also hated the thought of having to tour again. There were plans to film a concert of the *Let It Be* material. Suggestions of locations included a Roman amphitheater in Tunisia, an ocean liner, the Houses of Parliament, a hospital, and even Liverpool Cathedral. George didn't want to play any of them.

There was wrangling over the Beatles' finances. Solicitors, accountants, and lawyers were hired to shore up Apple's crumbling fortunes. This too offended George. In the early days he'd always been the Beatle most interested in money—at least the one keenest to discuss it—but now he displayed detachment. He contrasted the venality of the record industry with the spiritual and artistic dedication of his Indian musician friends. "Although we'd all been plugging into the peace [while in India] things were splitting off and racing off down a blind alley," he said. "If everyone had 'got it' while in

Rishikesh, they would have been meditating more and not getting into so many distractions. Or, if we had to get involved more with outside matters, meditation would have helped handle it. Then Apple might have turned into all the things it could, and should, have been. Instead, we all went crazy."

These beliefs, combined with his naturally laid-back nature and the fact that he was the youngest Beatle, led him to feel isolated even within the group. The sound tapes made by the crew that filmed the *Let It Be* sessions reveal that in the conversations between songs George frequently tried to introduce new material that was eventually ignored. The more powerful personalities of John and Paul predominated, even though "While My Guitar Gently Weeps" had been one of the stand-out tracks of *The Beatles*.

It's now known that George was already writing songs that he would keep for *All Things Must Pass*, his first solo album. The title track, based on one of Timothy Leary's *Psychedelic Prayers*, was offered to the Beatles during the *Let It Be* sessions, as was "Hear Me Lord," a song that Prabhupada must have been told about in January 1969 because in a letter to the London devotees he commented "I am so glad that Mr. Harrison is composing songs like 'Lord whom we so long ignored.'" If George was to remain in music he intended to use his songs to raise Krishna Consciousness. There was not much scope for this within the Beatles.

"All that sort of Beatle thing is trivial and unimportant," he said. "I'm fed up with all this 'me,' 'us,' 'I' stuff and all the meaningless things we do. I'm trying to work out solutions to the more important things inside." Those who became totally committed to the International Society for Krishna Consciousness renounced the world. The women didn't wear makeup or style their hair. The men shaved their heads and wore simple cotton dhotis. They had few material possessions, lived simply, forsook alcohol and drugs, believed that sex should be used only within marriage for procreation, and chanted "Hare Krishna" for long periods at a time.

In common with many fundamentalist religions, it was dualistic. The spiritual world was good but could only be approached by turning off the intellect. The material world was bad and worked against our desire to be fully realized. Material things, including our own bodies, were full of traps and temptations. "Each person has to burn out his own karma," George said, "and escape from the chains of *maya*, reincarnation, and all that." Not surprisingly his interest in everything surrounding the Beatles waned. As he began to spend more time chanting and avoiding the world, his marriage to Pattie began to suffer. Their mutual friend Eric Clapton later commented, "All she wanted was for him to say 'I love you,' and all he was doing was meditating."

George's belief was essentially life-negating because everything received through our senses and evaluated by our minds he now viewed as an enticement to remain in the world of illusion. Whereas Christians viewed their bodies as marred because of sin but wonderful because they were given by God, George adopted a low view of his physical self. "This impermanent body," he said, "a bag of bones and flesh, is mistaken for our true self, and we have accepted this temporary condition to be final."

His most successful song from this period, "Something," was assumed to be about Pattie, but when he first played it to a group of Krishna devotees that he'd invited down to Esher for the evening, he told them it was actually about Krishna. He was imaging it saying, "Something in the way he moves . . . ," but realized he could never sing that on a Beatles album. "I had to say 'she,'" he told his friends, "otherwise they'd think I'm a poof."

Despite his happy-go-lucky exterior Ringo was an idealist and a believer that peace would slowly be ushered in as the baby boomers took over positions of power. "The young people all want peace, and they'll get it if they just wait because we're going to outlive them all. The people in power now are going to die and not be thought of again."

Although no longer a practicing meditator, he still clung to the Hindu ideas he'd been introduced to in Rishikesh. In an interview in November 1969 he said that although Maharishi wasn't the one for him he'd learned a lot and believed that someone else would come into his life and take him on further in his spiritual journey. "In the end I'll find him. I believe that if it's my time to find out, I'll find out. I believe in reincarnation. You come down to do something. I just follow the path. After this life I'll go somewhere else and I'll get taught something else. There are a lot of stages, and in the end you become one with the god-figure. Then you don't come back anymore. That's when you live in ecstasy, you know; in heaven. I don't think there's anything beyond that, beyond actually being one with God. You just have to keep hoping and praying."

Never convinced by Hinduism, John was now embracing what he called "Yoko's type of Zen." Yoko was introduced to both Christianity and Buddhism as a child and had been part of the New York avant-garde art scene of the late 1950s and early 1960s when Zen was an attractive alternative to young Americans because it promised enlightenment but had no dogma, no commandments, no heaven, no hell, and no God. One of the most influential promoters of Zen in the West was Alan Watts, an ordained minister who became dean of the American Academy of Asian Studies in San Francisco. With his intimate knowledge of Christian theology he was able to explain

Eastern thought to the Western mind. In his 1958 booklet *Beat Zen, Square Zen, and Zen* he explained that Zen had many affinities with European existentialism. "Above all," he wrote, "I believe that Zen appeals to many in the post-Christian West because it does not preach, moralize, and scold in the style of Hebrew-Christian prophetism."

Zen's emphasis on living in the moment without concern for the past or future was close to John's natural inclination. Since we can never know for certain why and how humans came into being, the best bet, he reasoned, was not to worry but to focus fully on the present. He believed that we were deprived of much contentment simply through worry about things which can never be known or over which we have no control. Watts published a collection of essays in 1960 called *This Is It*. In the title essay he said, "The central core of the experience [of cosmic consciousness] seems to be the conviction, or insight, that the immediate *now*, whatever its nature, is the goal and fulfillment of all living."

Another aspect of Zen that appealed to John was the high priority given to contemplation. Western culture, with its emphasis on productivity, attached guilt to sitting and doing nothing. Value and identity were consequently bound up with what we do. For followers of the Zen way there is value in just being, of watching our own thoughts without allowing those thoughts to grasp hold of anything. Given the evidence of "I'm Only Sleeping" and "Good Morning Good Morning," John was already accomplished in this practice. (He would later write "Watching the Wheels" for the *Double Fantasy* album, a song in which he justified his idleness and refusal to join in "the game.")

The postwar Western interest in Zen affected the work of musicians like John Cage and La Monte Young, poets like Allen Ginsberg and Gary Snyder, the painter Jackson Pollock, and Beat novelist Jack Kerouac. It encouraged an approach to art that valued spontaneity over premeditation, simplicity over complexity, the random over the carefully chosen, stream of consciousness over logical, linear thought. "Revolution 9" on *The Beatles*, which was compiled from arbitrarily cut-up tapes of pre-recorded music (and voice), was one of the earliest examples of how Yoko's Zen approach affected John. Zen spoke of the "absurdity of choosing" (*The Way of Zen*, Alan Watts, 1957), and John Cage's use of chance in composition was, in his own words, "an affirmation of life—not an attempt to bring order out of chaos or to suggest improvements in creation but simply to wake up to the very life we are living, which is so excellent once one gets one's mind and desires out of the way." For the *Let It Be* tracks "Dig a Pony" and "Dig It" John used free association techniques to build the lyrics with no concern for literalism. Because Zen questioned the categorizations that appeared normal to the Western mind, it opened up the possibility of incorporating natural sounds into music, dripped or flicked paint into art, or common speech into poetry. Why should a plucked guitar string be considered more musical than a hammer hitting an anvil or the sound of industrial machinery grinding? In 1969 John said, "I can groove to the sound of electricity in the house, or the water pipes."

Another aspect of Zen art was minimalism. Zen drawings used brisk lines to capture the essence. Zen poetry used few words. After John met Yoko he halted the often florid writing of his psychedelic period and simplified both his music and his lyrics. He explained the transition in this way: "When you get rid of a whole section of illusion in your mind you're left with great precision. Yoko was showing me haikus in the original Japanese. . . . To me, the best poetry is haiku; all the best paintings are Zen."

The new compositions were sparse, heavy on repetition, and adjectives were all but eliminated. The classic of the new genre was "I Want You," released on *Abbey Road* in 1969. The lyrics consist of not much more than the title and the additional line "I want you so bad" repeated eight times. In common with Zen poetry it said what it needed to say in as few words as possible and allowed the listener to fill in the spaces. When John heard that it had been mockingly read out on a TV program as if it were poetry, he responded, "That's all it says, but it's a damn sight better lyric than 'I Am the Walrus' or 'Eleanor Rigby' because it's a progression to me. And if I want to write songs with no words or one word—maybe that's Yoko's influence."

Dan Richter, an American mime artist who met Yoko in Japan when he was studying Noh Theater, moved into Tittenhurst Park in 1968 where he oversaw John and Yoko's joint artistic output for the next four years. "Zen is a large part of Japanese culture, and particularly Japanese aesthetic culture," he says. "You can't be a Japanese artist and not be influenced by Zen, and John was married to an important Japanese artist and was her collaborator. Yoko used minimalism in almost everything she did, still does, and that was a great influence on John. Once Yoko turns up, you start seeing that in all his work. In many ways Yoko was the teacher and John was the student. She was teaching him how to be a sophisticated artist."

Yoko discouraged John from theistic religion, arguing that our need for saviors and spiritual leaders resulted from inadequate parenting. We seek in Christ or Krishna, Billy Graham or Srila Prabhupada, what was lacking in our fathers. Buddhism discouraged leadership, and the role of the Zen master was simply to help students realize their innate Buddhahood. "They want to rely on their father," Yoko said of those who sought leaders. "It's not just learning the rules, which is very crude—it's adoration. There's no difference between that and adoring Hitler. It's a very dangerous game to play."

This was a potent argument in John's case. It would imply that his continuing quest for guidance, meaning, and approval was the result of his father's absence during his infancy and the later separation from his mother. Yoko was suggesting that his energy would be better spent on healing his psychological wounds and letting go of the pain rather than on trying to find God. His need for religion was in direct proportion to his suffering. Had this been why the least anxious Beatles, Paul and Ringo, had also been the least interested in religion?

As his faith in psychedelic religion cooled, a passion for politics took its place. Before his LSD experience he hadn't shown much interest in political affairs other than displaying an ingrained dislike of authority. His standard reply to questions about politics was that it was "boring" and his favorite political party was the one that would allow him to keep the most money. For the first time, in 1966, he expressed an interest in international events. In Japan, after being asked what he was looking for next, he answered "Peace." Questioned about Vietnam, he said that the Beatles thought about the war every day "and we don't agree with it. We think it's wrong. . . . That's all we can do about it—say we don't like it."

Many on the radical left disagreed with the view that drugs could change the world: opium becoming the religion of the people was as bad as religion becoming the opium of the people. They thought that the Beatles could do more than express disapproval. It was time for them to take sides. Their influence could be invaluable in raising awareness of issues. John in particular was pursued by activists who wanted him to support their causes. He addressed them in "Revolution," saying that although he sympathized with their call for change, he didn't believe in violent revolution. He remained a pacifist. "I think you should do it by changing people's heads," he said in December 1968. "They're saying we should smash the system. Now the system-smashing scene has been going on forever. What's it done? The Irish did it, the Russians did it, and the French did it, and where's it got them? It's got them nowhere."

The root of aggression, he alleged, was in the mind. People fought because they were repressed or denied love. There was no original sin or spiritual evil, just people who'd gotten messed up. The solution, in the words of his song "Revolution," was to "free their minds." Art was one of the ways this could be achieved. It could create a new state of awareness. "You can change people," he said. "You can change their heads. I've changed a lot of people's heads. A lot of people have changed my head just with their records, apart from anything else they do. I believe in change. That's what Yoko and my scene is: to change it like that."

He wrote campaigning songs that he recorded as the Plastic Ono Band, including "Give Peace a Chance" and "Power to the People." "Give Peace a

Chance" was built from a casual remark made to him by a Canadian rabbi, Abraham Feinberg, during his Bed-in with Yoko in Montreal. After listening to the couple's concerns the rabbi said, "John, we really have to give peace a chance." "Come Together," the opening track on *Abbey Road*, started as a song for Timothy Leary's 1969 campaign for the governorship of California. The title was the name of the forty-fifth hexagram of the *I Ching*, and Leary's slogan, "Come together. Join the party." "John wrote a version of it and gave a tape to Paul Williams of *Crawdaddy* magazine who played it on alternative radio stations in California," said Leary. "Then, in 1970, I got put in prison so I couldn't run, and the Beatles released it commercially. It was much better than the campaign song, which was just John on guitar fooling around with me. The final version was really wonderful."

The spur to his high-profile peace campaigning was a letter from the film director Peter Watkins, then best known in Britain for his polemical television drama *The War Game*, which had been banned by the BBC for being too alarmist. Watkins asked him candidly what he was doing to fight war and promote peace. He argued that John and Yoko had a responsibility, as media figures, to come out and do something. Says John, "We sat on the letter for three weeks thinking 'Well, we're all doing our best'—you know, 'All you need is love, man' and all that. Finally we came up with the bed event."

The Bed-In for Peace was the first in a series of happenings designed to tease, bemuse, and outrage. It was a Zen approach to campaigning that provoked rather than challenged. In Amsterdam (March 1969) and then in Montreal (May 1969) John and Yoko stayed in their hotel beds twenty-four hours a day and invited the world's press into their suites to interview them. In this way the media got its sound bite and John and Yoko transmitted their ideas about peace. In Montreal they recorded "Give Peace a Chance" in bed surrounded by friends such as Leary, Rabbi Feinberg, and members of ISKCON.

John and Yoko also showed concern for the Nigerian civil war being fought over the independent state of Biafra. Photos of starving Biafran children with swollen stomachs had touched the conscience of the West, and when John returned his MBE (Member of the British Empire) award that had been given to each of the Beatles by the Queen in 1965 he referred to Biafra in his cover letter. Francis Wyndham, then working as a writer on the *Sunday Times Magazine*, had reported on the conflict, and when he returned from Nigeria in the summer of 1969 John and Yoko invited him to Apple so that they could quiz him about what he'd seen.

"Yoko was pregnant, and she told me, 'I thought it would be rather great to have the child in Biafra,'" Wyndham remembers. "I thought the idea was raving mad. It was a very poetic idea, but Biafra was full of starving babies with wonderful nuns trying to help them. You could only go into the country illegally. Mercenary pilots would fly you in without any lights, and as you passed anything you'd be shot at. I remember that the questions that she asked me were all very intelligent and as a result of my answers she didn't go." On October 9 Yoko was rushed to King's College Hospital, London, for emergency blood transfusions. Three days later she miscarried the child.

It was sometimes difficult to keep up with John's changing views. He'd renounce all drugs and then snort heroin to the point of addiction. He'd call for revolution and then attack revolutionaries for being destructive. He'd sneer at religion and then devour religious literature or become totally enslaved to the advice of psychics. He'd praise Karl Marx, the father of communism, while living in a mansion in the stockbroker belt. He'd tell people that they didn't need leaders and then write songs telling people how to behave, "changing their heads" as he would describe it.

Yoko introduced him to macrobiotics, a system of eating promoted in the West by George Ohsawa's 1960 book *Zen Macrobiotics*. The premise of the system was that everything was composed of the opposing forces of yin and yang. Some foods were designated yin, some yang, and some were considered to have both yin and yang. The ideal was a diet with a perfect balance of the two forces. This meant eating a lot of grain (up to 60 percent of total intake), sea vegetables, and root vegetables while avoiding meat and dairy products, out-of-season fruits, additives, preservatives, and caffeine.

The Beatles were already familiar with the concept of "yin" and "yang." The circular Yin Yang symbol was prominently displayed among the flowers and balloons at the televised recording of "All You Need Is Love" on June 25, 1967. Paul's "Hello Goodbye" released as a Beatles single in November 1967 played with opposites:

> You say yes, I say no
> You say stop, I say go, go, go. Oh, no.
> You say goodbye and I say hello.

"The answer to everything is simple," Paul told *Disc* when discussing the single. "It's a song about everything and nothing. Stop-go. Yes-no. If you have black you also have white. That's the amazing thing about life, all the time."

John had given up eating meat after being told, probably by Maharishi, that the fear experienced by the animal as it died would be transferred to him. The macrobiotic diet was vegetarian, and he believed that it gave him the clarity of mind to experience the same cosmic consciousness he'd discovered through meditation. "I was 100 percent saying meditation could do it," he said in 1968. "I still believe that people can become aware of this with acid, meditation, and macrobiotic diet. So that's what I'm doing now, and the combination is the best thing I've come across so far."

He even invested in an Orgone Accumulator, which was a metal box insulated with organic material designed by the controversial doctor and author Wilhelm Reich (1897–1957) to trap positive energy. Reich's theory was that traumatic experiences in our lives blocked the natural flow of life energy and that this led to physical and mental disease. The Orgone Accumulator promised to improve the flow and release energy blocks. "It gathers atmospheric energy," said John. "Just the general vibrations that are in the air. You sit in it and it gathers energy. It charges you up."

John was consistently attracted to the inexplicable and the unknown. His enduring contempt for conventional thought meant that he rarely dismissed a theory simply because it flew in the face of science or reason. Perhaps his most bizarre inquiry was into the possibility of being trepanned—having a small hole drilled into his skull to bring about a permanent state of expanded consciousness. In Amsterdam he had met Bart Huges, a failed medical student turned research librarian, whose theory was that by walking upright humans had lost full consciousness. When we stand, our brains don't get enough blood to function at their maximum potential. As Huges's leading disciple, Joey Mellen, explains: "Trepanning puts more blood in the brain. When you're born the plates of your skull aren't joined together. When they are completely sealed it suppresses a pulsating in the brain's arteries. The capillaries then shrink. You lose blood volume from the brain when you grow up. That is why children are 'higher' than grown-ups. It's at the age that the plates seal—between eighteen and twenty—when people start to drink and take drugs in order to get high. They're trying to regain the consciousness they had as children."

John felt this had been true for him. He'd had more of a sense of wonder as a child in Scotland or playing in the gardens of Strawberry Field than when he was an adult. He'd referred to this in his writings to Stuart Sutcliffe and his line in "She Said She Said": "When I was a boy everything was right." Huges, who'd developed his theory during a mescaline trip in 1962, had devised a scroll pointing out the similarities between the states of consciousness gained from LSD, headstands, yoga, marijuana, and trepanation. Mellen had discussed these ideas with Paul and John Dunbar when they'd dropped into the World Psychedelic Centre in Pont Street in 1966, but Dunbar had scoffed at the comparisons. "It was using schoolboy biology to explain the effect of acid," says Dunbar. "To people without a science background it seemed acceptable, but I thought it was bollocks really." John didn't go through with the trepanning, although he did suggest it to the other Beatles. "This wasn't a joke," remembered Paul. "This was like, 'Let's go next week. We know a guy who can do it and maybe we could all go together.' So I said, 'Look. You go and have it done. If it works, great. Tell us about it, and we'll all have it.'"

Paul was as unlikely to contemplate having holes drilled in his head to expand his consciousness as he was to shave his head and devote his life to Krishna. His biggest project in 1969, as evidenced by the chat between songs on *Let It Be*, was keeping the group together. He was the one who was most proud of being a Beatle, most accepting of the business deals, the performances, and the public relations that were necessary to keep the enterprise alive, and keenest for the group to progress even further. His lack of introspection meant that he didn't create the ruminative songs that John and George were known for, but it also meant that he was stable and outward looking. He was solid and dependable.

Two years before meeting Linda, on the advice of the Beatles' accountants he had bought a dilapidated Scottish hill farm on the promontory of Kintyre. It was a way of spending money, not a desperately needed second home, and he had rarely visited it. There was no furniture other than wooden potato boxes, rats had nested in the walls, and it was completely isolated. Linda, however, immediately fell in love with it. She liked the outdoors, and after time spent in New York's fast lane was ready to enjoy a quieter life.

Having Linda around brought Paul a sense of completion. He was ready to settle, and the theme of home and returning to his roots began to crop up on the songs for *Abbey Road*. Although no one knew they were recording the last Beatles album, there was a sense of finality about it. Songs like "You Never Give Me Your Money" and "Carry That Weight" (both written by Paul) alluded to the business troubles that were enveloping them. George's "Here Comes the Sun" reflected on a day when he was able to escape the meetings and hang out in Eric Clapton's country house. In "Golden Slumbers," his adaptation of Thomas Dekker's seventeenth-century lullaby, Paul added poignant lines about the fact that there had once been a way to return home, implying that it was now too late.

By 1969 there was a universal sense that the countercultural dream wasn't becoming a reality. The lifting of traditional restraints had led to increased acceptance of lifestyles previously considered aberrant and an explosion of creativity in the popular arts, but there were no mutually agreed limits. Life had swung from strict regimentation to wild improvisation. The Beatles typified the new outlook. From the high heels and long hair of 1963 to the drugs and nudity of 1968, they had repeatedly challenged convention. "Freedom," said John, "is not being told what to do."

Yet there was evidence that the destruction of long-established values had also caused damage. Unprecedented numbers of young people were discovering that although drugs did encourage a certain fluidity of imagination and conscience, they could also enslave. Many people, dismissed in hippie terminology as "acid casualties," had damaged their minds through LSD use. The idea of the religious supermarket where people shopped for a spirituality that fitted their requirements or constructed their own from the best bits of several other traditions led to the rise of dubious cults that exercised mind control.

One event seemed to sum up everything that was going wrong and came to mark the end of hippie optimism. On August 9 and 10, 1969, there were seven horrific murders in Los Angeles, all of which were later found to have been committed by followers of Charles Manson, on his orders. On August 9 the actress Sharon Tate and four of her friends were stabbed, shot, strangled, or beaten in her Benedict Canyon home. On the next day Leno and Rosemary LaBianca were stabbed at their home in Los Feliz. One of the clues that linked the murders was that in both cases words were scrawled in blood on walls or doors. At the Tate residence it was simply "pig." At the LaBiancas, "death to pigs" and "healter [sic] skelter."

Although not given much prominence in the immediate investigation, the daubing would eventually lead to a major breakthrough. Manson, it turned out, was a huge Beatles fan. He also had an apocalyptic vision that was drawn in part from their songs and in part from the Revelation of St. John, the final book of the New Testament. In fact, as far as he was concerned, St. John had predicted the Beatles. They were the four angels "standing on the four corners of the earth" in chapter 7, as well as the locusts of chapter 9 who had faces that were "as the faces of men. And they had hair as the hair of women." Manson thought that the Beatles were addressing him in their songs, urging him to bring on the end of the world.

Manson was an example of someone who took every freedom on offer and pushed it to the limit. He had long hair, lived in a desert commune, played rock 'n' roll, wrote songs, dropped acid, practiced free love, and had a great interest in Eastern religion and the occult. He also had a vision of a future holocaust in which black Americans would rise up and wipe out the whites, take over the country, and then lose interest in governing. The Manson Family, therefore, would sit out this revolution in an underground hideout, and take over when the blacks gave up. The murders were an attempt to hasten the revolt. They hoped that the rich white community would suspect blacks and go after them in revenge, thus fomenting a racial war.

Was Manson a madman who happened to have adopted hippie garb or a hippie whose involvement with acid and esoteric religion had sent him mad? Some of his views bore a similarity to views that John and George had expressed. Manson believed that everything was good because all was one.

There was no absolute right and wrong. (George: "If you get to a state that is beyond this relative field, then there's no such thing as good or bad.") Whatever you did was what you were supposed to do because it was your karma. Manson said that there was no such thing as death; death was just a change of form. (George: "There's no such thing as birth and death.") Yet at the same time Manson denounced people for killing snakes or picking flowers. When he was on LSD he encouraged his followers to destroy their egos.

What was salutary about Manson's example was that he took psychedelic religion to its logical conclusion. There was not even the vestige of Christian morality to hold him back. He taught his followers that as we were all part of a cosmic unity and all that we consider to be real is in fact illusion, there was nothing wrong in terminating a life. A person whether alive or dead was still part of the cosmic whole. Death was no big deal. (In 1969 John said, "I'm prepared for death because I don't believe in it. I think it's just getting out of one car and going into another.") One of the girls who killed for Manson subsequently argued that her actions couldn't be evil because she'd felt so right when she was doing it. R. C. Zaehner, Oxford professor of Eastern religions and ethics, commented at the time: "Manson, far from being mad, seems to have had a lucidly logical mind. He took the ambiguities and ambivalences of Indian religion as transmitted to him seriously but drew conclusions that were the exact opposite of conclusions conventionally drawn."

To Manson *The Beatles* (The White Album) was a prophetic work. In part it was a personal message to him—he had tried several times to contact the Beatles by phone—and in part a message of insurrection to the black community. Once he had designed his black-on-white scenario a huge chunk of the album seemed to support his view. "Blackbird" urged black radicals to start spreading their wings. "Piggies" was a veiled attack on the white bourgeois who needed to be whacked. "Happiness Is a Warm Gun" encouraged the militants to get armed. "Revolution" was John asking Manson to see his plans. "Honey Pie" was a request to hear his unreleased music, his "Hollywood songs." "Helter Skelter's" portrayal of someone coming down from the top to the bottom was a reference to the caves in which the Manson Family would hide during the race war.

Everywhere Manson looked on the album there were references to Manson. Even songs such as "I Will," "Yer Blues," and "Don't Pass Me By" were begging letters to him from the Beatles. "Revolution Number 9," the only track without lyrics, was Revelation 9 translated into sound effects of the coming conflagration. Why else would John have included gunfire, the noise of squealing pigs, and a man's voice screaming "Rise!"—a clear call in Manson's mind for the uprising to begin.

The Beatles was constantly on the turntable at the desert ranch, and Manson would explain every detail of the lyrics to his followers like an inspired end-times evangelist. When they eventually killed for him, they felt as though they were fulfilling Beatles' prophecies. The "pigs" and "rise" daubing referred to "Piggies" and "Revolution Number 9." They stabbed the LaBiancas with knives and forks because that's what the pigs in George's song used. A door at the ranch was painted with words from two Beatles' songs—"Helter Skelter" and "You Never Give Me Your Money."

The Beatles were bemused and outraged at the way in which their songs had been used. All they could do was shake their heads and point out that they had never imagined them being taken as instructions for a bloody revolution. Worryingly, Manson had been on the fringes of the music business. He'd written songs with Beatle-like titles such as "Ego," "I'll Never Say Never to Always," "Cease to Exist," and "Mechanical Man." He had pitched his songs to Terry Melcher, son of the actress Doris Day, and had befriended Beach Boy Dennis Wilson. He'd even had demo disks made. "If I learned anything from the whole Manson episode," said Paul, "it was not to read too much meaning into songs because that can get fairly freaky."

Another incident in 1969 was more benign, but no less worrying. In October a rumor was started in America that Paul had died in a car accident. It began as a phone call to a DJ but was followed up by a student journalist, Fred LaBour, who wrote a mischievous piece for a university magazine putting forward the case that Paul had died in November 1966 and had been replaced by a look-alike named William Campbell. He then listed the clues. In the centerfold photo of *Sgt. Pepper*, Paul was wearing a badge that read O. P. D., which stood for Officially Pronounced Dead. On the back cover George, John, and Ringo look forward while Paul turns his back. Clues multiplied throughout the lyrics. On the final track the man who "blew his mind out in a car" was, of course, Paul.

There were clues on *Magical Mystery Tour* and *The Beatles*. A voice said "I buried Paul" at the end of "Strawberry Fields Forever." The cover of *Abbey Road* was replete with symbolic references. John, dressed in white and representing God, led the group across the zebra crossing. Behind him was Ringo, dressed in black. He's the undertaker. Then came Paul (actually William Campbell). He's the only Beatle without shoes, symbolizing death. Behind him came George in denim jeans and a work shirt. He's the grave digger.

Although LaBour's article was written as a joke, it was widely reported, and Beatles fans subsequently found even more clues to support the thesis. By the end of 1969 almost one hundred clues had been discovered, apparently giving the story plausibility. A reporter from *Life* magazine was eventually dispatched to Britain to determine whether Paul was alive or dead. He and Linda were found on their farm in Kintyre and a front-cover story, complete with new photographs, was published on November 7, 1969. However, even this didn't deter some of the conspiracy theorists who argued that the "Paul" who'd been interviewed was simply an actor cooperating in the conspiracy.

The appetite for such hidden meanings was proof of a need for mystery and revelation that modern secularism hadn't been able to fulfill. Ignorant of Holy Writ, which could bear deep textual analysis, a generation had trained its spiritual curiosity on pop culture, asking it to offer enlightenment and guidance as well as entertainment. Artists like Bob Dylan and John Lennon, who hadn't taken up music with any intention of becoming spiritual leaders, were unqualified for the responsibility. They were too aware of their own inadequacies and their own need to discover the light.

The Beatles' penultimate single, "Let It Be," sounded like a valediction. It emerged from the bitter conflicts engulfing Apple and the disintegration of the group that Paul loved so much. It was a word of solace, a word of wisdom, written to himself and the "broken-hearted people" of the world. The simple message was, "Let it be." As with the best of Paul's songs, it was probably intended to have many possible interpretations, but it was undeniably a salvation song. The world is broken, troubled, dark, and cloudy, but there is hope. There is an answer. If this answer is heeded, there will be light and the darkness will roll away.

Billy Preston's gospel-style organ made it sound like a Christian hymn. Some of the song's most ringing phrases could be found in the Bible: "times of trouble" (Ps. 10:1), "the brokenhearted" (Luke 4:18), and "a light that shines" (John 1:5). It sounded a bit too Christian for John, who attempted to undermine its importance during the final sequencing by preceding it with the childish request, "And now we would like to do 'Hark the Angels Come,'" probably a reference to Charles Wesley's "Hark, the Herald Angels Sing," which he sang as a choirboy at St. Peter's. Should that have proved ineffective, he followed "Let It Be" with a brief rendition of "Maggie May," a traditional Liverpool song about a Lime Street whore who robbed sailors.

The song's reference to "Mother Mary" was to Paul's mother, whom he had dreamed of during the troubles. But Paul was aware of what he later called the "quasi-religious" implications. This was heightened by the fact that Mary's words of submission to the angel who informs her that she will give birth to the savior of the world, according to the Gospel of Luke, contained the words "be it unto me according to thy word," a phrase not too dissimilar to "let it be."

However, rather than submission to God, the phrase could be taken in the Buddhist or Hindu sense of not holding to the material world. In this sense "let it be" would mean "let it go" or "don't get attached." The *Bhagavad Gita* said, "By working without attachment, one attains the Supreme." Buddha said, "Let go the past. Let go the future. Let go the present." Paul may have reluctantly come to the realization that the only way out of the problem of the ownership and financial management of the Beatles was for all involved just to release their grip.

For anyone who had invested hope in the Beatles, the final year of their career was a series of disappointments. The years of exploration appeared to have left them pretty much where they started. The love that they had said could change the world couldn't even keep the group together. John and Cynthia had divorced because of his adultery with Yoko. Paul and Jane Asher broke up the same year. Apple, the microcosm of the alternative society, had to let go of everything but its record label. In Derek Taylor's opinion, they had become "confused, then overwhelmed." He concluded, "It was beyond the powers of any of us to run a company based on 'controlled weirdness' when the owners of the power, the name, and the money, were either present and interfering, or absent and complaining. There never was a time in all of Apple when unanimity was achieved on anything except that it was A DRAG."

The Beatles' final two albums were recorded over an eight-month period during 1969 but were released in reverse order because *Let It Be* had to coincide with the premiere of the documentary film of its recording. The overwhelming feeling at the end of it all was not of a triumph at having discovered a new way of living and a fresh view of reality but of tiredness at having exhausted so many solutions in such a short time. George said that being in the Beatles was like living ten years within every twelve-month period. Within six years of Beatlemania breaking out they were a spent force.

What was striking about *Let It Be* and *Abbey Road* was the ordinariness of their concerns. They were no longer trying to change their heads, let alone the world. The visionary euphoria of 1965 through 1967 had disappeared, and in its place were worries about money, privacy, home, business, and girlfriends. The sentiments of "Love Me Do" were restated in "I Want You," but the difference was that "I Want You" was desperate and dependent and didn't mention the word "love." The relationships that had once been meant to make John feel so good were now merely to prevent his feeling so bad. In his case Preludin had been replaced by heroin, "A Hard Day's Night" by "Cold Turkey."

There was a yearning on both albums to return home, whatever "home" might have meant. They knew that they couldn't literally return to Liverpool and become an anonymous quartet, but they missed the excitement and freshness of those days. One of Paul's ideas was to tour village halls under a pseudonym such as Ricky and the Red Streaks so that they could again experience the audience energy that they'd once thrived on. *Let It Be* was one other such attempt to get back to where they once belonged. The songs were uncomplicated, the film demystified the creative process, and "Get Back" was a return to the pumping rock 'n' roll that they'd learned at the Cavern and in Hamburg. The advertisement for the single conveyed the spirit. It was headlined "The Beatles as nature intended."

The last song the Beatles recorded was George's "I Me Mine," a song about possessiveness and "the problem of ego" written while arguments were raging about ownership of copyrights and even the Beatles' name. He said, "I looked around and everything I could see was relative to my ego. You know, like 'that's *my* piece of paper' and 'that's *my* flannel,' or 'give it to *me*,' or '*I* am.' It drove me crackers. I hated everything about my ego. It was a flash of everything false and impermanent which I disliked."

The final album to be released, *Let It Be*, had the faces of all four Beatles on the front but appropriately they were individual shots. A thin line divided them. The cover was edged with black.

Chapter Ten

Carry That Weight

I'm a pagan—a Zen pagan to be precise.
—John Lennon, 1979

I am actually practicing to be more spiritual, to be a better human being. I try to do that more on a daily basis.
—Ringo Starr, 1998

With life and all the stuff I've been through, I do have a belief in, I don't know what it is—in goodness, in a good spirit.
—Paul McCartney, 1989

Everything else can wait, but the search for God cannot wait.
—George Harrison, 1998

What John, Paul, George, and Ringo did after the breakup can't be strictly categorized as part of Beatles lore, but it's worth considering because their paths after 1970 represent different ways in which they sought to apply the gospel they had promoted during the 1960s. Each of them was deeply affected by the ideas and practices he had followed as a young man.

Paul's interest in religion was never rekindled after he left the Maharishi's ashram in 1968. He remained the "flabby agnostic" that Maureen Cleave detected in 1963. "I don't like religion as such because there are always wars with every religion," he said in 1989. However, although Paul was often perceived as the straight man in contrast to surreal John and mystical George, he had absorbed many hippie elements into his lifestyle. While George lived in a mansion in Henley-upon-Thames and John in a multimillion-dollar apartment overlooking Central Park, Paul's base was an organic farm in unfashionable East Sussex. He sent his children to state schools, was a heavy user of marijuana, painted, wrote poetry, loved nature, sang songs for peace, supported

173

Friends of the Earth, and retreated to a remote cottage in the Scottish mountains for his holidays.

The closest thing to a religion in his life has been vegetarianism, his concerns for animal rights, and environmentalism. He not only chooses to eat vegetarian food but campaigns against meat eating with fundamentalist fervor. Like religion, these causes involve issues of purity (of the body), sanctity (of all life), and salvation (of the planet). For Paul this is not just a personal preference but a question of right and wrong. "If anyone wants to save the planet, all they have to do is just stop eating meat," he said in 2001. "That's the single most important thing you could do. Vegetarianism takes care of so many things in one shot: ecology, famine, cruelty."

As with any fundamentalism, his conviction requires preaching to the unconverted, and forbidding any wrongdoing in areas under his jurisdiction. During his 1993 world tour a shocking visual presentation on animal abuse and mutilation was projected on a screen before the band came on stage. In his 2004 tour he forbade any member of his touring party to eat meat during work time. A spokesperson was quoted as saying, "We can't control what they [the employees] do in their spare time."

Although he often dates his conversion back to a day when he and Linda were eating lamb and looked out of the window at their own lambs frolicking in the field, the roots go back to his experiences with LSD and Eastern religion. When tripping he'd become persuaded of the interconnectedness of all things, and this view received confirmation from the Maharishi. By December 1967 he was already "sympathetic" to vegetarianism although still partial to bacon for breakfast. "If you've ever opened an egg," he told *Disc and Music Echo*, "and seen a little chicken in there, you'll know what the feeling behind this is. We [himself, John, and George] have decided we don't need meat. There's no need at all to eat it—a lot of people say it's no good for you."

Hinduism offers five main reasons for not eating meat: dharma (Ahinsa, the law of noninjury), karma (by involving yourself in pain and death you will in turn experience suffering), spirit (the anxiety felt by the slaughtered animal enters the body of the eater and affects the consciousness), health (the vegetarian diet is purer), and ecology (killing animals disturbs the balance of life). The *Mahabharat* states: "He who desires to augment his own flesh by eating the flesh of other creatures lives in misery in whatever species he may take his birth" (115.47).

It was the Hindu view that took John into vegetarianism. In 1968 he told an interviewer, "If you are what you eat, I don't want to be a pig or a cow. It's as simple as that. I believe that the vibration of the animal coming off on you . . . any vibration an animal has—dying in fear, pain or whatever situation it died in—I believe it will rub off on you. It's a lot of hokey pokey and magic, but I believe in that too."

With songs like "Give Ireland Back to the Irish" (1971), "Ebony and Ivory" (1982), "Pipes of Peace" (1983), and "Peace in the Neighbourhood" (1993) Paul kept the flag flying for love, peace, and understanding, but the sentiments were never more than vague hopes that people would be nicer to each other. There was no accompanying social, political, or spiritual vision, and because of this they were not treated as seriously as the songs of John and George that addressed similar issues.

His *Liverpool Oratorio*, premiered at Liverpool Cathedral in 1991, used a form of religious music developed in the eighteenth century by musicians such as Handel (a church oratory was a building used for religious music and plays), but although Paul made mention of "blessings," "heaven," "virtue," "the light," "eternal love," and even "salvation," his oratorio was strictly secular. It was really an expression of the belief he'd come to as a schoolboy at the Liverpool Pierhead when he'd decided that God and the devil were good and evil endowed with personalities. In fact, this aphorism is played with in the final movement.

So when he wrote of "living in God forever," he meant living in the good forever, and when he wrote of having found salvation in "his eternal love," he meant being saved by love itself. After all his spiritual meandering he'd returned to the core beliefs of his father that all you needed was love, decency, honesty, hard work, and toleration. If he worshiped anything it was these values, the values of his childhood. "They're just ordinary people," he said at the time, "but I'll tell you, I've met world leaders and famous people in most countries, but I've never met anyone as interesting, caring, wise, and with as much common sense as the members of my Liverpool family."

Ringo, whose interest in religion was superseded by his interest in booze and partying, was more forthcoming on the subject of spiritual values after being treated for alcohol dependency in 1988. With his wife, the actress Barbara Bach, he spent five weeks in the foothills of Arizona's Santa Catalina Mountains at the Sierra Tucson treatment center where the cure was based on the twelve steps of Alcoholics Anonymous. The steps begin with an admission of powerlessness and go on to invoke "a power greater than ourselves" to aid recovery. Although the power is not specific to a particular religion— "God as we understand him" is the given definition—he is a God who hears prayers, removes faults, strengthens determination, and reveals his will.

On his 2005 album *Choose Love* Ringo's song "Oh My Lord" was a confession of his need to be loved by God. He composed it at the piano and said that the chords, words, and melody came to him simultaneously. "We were talking about 'It Don't Come Easy,'" he said. "George and I wrote that song and

he produced it, and he was trying to throw in Hare Krishna and God and everything and at that time of my life I would say, 'No, no, no. That's you. I don't
sing these songs.' Now I have no problem saying it. People change. You just
change on this long and winding road we're on. Some things become easier."

In his contribution to the *Anthology* book he said he was now "comfortable
with my spirituality" but that he'd had to go through a lot of turmoil to get
there: "No growth without pain is always the question and the answer. There
is a lot of banging your head against the wall when you could be actually
walking through the door. But that's what we all are—little human beings.
God saved my life. I've always felt blessed, but there have been times when
I've got crazier and crazier and forgot about that blessing."

George was the most unwavering in his beliefs. When he first espoused
Hindu thought it was generally assumed to be another fad, but from the earliest days he was adamant that he would stick to it for his lifetime. Although
Lord Krishna was the focus of his prayer and worship, he never joined a religious order or participated in regular group worship. His main spiritual practice was meditation and chanting, which he attempted to do for at least two
hours a day when he wasn't working. He said he felt closest to God when surrounded by nature, which was the main reason he developed the extensive
gardens at Friar Park and spent so much of his time digging, cutting, planting, and pruning.

While with the Beatles he stockpiled songs that were ignored or passed
over by John and Paul, and in 1970 he had enough material for the triple
album *All Things Must Pass*, which was suffused with the beliefs that he'd
had to hold back. "Beware of Darkness" spoke of the dangers of *maya* (illusion). "Awaiting on You All" claimed that you didn't need the church or
rosary beads to reach God; all you needed was to chant "the names of the
Lord." "Art of Dying" dealt with reincarnation, and the title track was based
on a Timothy Leary poem collected in *Psychedelic Prayers* (1966), which was
itself a paraphrase of part of the twenty-third chapter of the *Tao Te Ching*.

The single released from the album, "My Sweet Lord," topped the charts on
both sides of the Atlantic. It was a song of praise to Krishna inspired by the
gospel song "Oh Happy Day," by the Edwin Hawkins Singers, which had been
a surprise hit in Britain during 1969. George consciously started the song in a
way that wouldn't offend Christian ears with the intention of seducing them
into singing the Krishna mantra. "My idea . . . was to sneak up on them a bit,"
he admitted. "The point was to have the people not offended by 'Hallelujah'
and then, by the time it gets to 'Hare Krishna,' they're already hooked. Their
feet are tapping. They're already singing 'Hallelujah' to lull them into a false
sense of security and then it suddenly turns into 'Hare Krishna.'"

His 1973 album, *Living in the Material World*, was even more devotional. The titles told the story: "Give Me Love (Give Me Peace on Earth)," "The Light That Has Lighted the World," "The Lord Loves the One (Who Loves the Lord)." Inside the sleeve was a reproduction of a painting of Krishna and Arjuna in their chariot taken from Prabhupada's translation of the *Bhagavad Gita*. The same year George bought a Victorian mansion with seventeen acres of land in Letchmore Heath, Hertfordshire, and donated it to the Krishna movement to be used as its British headquarters.

His relationship with Ravi Shankar grew stronger and more intimate over the years. In 1971 Shankar asked him for help in raising awareness of and money for Bangladeshi refugees fleeing civil war. Within months George was able to put on a star-studded event at Madison Square Garden that became an album and a movie. It raised $15 million for UNICEF and focused world attention on the country's plight. Three years later, after George had produced two albums for him, Shankar and a group of his musicians became the support act on his poorly received *Dark Horse* tour of America.

His natural reluctance to be in the spotlight found support in religious beliefs that promoted detachment from the world. He rarely played live, avoided talking about the Beatles, never appeared on the celebrity circuit, and was at his happiest behind the high walls of Friar Park, the huge Victorian folly he bought in 1971 for two hundred thousand pounds. Although he enjoyed the spoils his Beatle years had provided, he didn't enjoy being an object of fascination. To him fame was a dangerous drug that inflated the ego and kept the subject in thrall to the world of illusion. It was no accident that the cover of *All Things Must Pass* featured him sitting on a lawn dressed in rubber boots, jeans, and an old hat, surrounded by garden gnomes. This was George Harrison sans glamor.

In some respects his expression of faith appeared similar to Christianity, and he was fond of quoting such Bible verses as "Seek and ye shall find" and "The kingdom of God is within." Despite his rejection of childhood church, many aspects of his religious life were remarkably similar to someone committed to a Catholic order. He spoke of his life as a preparation for death, shunned the glamor of the world, placed a high importance on humility, believed in love, donated regularly to a wide range of charities, chanted daily with the assistance of prayer beads, adorned his walls with religious paintings, and believed in the power of God's name.

Surprisingly, in light of his distaste for the Catholicism of his childhood, he claimed in 1968 that his initial problem when considering Hinduism was in reconciling it with the story of Christ. It was only when he read *Autobiography of a Yogi* that he was able to conclude that everything that was great about Christ was because he was an avatar. "I didn't believe in Christianity that way it had been taught to me," he told Art Unger. "My concept of Christ was that he was two thousand years ago and that I couldn't be like him or couldn't put [his teachings] into practice in this modern environment we live in. I couldn't see the connection between what he was saying and what we're doing now. But . . . through his book Paramahansa Yogananda, who was a fully realized person, was able to tell about Christ's life and teachings that brought him [Christ] more into today."

George then viewed the Bible through the lens of Hinduism. When Christ was baptized by John, "That was his initiation, when he received his mantra." When Christ said, "The kingdom of God is within," he was recommending deep meditation techniques. His death and resurrection were proof that he was fully realized because a fully realized person can move outside the physical body with ease. "If you can imagine your physical body being an overcoat on your true self," he said, "they get to the point where they can take that over-coat off and go wherever they want to go."

Yet, despite this appreciation for Jesus, he maintained a beef against Christianity and the established church. "He embraced the essence of all religions," said his second wife, Olivia, "although he had little patience for organized religions or dogma that espoused guilt, sin, or mystery." In 1978 he rescued the Monty Python film *The Life of Brian* when EMI withdrew its financial backing at the last minute. Although avowedly not intended to be blasphemous—Brian is not actually Jesus; he just happens to have been born near the stable at the same time—it became notorious for its closing scene in which crucified men sang "The Bright Side of Life." It's difficult to imagine George spending £4 million on a comedy about someone "almost identical" to Lord Krishna.

In 1982 Mukunda, one of the first Krishna followers to befriend George, asked him what was the difference between the God of the Bible and the Krishna of the *Bhagavad Gita.* "When I first came to this house it was occupied by nuns," George said. (Between the years 1953 to 1970 Friar Park was used as a school run by the Salesian Sisters of St. John Bosco.) "I brought in this poster of Vishnu. You just see his head and shoulders and his four arms holding a conch shell and various other symbols, and it has a big OM written above it. He has a nice aura around him. I left it by the fireplace and went out into the garden. When we came back in the house they all rounded on me, saying, 'Who is that? What is that?' as if it was some pagan god. So I said, 'Well, if God is unlimited he can appear in any form, whoever way he likes to appear. This is one way. He's called Vishnu."

In September 1991, twenty-three years after leaving Rishikesh, he flew to Vlodrop in Holland with Indian-born, holistic-healing proponent Deepak Chopra for a reconciliatory meeting with Maharishi. According to Chopra,

George arrived with a rose and said that he had come to apologize. "For what?" Maharishi asked. "You know for what," George said. He then told Maharishi about the gossip and intrigue that had caused him and John to leave the ashram. Maharishi told George that he thought that the Beatles were "angels on earth. It doesn't matter what John said or did, I could never be upset with angels." According to Chopra, George broke down and wept at this. The two men parted by expressing love toward each other. A few days later George called Chopra and said, "A huge karmic baggage has been lifted from me, because I didn't want to lie."

It was probably this meeting that led George to perform at the Royal Albert Hall in London on April 6, 1992, in a benefit concert for the Natural Law Party, a political party formed by Maharishi's followers that had fielded 310 candidates in the British election. In a statement George said: "I will vote for the Natural Law Party because I want total change and not just a choice between left and right. The system we have now is obsolete and is not fulfilling the needs of the people." (The Conservative Party under Margaret Thatcher won the election with over 14 million votes. The Natural Law Party failed to win a single seat and picked up only 62,888 votes nationwide.)

In 1997 he was operated on for throat cancer and four years later for lung cancer, but he wasn't cured. In November 2001, now suffering from a brain tumor, he left a hospital in New York to come to Los Angeles to die. Believing that the nature of his next reincarnation was dependent on the state of his soul at the moment of death, he surrounded himself in his final days by his family, Ravi Shankar, and two devotees of Krishna whom he had known for over thirty years, Shyamasundar das and Mukunda Goswami. Ravi played his sitar while Shyamasundar and Mukunda chanted the Hare Krishna mantra. After his death on November 29, the two devotees issued a news release that claimed George had "done more than any single popular cultural figure during these past few decades to spread spiritual consciousness around the world. He transferred his perceptions of a state of being beyond and higher than ordinary consciousness into the words and music that altered millions of lives."

Newspaper reports claimed that he had a sacred leaf placed in his mouth and was sprinkled with holy water. Rumors suggested that his ashes had been taken to Switzerland or scattered on the River Ganges. All accounts agreed that he had a dignified death in keeping with his ambition to finish well. It was the moment he had spent thirty-six years preparing for. Olivia's official statement read: "He left this world as he lived in it, conscious of God, fearless of death and at peace, surrounded by family and friends." His posthumous album, *Brainwashed*, recorded as he was dying, shows that his final thoughts were about God, worship, reincarnation, and the karmic wheel. One of his legacies was the Material World Charitable Foundation, established in 1973, dedicated to sponsoring "diverse forms of artistic expression and to encourage the exploration of alternative life views and philosophies." It has also poured money into a range of causes from Greenpeace and Friends of the Earth to hospitals, medical research, and youth clubs.

Two years after George's death his son Dhani said, "My dad was constantly re-evaluating his thinking. He was always saying, 'The most important thing is, Who am I? What am I doing? Where am I going? Why am I going anywhere?' And to even ask those questions—some people haven't even begun. So a lot of the music is just posing questions—maybe to himself. Or maybe he's posing the questions in his music because he's already found the answer for himself."

John's life after the Beatles was a complete contrast to George's. Although similarly curious about the meaning of life and attracted to alternative spiritualities, he would flit from view to view without developing a complete understanding or making a commitment. A comment he made in 1968 with reference to the idea that the fear experienced by animals in death is passed on to the eaters of meat—"I believe in everything until it's disproved"—could well have been his motto.

Having spent the sixties expunging the beliefs of his early years and then systematically destroying his ego with LSD, he was spiritually empty during the Beatles' final year. Yoko became his only certain belief. His contribution to the group dropped dramatically, leaving Paul to be the organizer of *Abbey Road* and *Let It Be* as well as the composer of most of their final singles: "Hello, Goodbye," "Lady Madonna," "Hey Jude," "Get Back," "Let It Be," "The Long and Winding Road."

In December 1969 John and Yoko flew to Denmark where they spent a month at an isolated farmhouse on the northern tip of the country with Yoko's ex-husband Tony Cox and his wife Melinda. Free of drugs, they were even trying to quit smoking and enlisted the help of the black activist and comedian Dick Gregory, who arranged for them to go on a series of fasts. Cox had recently cut his hair short "to get a fresh perspective on life," and John and Yoko followed suit. It was a dramatic change for a Beatle whose identity for so long had been bound up with being a "longhair," yet it was indicative of his desire to change.

Cox was interested in exploring Christianity, and mealtime discussions inevitably turned to religion. John seemed open to the subject and readily talked about God, but Yoko was constantly uneasy. The concept of a personal God seemed alien to her. Yet she considered herself to be someone committed to discovering truth, and things had become desperate for them as a couple.

Early in 1970 a publicist at the New York publishing company G. P. Putnam sent John a copy of a new book, *The Primal Scream: Primal Therapy, the Cure for Neurosis*, by California psychotherapist Arthur Janov, hoping that John might review or at least endorse it. The package arrived at Tittenhurst Park, and both John and Yoko avidly read it. They were impressed with Janov's claims to be able to rid people of neuroses by helping them relive their past emotional pain.

Janov's theory was that adult neuroses are built on early childhood trauma. Even though hidden from the conscious mind, these early experiences continue to exert control through fear. He believed that the only way to deprive them of their power was to dig deep and relive the anxieties. "I believe that the only way to eliminate neurosis is with overthrow by force and violence," he wrote. "The force of years of compressed feelings and denied needs; the violence of wrenching them out of an unreal system."

The theory made sense to John. He'd been hurt in his childhood by the rejection of his father and the removal from his mother's care, and his character had been formed by this pain. In order to survive he had to ignore his feelings and live by the code of behavior authorized by his Aunt Mimi. He learned that to act on his feelings was not socially acceptable, and he therefore suppressed them. They would rise to the surface only when he was angry or drunk. The moments in his songwriting that he'd always been most proud of were those when he'd let his feelings dominate—"In My Life," "Help," "Strawberry Fields Forever."

If Janov's theory was true, John had a huge reservoir of unexplored and unexpressed feelings that could be responsible for his bitterness, pessimism, jealousy, cynicism, violence, lack of confidence, and even his need to find strong male figures to look up to. Maybe he didn't need salvation from sin, release from the world of illusion, or increased blood flow to the brain but purgation of bad memories and a reconnection to his feelings.

In March 1970 Yoko phoned Janov and invited him to come to Tittenhurst to begin immediate therapy with her and John. When he arrived, Janov was shocked to see John's condition. It was as if he had been through a complete nervous breakdown. He had ended up locking himself in. "He couldn't get out of his house," says Janov. "He couldn't get out of his room. He was in very bad shape. He'd had a lifetime of pain. The drugs he was taking didn't do him much good because they opened him up. After a while his defenses just crumbled. He couldn't function anymore."

The primal therapist's job was simply to prompt him to explore his more painful memories. How had his relationships been with his father, mother, Mimi? When had he last cried? Had he ever felt lonely as a child? The early sessions took place in the partly built recording studio at Tittenhurst. Then they moved to a London hotel until they all left for Los Angeles on April 23, 1970. John and Yoko rented a home on Nimes Road in Bel Air where they were treated on a one-to-one basis for four months while also attending group sessions at the Primal Institute in West Los Angeles.

"I've rarely seen pain like John's, and I've seen a lot of pain," says Janov. "It was mostly about his mother but quite a bit about Brian (Epstein) that I can't talk about. Also his relationship with Mimi. Mimi had been tough on him. There was almost more pain than you could possibly imagine. It would put him on the floor, and he'd lay there writhing around. He would scream, but he told me that he hadn't known how to scream. Yoko had had to teach him."

It was while undergoing Primal Therapy that John wrote his first solo album, *Plastic Ono Band*, every track of which revealed the pain that had recently been exposed. There hadn't been a rock album with such naked emotion before. He sang about rejection and loneliness, fear and isolation, about the departure of his father and the death of his mother, about the pressure of fame and the destructiveness of drugs. Phil Spector's deliberately primitive production and the anguished vocals on "Mother" gave the impression that the recording had been an extension of the therapy. It soon became known as the Primal Album.

Three of the songs gave his revised view of religion. Only the year before he had spoken enthusiastically about God as "a power that we're all capable of tapping" and, asked whether he believed in an afterlife, said he definitely did because, "In meditation, on drugs, and on diets, I have been aware of soul and have been aware of the power." Now he was adamantly atheist. Religion in general was a drug ("Working Class Hero"), Krishna was pie in the sky ("I Found Out"), and God was a concept by which we measure our pain ("God").

Dominating the album was the theme that he needed to feel his own pain or else face a life of seeking refuge in fantasy. The particular fantasies he isolated—sex, drugs, television, and religion—had long been his favorites. The song "God," probably based on his memory of the fourth-century Nicene Creed still used in the Church of England ("We believe in one God . . ."), listed fifteen things he'd lost faith in, starting with magic and ending with the Beatles. Nine of the fifteen were connected with religion. His conclusion was that all he now believed in was himself and Yoko because that was "reality." The song ended with the assertion that "the dream" was over, meaning the dream of the Beatles as savior figures.

Although Janov didn't attempt to talk patients out of their personal religious beliefs, it's clear from *The Primal Scream* that he was no fan of God. (John once said that Janov believed that religion was "legalized madness.")

In two pages of *The Primal Scream* given to his views on Transcendental Meditation, Janov recounted the story of a patient, a senior Vedanta monk, who had been meditating for twelve years. "But the final result of all this bliss," Janov wrote, "was a complete breakdown and the need for therapy. Perhaps this deserves some explanation. I think that the state of bliss comes from a complete suppression of self, giving oneself over to a fantasy (deity) of one's own creation, a merging with this product of one's imagination, and a loss of reality. It is a state of total unreality, a socially institutionalized psychosis, as it were."

This would have chimed with John's experience and with Yoko's skepticism about gurus. Although Janov never discussed specific religions with John, they did discuss God. "He asked me why people believed so fervently," Janov says. "I said, look at their pain. The more pain they're in, the more they're going to believe. It's the transformation of that feeling, of the need. 'I need protection,' 'I need love'—and there it is. John said, 'You mean that God is a concept by which we measure our pain?' I'd seen this with people who came to me for therapy. I had a Muslim come in with a prayer rug and one day he just stopped. I asked him why he'd stopped praying, and he just said, 'I fell in love with my pain.' It made sense."

To promote *Plastic Ono Band* John gave an extensive interview to *Rolling Stone* publisher Jann Wenner that was the frankest and most revealing insight into the Beatles thus far. He argued that nothing had changed in Britain because of the Beatles except that there were "a lot of middle-class kids with long hair walking around London in trendy clothes." In that sense, the Beatles were a myth, he said, and he no longer believed in myths. Picking up where he had left off in "God," he said, "I don't believe in it. The dream is over. And I'm not just talking about the Beatles. I'm talking about the generation thing. The dream is over. It's over and we—well I have anyway, personally—gotta get down to so-called reality."

In a radio interview given in December 1970 John said that Primal Therapy had provided him with a mirror in which to see himself. "I had to look into my own soul," he said. "I wasn't looking at it from a mystical perspective which tended to color things or from a psychedelic perspective or being a famous Beatle perspective or making a Beatle record perspective. All those things gave a color to what I did. This time it was just me in a mirror, and so it came out like that."

His next album, *Imagine*, recorded at Tittenhurst in 1971, continued the ruthless self-examination, but this time with more melodic flair. Although prompted by his experiences in Primal Therapy, it involved the same approach to writing that he had started with "Help!" and "In My Life." At the root was the idea that confession led to self-knowledge, which in turn led to wholeness.

While shining a light into the dark corners of his psyche in songs like "Jealous Guy" and "Crippled Inside," he also shone it on the world outside. He demanded truth of himself, and also of others. "Give Me Some Truth" was a sharp, polished attack on politicians—America was still involved in Vietnam—accusing them of everything from condescension to neurosis.

The title song encapsulated his utopian dream. In essence it was no different from most people's: the best of all possible worlds was one without fear, war, greed, hunger, or hatred. In place of division he wanted unity, brotherhood, and shared wealth. It parallels the new heaven and the new earth that he would have read about in chapter 21 of the book of Revelation: "And God shall wipe away all tears from their eyes; and there shall be no more death, neither sorrow, nor crying, neither shall there be any more pain: for the former things are passed away" (v. 4).

He differed from the biblical vision in attributing humanity's problems to national borders, personal ownership, and religious belief where the Bible blamed fallen nature, rebellion, and spiritual evil and argued that religion, national borders, and personal possessions were some of the ways in which the progress of evil could be slowed down.

The song started with the arguments of existentialism. He believed, correctly, that the notion of heaven and hell hinders people from simply "living for today." The possibility makes people look back to their past sins and forward to the final judgment. The present is lived in the light of both. Saint Paul would have agreed with John in this respect. He said that if there was no resurrection of the dead, we might as well indulge our appetites to the fullest because "tomorrow we die." John summed up the song as "Antireligious, antinationalistic, anticonventional, and anticapitalistic." He reckoned that it broke into the mass market, where "God" had been perceived as too "heavy," because unlike the earlier song it was "sugar-coated."

The title provided the key. John didn't use the word "imagine" to mean simply "suppose" or "assume." He believed in imagination as a form of magic; if enough people believed something to be true, the reality would manifest itself. One of the inspirations behind the song was a book on prayer that Dick Gregory had given him. Gregory can no longer remember the title or the author but knows that John would call him to discuss the theories it was promoting. "It spoke about forgiveness, love, and the power of the mind," he says. "It had prayers in it, but not the kind that you would hear in a church. They were the prayers of the power within, the power that you can't release if you are holding hatred, bitterness, or pain." This was the concept behind the 1969 "War Is Over—If You Want It" campaign, when he and Yoko had posters put up at significant sites in ten world cities announcing WAR IS OVER! IF YOU WANT IT. Four years later this concept informed the creation of their "conceptual country" called Nutopia. "Citizenship of the country can be obtained by declaration of your awareness of NUTOPIA," they said in an advertisement. "NUTOPIA has no land, no boundaries, no passports, only people. NUTOPIA has no laws other than cosmic. All people of NUTOPIA are ambassadors of the country. As two ambassadors of NUTOPIA, we ask for diplomatic immunity and recognition in the United Nations of our country and our people."

The fullest explanation of their theory came in May 1979 when they paid for a full-page announcement on the back page of the *New York Times* headed "A Love Letter from John and Yoko to People Who Ask Us What, When and Why." It was their defense against accusations that they were artistically and politically inactive, hiding in their luxury apartment without a care for the world. The case they put was that "our silence is a silence of love and not indifference." They were spending their time making good wishes. "We are all part of the sky, more so than of the earth. Remember, we love you."

The crux of the argument was that they had the power to effect change through mind power. "More and more we are starting to wish and pray. The things that we have tried to achieve in the past by flashing a V sign, we try now though wishing. We are not doing this because it is simpler. Wishing is more effective than waving flags. It works. It's like magic. Magic is simple. Magic is real. The secret of it is to know that it is simple, and not kill it with an elaborate ritual which is a sign of insecurity. . . . Everyone has goodness inside, and . . . all people who come to us are angels in disguise, carrying messages and gifts to us from the Universe. Magic is logical. Try it sometime."

It sounded as though they were suggesting a sprinkling of fairy dust and a wave of a wand would sort out the world's problems, but subsequent revelations by former employees have shown that John and Yoko came to believe in magic in a literal sense. After 1975 John sought guidance through using a wide range of occult practices from astrology and séances to numerology and directionalism.

Following his bold atheistic statements in "God" and "Imagine" in the early 1970s, John abandoned the spiritual in favor of the political. On moving to New York he associated with the young left-wing radicals Jerry Rubin, Abbie Hoffman, and Rennie Davis, who were then seen as the scourge of the establishment. His 1972 album *Some Time in New York City* was almost exclusively political, lending moral support to feminists, Irish Nationalists, and

Black Panthers, among others. Asked in 1971 if he was becoming increasingly radical and political, he said, "In my case I've never *not* been political, though religion tended to overshadow it in my acid days, around 1965 or 1966. That religion was directly the result of all that superstar shit. Religion was an outlet for my repression."

Yet, despite giving the impression of being at home in a world with no supernatural dimension and of having purged himself of all "myths," he was still interested in the subject of spirituality and particularly in techniques that promised to harness power. Part of him wanted to be a hardheaded materialist, but another part still believed in mystery. His intellect told him to trust in reason alone, but his soul was moved by mysticism, surrealism, and the paranormal.

John Green, a psychic hired in 1975 for twenty-five thousand dollars a year, said that Yoko provided John with an "occult education." Green offered psychic advice, acted as a medium, and read tarot cards for them. He was involved in all their major decisions. When, at the start of their business relationship, he asked John what he wanted out of it, John apparently answered, "Whatever I want. Change the world, whatever. I always had the plan, but I never had the power. I thought I did. Big star, big deal. No one listens when they don't have to. It's too much work."

For someone from John's background the occult smacked of the forbidden. The Latin origins of the word suggest that which is concealed. Occultism looks into things hidden from the normal consciousness. The Old Testament commands the obedient Jew not to be "an observer of times, or an enchanter, or a witch, or a charmer, or a consulter with familiar spirits, or a wizard, or a necromancer. For all that do these things are an abomination unto the Lord" (Deut. 18:10–12). But for Yoko there was no such forbidding.

A close friend of Yoko's who knew her in Tokyo and New York says, "Magic was part and parcel of the culture she grew up in. It was a part of everyday life. I don't think she would ever consider herself a practicing Buddhist. On one occasion we went to a Buddhist temple and she prayed there, but her background was in ancestor worship and many gods. She practiced numerology and astrology. She believed in a spirit world where spirits were coming and going and there were spirit gods who could help you and also in reincarnation. When I knew her she believed in these things."

The exercises that Yoko recommended for John ranged across a variety of occult disciplines but were all designed to maximize his power and provide him with guidance. Although John never spoke publicly about these activities, they were revealed in four books after his death: *Dakota Days*, by their psychic, John Green; *John Lennon: Living on Borrowed Time*, by their aide,

Frederic Seaman; and two books by writers who saw Lennon's detailed personal diaries from the 1970s, Geoffrey Giuliano's *Lennon in America* and Robert Rosen's *Nowhere Man*. Although these books differ on details and all were prevented from using direct quotes, they all agree that John became increasingly dependent on and subservient to Yoko and, as a result, dependent on the guidance of occultists.

In 1976, for example, he consulted psychics, meditated to arouse the "kundalini serpent" that he believed existed at the base of his spine, practiced self-hypnosis and past-life regression (in one session believing he was a Neanderthal man, in another a Crusader), had his cards read, devoured Patric Walker's horoscopes in *Town and Country*, and obeyed Yoko by traveling in an easterly direction around the world to get rid of "bad karma." He was also deeply involved in numerology, studying *Cheiro's Book of Numbers*. Robert Rosen reported: "John and Yoko were unable to walk out of the house without finding mystical significance in every license plate, address, and street sign." John believed that his life was governed by the number nine, a number that signified spirituality. He was born on the ninth of October when his mother was living at 9 Newcastle Road. Brian Epstein had first seen the Beatles on the ninth of November. The first contract with Parlophone was signed on the ninth of May. On the cover of his 1976 diary he had pasted the Magician card from a tarot pack. On the face of the Magician he had superimposed a photo of himself.

In March 1977 Yoko traveled with John Green to Catagena in Colombia to meet a witch who had been recommended to her as someone "who could do anything." Green had to accompany her to check out the witch's validity. Yoko paid the witch sixty thousand dollars to perform a series of rituals culminating in the sacrifice of a dove. When they returned to New York, Yoko insisted that they had to fly via Los Angeles and Alaska to avoid having to fly in a northeasterly direction because she believed this would bring her bad fortune.

Next came one of the most extraordinary turnabouts in John's life. A television addict for many years (it was his way of looking at the world since he could no longer walk around anonymously), he enjoyed watching some of America's best-known evangelists—Pat Robertson, Billy Graham, Jim Bakker, and Oral Roberts. In 1972 he had written a desperate letter to Roberts confessing his dependence on drugs and his fear of facing up to "the problems of life." He expressed regret that he had said that the Beatles were more popular than Jesus and enclosed a gift for the Oral Roberts University. After quoting the line "money can't buy me love" from "Can't Buy Me Love" he said, "It's true. The point is this, I want happiness. I don't want to keep on with drugs. Paul told me once, 'You made fun of me for taking drugs, but you will regret it in the end.' Explain to me what Christianity can do for me. Is it phoney? Can He love me? I want out of hell."

Roberts sent him a copy of his book *Miracle of Seed Faith* and several letters explaining basic Christian beliefs. In the second of his letters Roberts said,

> John, we saw you and the Beatles on television when you first came to America. Your talent with music was almost awesome and your popularity touched millions. Your influence became so widespread and powerful that your statement—the Beatles are more popular than Jesus— might have had some truth in it at that moment. But you know, our Lord said, I am alive for ever more. People, the Bible says, are like sheep and are often fickle, following this one day and something else the next. However, there are millions who have received Jesus Christ as their personal Savior and have been filled with the Holy Spirit. They love him. To them He is the most wonderful and popular man who ever lived because he is the Son of God and His name endures.
>
> I thank God that you see this, John, and finally regret thinking any man or group could be more popular than Jesus. Jesus is the only reality. It is Jesus who said "I am the way, the truth, and the life." So, you see, your statement that because of your hard background you've never wanted to face reality is actually really saying you've never wanted to face our loving Lord. What I want to say, as I tried to say in my other letter, is that Jesus, the true reality, is not hard to face. He said, "Come unto me all ye that labour and are heavy laden, and I will give you rest. ...For my yoke *is* easy, and my burden is light." You said, John, that you take drugs because reality frightens you. Remember as you open your life to Jesus, He will take all the fear away and give you peace. Peace that passes all understanding.

This correspondence and his exposure to TV evangelism didn't appear to have any effect until he suddenly announced to close friends in the spring of 1977 that he'd become a born-again Christian. He had been particularly moved by the U.S. television premiere of Franco Zeffirelli's *Jesus of Nazareth*, starring Robert Powell as Jesus, which NBC showed in two three-hour segments on Palm Sunday, April 3, 1997. A week later, on Easter day, he took Yoko and Sean to a local church service.

Over the following months he baffled those close to him by constantly praising "the Lord," writing Christian songs with titles like "Talking with Jesus" and "Amen" (the Lord's Prayer set to music), and trying to convert nonbelievers. He also called the prayer line of *The 700 Club*, Pat Robertson's program. The change in his life perturbed Yoko, who tried to talk him out of it. She reminded him of what he'd said about his vulnerability to strong religious leaders because of his emotionally deprived background. She knew that if the press found out about it they would have a field day with another John and Jesus story. John became antagonistic toward her, blaming her for practicing the dark arts and telling her that she couldn't see the truth because her eyes had been blinded by Satan.

Those close to the couple sensed that the real reason she was concerned was that it threatened her control over John's life. If he became a follower of Jesus he would no longer depend on her and the occultists. During long, passionate arguments she attacked the key points of his fledgling faith. They met with a couple of Norwegian missionaries whom Yoko questioned fiercely about the divinity of Christ, knowing that this was the teaching that John had always found the most difficult to accept. Their answers didn't satisfy her, and John began to waver in his commitment.

In an unpublished song, "You Saved My Soul," he spoke about "nearly falling" for a TV preacher while feeling "lonely and scared" in a Tokyo hotel. This must have referred to a trip to Japan at the end of May when he stayed at the Okura Hotel for over two months while Yoko visited relatives. Feeling isolated because of the language barrier, he locked himself away in his room for long stretches of time. At night he suffered terrifying nightmares. According to John Green, who makes no mention of the born-again period in his book, John told him, "I'd lie in bed all day [in Tokyo], not talk, not eat, and just withdraw. And a funny thing happened. I began to see all these different parts of me. I felt like a hollow temple filled with many spirits, each one passing through me, each inhabiting me for a little time and then leaving to be replaced by another."

The image was remarkably like one suggested by Jesus and recorded in Luke 11. It's hard to imagine that John was unfamiliar with the passage. Jesus was warning of the danger of merely ridding oneself of evil spirits without taking in the good. He says that an unclean or evil spirit, finding nowhere to rest, will return. "And when he cometh, he findeth it swept and garnished. Then goeth he, and taketh to him seven other spirits more wicked than himself; and they enter in, and dwell there: and the last state of that man is worse than the first."

Whatever happened in Tokyo, it marked the end of his personal interest in Jesus. "You Saved My Soul" said that he "nearly" fell for the TV preacher, but that Yoko "saved me from that suicide." So the salvation of the title refers to being saved *from* God, not *by* God. Yoko had again become the captain of his soul, the mistress of his destiny. Yet his life didn't improve. He sank into a depression, concerned that his creativity had deserted him and that he had no real purpose in life. The only real joy he experienced came from spending time with his son, Sean.

His life was out of his control. He worried about his health and his eyesight, about making the right investments with his money, about his personal safety.

The only way out, as far as he could see, was to pay for the services of people who claimed to see into the future. But then, which ones could he trust? If the advice of the tarot card reader contradicted that of the astrologer, which should he follow? Instead of the freedom he wanted when he broke away from the Beatles, he was now completely enslaved. He couldn't travel anywhere without advice from a directionalist, do deals with anyone without knowing their star sign, or make plans for the future without consulting the *I Ching*.

In January 1979 he and Yoko traveled to Cairo, having heard that there was a major illicit archeological dig taking place. Both of them believed that ancient Egyptian artifacts contained magical powers, and Yoko had dedicated one of the rooms in their apartment to Egyptian artifacts. "I love Egyptian art," she said. "I make sure I get all the Egyptian things, not for their value but for their magic power. Each piece has a certain magic power." They stayed at the Nile Hilton and toured the pyramids, but when word got out about their intentions they were prevented from visiting the dig.

By the time Frederic Seaman became John's personal assistant in February 1979, John's main interest was reading books on religion, psychic phenomena, the occult, death, history, archeology, and anthropology. Specific books Seaman can remember him asking for included *Rebel in the Soul: An Ancient Egyptian Dialogue Between a Man and His Destiny*, by Bika Reed; *Drawing Down the Moon: Witches, Druids, Goddess Worshippers, and Other Pagans in America Today*, by Margot Adler; and *Practical Occultism*, by (Madame) H. P. Blavatsky. He also listened to a thousand dollars' worth of taped lectures by Alan Watts.

Vacationing in Florida in the spring, he again watched *Jesus of Nazareth* on its by now regular Easter showing, but his reaction was completely different from the one he had had two years before. He kept joking that they should just get on with it and fast-forward to the crucifixion. Seaman, who was present with John's sons, Sean and Julian, recalled, "John began working himself up into a tirade against Christianity, saying that it had virtually destroyed what was left of pagan culture and spirituality in Europe—a great loss to civilization." He then announced that he was now a "born again pagan."

Later in the year Bob Dylan recorded *Slow Train Coming*, a gospel album born out of personal experience. Dylan told Robert Hilburn of the *Los Angeles Times* that he'd recently accepted that "Jesus was real. . . . I had this feeling, this vision and feeling. I truly had a born-again experience, if you want to call it that. It's an over-used term. But it's something that people can relate to." Hilburn asked him what "born again" meant. "Born once," he answered, "is born from the spirit below, which is when you're born. It's the spirit you're born with. Born again is born with the Spirit from above, which is a little bit different."

Slow Train Coming was a direct and challenging album. Unlike most gospel recordings, it didn't simply praise Jesus but attacked opposition to him, whether that was religious syncretism, false saviors, or lack of commitment. It was addressed to people like John. In "Precious Angel," the first single, Dylan sang, "Ya either got faith or ya got unbelief and there ain't no neutral ground.' In the title track he sang of "Fools glorifying themselves, trying to manipulate Satan."

Dylan's transformation took John completely by surprise. After all, Dylan had been the Beatles' only peer and remained someone whom he deeply respected. What made it particularly galling was that everything Dylan sang about on the album was delivered with a confidence that had always seemed to elude John. Dylan seemed certain that his sins were forgiven, his eternal security was assured, and that God was actively involved in his life.

When asked in 1980 about his response to Dylan's conversion, John was less than honest. He said he was surprised that "old Bobby boy did go that way," but "if he needs it, let him do it." His only objection, he said, was that Dylan was presenting Christ as the only way. He disliked this because "There isn't one answer to anything." This is why he favored Buddhism. It didn't proselytize. In what can now be seen as an allusion to his own born-again period, which hadn't yet been made public, he said, "But I understand it. I understand him completely, how he got in there, because I've been frightened enough myself to want to latch onto *something*."

His private feelings about the conversion were expressed in his songwriting. He was particularly incensed by the track "Gotta Serve Somebody" because it opposed his view that there was no single truth. The song said, as bluntly as possible, that whatever your station in life, you were either serving God or the devil. This wasn't an avoidable choice. John wrote a riposte titled "Serve Yourself," arguing that no one can save you. The only person you have to serve is yourself. "He was kind of upset [about Dylan's song] and it was a dialogue," said Yoko in 1998. "He showed his anger but also . . . his sense of humour."

In 1980, just as John returned to the recording studio for the first time in five years, another spiritually disturbed individual was planning his downfall. Mark David Chapman, a twenty-five-year-old maintenance engineer, had become fixated on him after discovering Anthony Fawcett's book *John Lennon: One Day at a Time* in his local library. A long-standing Beatles fan, he suddenly decided that John was a hypocrite, a man who had encouraged people to distrust the system but who was now a serious investor living in one of New York's most expensive apartment buildings. It quoted John saying, "I've bought everything that I could buy. . . . There's nothing else to do, once you do it. So I just live however makes me most comfortable." The photos in the book, some of them showing John casually posing on the roof of the Dakota, reinforced Chapman's sense of inadequacy. He, Mark Chapman, was nobody, and John was someone known to the whole world. The thought came to him that if he killed John, John would become nobody, and he would become known to the whole world.

Chapman had idolized the Beatles and listened carefully to their words. He'd taken LSD and dressed like a hippie. Then in 1971 he'd become a born-again Christian, identifying himself with the Jesus Freak movement. It was around this time that he took offense at what John had said about the Beatles and Jesus and also at the sentiment of "Imagine" and "God." Who did John think he was to discount religion and to say that he did not believe in Jesus or the Beatles? Friends at the time remember Chapman singing "Imagine" but instead of the line "imagine there's no heaven," he substituted "imagine John Lennon's dead."

The new fixation with John was coupled with a deep identification with Holden Caulfield, the fictional hero of J. D. Salinger's classic 1951 novel *The Catcher in the Rye*. Caulfield abhorred what he called "phoneys," and Chapman thought that John was just such a phoney. He'd seen recent pictures of John in the recording studio and read a story in *Esquire* that reported on his real estate investments. Here was the man who urged people to imagine having no possessions owning Holstein cows, farmland in the Catskills, a boat, a gabled shorefront home surrounded by trees on Long Island, and a mansion in Palm Beach, Florida.

Psychiatrists have so far been unable to categorize Chapman's condition. He has spoken with precision about the processes of thought that led him to kill but with chilling detachment. He has told how he sat in his apartment in Honolulu in October 1980, naked but for a set of headphones, playing the albums of the Beatles and praying to Satan for the courage to kill John. "I ask only that you give me the power to kill John Lennon. Give me the power of darkness. Give me the power of death. Let me be a somebody for once in my life. Give me the life of John Lennon."

He told writer Jack Jones that he experienced an inner battle. Sometimes his good side would tell him to dismiss such evil thoughts and then he would have to pray to Satan again to suppress the good. He came to New York with the express aim of killing. He scattered clues wherever he went, writing the word "Lennon" after "The Gospel according to John" in his hotel Bible and telling a shop assistant that she would soon be reading about him in the paper.

On December 8, 1980, Mark Chapman's good side was defeated. He lay in wait outside the Dakota building. When John and Yoko returned from a night out, he let them walk past him, took aim with his Smith and Wesson .38 revolver, and fired four shots into John's body. The hollow-point bullets tore into the main arteries in his chest and destroyed his vocal cords. The voice of a generation couldn't even give his name to the police officers who picked him up in their car. He was dead before he reached Roosevelt Hospital, and no amount of cardiac massage could revive him. The Beatles had broken up in 1970, but only now was it truly over.

Chapman said that a voice in his head gave the final instruction. "Do it! Do it! Do it! Do it! Do it!" it said. John didn't believe in an actual devil, but he believed in evil. He once spoke of "the power of the devil or whatever you call it," adding, "it doesn't matter to him. Either way he gets his kicks. And his kicks are control or destruction. If he can't control, he destroys."

Chapter Eleven

What Goes On

This isn't show business. It's something else. This is different from anything that anybody imagines. You don't go on from this. You do this, and then you finish.

—John Lennon, 1963

Adults set up a lot of things they think kids should have respect for. We're just trying to find things for ourselves. We haven't found many things to respect yet.

—Ringo Starr, 1965

The more I go into this spiritual thing, the more I realize that we—the Beatles—aren't doing it, but that something else is doing it.

—George Harrison, 1967

We just happened to become leaders of whatever cosmic thing was going on. We came to symbolize the start of a whole new way of thinking.

—Paul McCartney, 2004

At the moment when Mark Chapman shot John Lennon I was in a plane high over America. I'd just traveled from California to Texas by car with the musician T Bone Burnett and had been staying at his home in Fort Worth when news came through that one of my closest friends had been killed in a car accident back home in Britain. I had had to cut my stay short to take part in the funeral and was flying to London from Dallas.

I was met at Gatwick Airport by my fiancée. As we drove out of the parking lot she said, almost casually, "John Lennon has just died." At first I assumed a car accident, an illness, or a heart attack. Then she told me he'd been "murdered," and I imagined that he must have been a victim of New York street crime. I turned on the car radio and listened to the news as it started filtering through.

Although it had been disturbing news to my fiancée, it didn't have the same impact on her as it had on me—if it had, that would have been the first thing she told me as I emerged from Arrivals. For her, as for many people, he was simply another celebrity. For me, he was someone who had loomed large ever since I entered my teens. I loved not only his music but his wit, insight, courage, honesty, and way with words. Although I wasn't a musician, the direction of my life had in part been shaped by his influence and that of the Beatles.

I had another reason for being stunned by the news of John's death. A few years earlier I had been approached by Tony Cox, Yoko's first husband, who wanted me to ghostwrite a book about his involvement on the avant-garde art scene of New York and London in the 1960s. Since absconding with his and Yoko's daughter, Kyoko, in 1970, Cox had been living as a fugitive, perpetually worried that Yoko had secret agents on his trail. He was living under an alias, had moved from country to country, and was paranoid about being spotted.

I didn't think the book was a sound commercial prospect at the time. It was the era of punk, when the 1960s was being ridiculed for its cranky concepts and wide-eyed utopianism. John was living in the Dakota Building overlooking Central Park, rarely venturing out, and since *Imagine*, he had made a series of disappointing albums. I didn't think publishers would get excited over a manuscript about Yoko's *Bottoms* film and her performance art, where members of the audience were asked to snip off pieces of her dress. So the project was dropped.

Then, in December 1980, things changed. I was hanging out with T Bone, who was moving back to Texas from Los Angeles. T Bone had played in Dylan's Rolling Thunder band, and Dylan was currently touring the West Coast. We went to see him in Santa Monica and then in San Diego. It was a controversial tour because he only played songs from his born-again album *Slow Train Coming* and his soon-to-be released *Saved*. These were no hits from the past. Audiences were booing him. Backstage at the Santa Monica Civic Auditorium, we found him surrounded by members of the Vineyard church where he had been attending Bible studies. They had their arms around his shoulders and were praying for him. After the San Diego gig I met him for the first time.

Somewhere on the journey I bought the latest copy of *Playboy* because of its exclusive lengthy interview with John. T Bone and I devoured every word of it. John might not have still been creating groundbreaking music, but we were interested to see "where he was at." He'd been a pioneer for our generation, checking out territory that lay ahead and reporting back. The interview with David Sheff didn't disappoint. John gave a commentary on many of the

Beatles' greatest songs, talked about his new lifestyle of baking bread and being a house husband, and explained the motivations for his creativity.

One quote jumped out at me. Sheff had asked about Yoko's estranged daughter, and John took the opportunity to make a personal appeal to Tony Cox. "If you're reading this, Tony, let's grow up about it. It's gone. We don't want to chase you any more, because we've done enough damage." One of my first tasks when I got back to London was going to be getting in touch with Cox to let him know about John's offer. Cox was hiding out in Amsterdam, and I was sure that he wouldn't have seen the interview.

When I did get back in touch with Cox, everything had changed. John was dead, and tribute magazines were pouring off the printing presses. His story was now extremely valuable. I spent months working on a series of in-depth articles with Cox, mostly meeting up with him in Amsterdam, but at the last minute, when the final story was written, he got cold feet. He didn't want to publish. It seemed that the story had become so much a part of his identity that he was reluctant to let it go. For a second time the project was abandoned.

I never discovered why Cox sought me out; why he thought I'd be an appropriate writer to help him tell his story. I think he may have known that I'd met Yoko. He knew that I'd written widely for the music press and had authored a book on Eric Clapton. He'd certainly made a good choice because I was steeped in the history of the Beatles and had stacks of reference material that went back to the first clippings I collected in early 1963.

I was absolutely the perfect age to enjoy the Beatles. Their career almost precisely spanned my teenage years, their first single being issued ten days after my thirteenth birthday and *Abbey Road*, the last album they recorded, coming out the day after my twentieth birthday. I heard "Love Me Do" on Radio Luxembourg while sitting in my bedroom one evening in 1962, and it registered with me as being strange. It wasn't just the slightly dragging vocal but the name of the group. Beatles sounded odd.

I think it's a Buddhist saying that "When the student is ready, the master appears," and it was certainly true of my generation. If, in September 1962, I had been asked to predict the ideal group for this point in history, I couldn't have begun to describe a musical phenomenon like the Beatles, yet when they came along they seemed to fit every requirement. It was as though they just *had to be*. And what made it all the more remarkable was that my experience was multiplied millions of times around the world in a short time. We all felt that aspirations we had barely recognized had been embodied in John, Paul, George, and Ringo.

For the first years of their recording career they influenced me more by style and attitude than the words. My earliest Beatles scrapbooks are dominated by large color photographs taken from magazines like *Fabulous* and *Boyfriend* and include almost no comments or quotes. I was more interested in the height of their Cuban heels or the fact that Paul wore a bracelet than I was in their views on God or the atom bomb.

Part of my interest was stirred by the evidence that girls liked them. Dot Webb and Veronica England taped color photos of them from *Boyfriend* magazine on the underside of their desk lids in our classroom at school. It therefore made sense that if a boy could look like a Beatle, he would get more female attention. The other part was stirred by their implicit rebelliousness. They were getting away with wearing hair and clothes that my parents and my teachers wouldn't tolerate. When I had Cuban heels fitted to my shoes my dad made me take them back to the repair shop to have the original heels replaced. Whenever my hair crept over my collar I was sent to the barber shop for a "trim." I wasn't allowed to buy a collarless Beatle jacket like the one Terry Moll had bought for the school dance because my parents thought it wasn't practical or long lasting. Dad didn't want me to buy a black turtleneck because it reminded him of the black shirts worn by the followers of the British fascist leader Oswald Moseley in the 1930s.

I've often wondered why these small acts of rebellion mattered. I wasn't unhappy at home; even less did I have a vision for restructuring society. I didn't hate the older generation. It was more a search for excitement. Rock music was like a splash of color in an otherwise sepia-tinted world. It was risk taking rather than safe, loud rather than soft, rude rather than polite. Like John, I'd grown up with the William books by Richmal Crompton, and William was bored by conformity and always looking for adventure and trouble, usually both at the same time. He hated having his hair combed, wearing a tie, or pulling his socks up. The Beatles seemed like a more grown-up version of William and his gang, the Outlaws.

The Beatles played twelve miles away in Northampton twice in 1963, but my parents discouraged me from going. Why would I waste my money on noise like that? Like most parents, mine didn't appreciate the sound. It was shouting, they said, not singing. I sat in the front room of our home on February 8, 1964, listening to reports of the Beatles' welcome in New York on BBC radio's *Saturday Club* and felt that it wasn't just the Beatles that were taking over the world but my generation. From now on we couldn't be ignored. I also felt that my taste in music had been vindicated. Up until then I'd been told that it was a passing fad. Now my intuition was proving to be right.

I don't know the exact moment when I started "listening" to the Beatles in the expectation of receiving some sort of guidance. I can remember feeling a slight thrill at the scene in *A Hard Day's Night* when they're in a train compartment and a city gent, played by Richard Vernon, sits between Paul and John. He wears a bowler hat and carries an umbrella, a briefcase, and a copy of the *Financial Times*. They are bareheaded and between them carry a ham roll, a camera, two bottles of Pepsi, a transistor radio, and a copy of the *Daily Mirror*. It was a classic stand-off between generations and cultures. He represented convention, age, privilege, power, and the City of London, whereas they represented nonconformity, youth, the working class, and the regions. Their only power, as Paul suggests, lay in their numbers: "There's more of us than you."

The dialogue that followed, scripted by Welsh-born Liverpudlian Alun Owen, succinctly painted the differences between the two ways of thinking. The Beatles want the window open, based on the fact that they're in the majority. The city gent wants it closed and argues for his rights. They want to play music. He wants silence. They don't like "his sort" because he's inflexible, posh, and stuffy. He doesn't like their "tone" because they're rude, noisy, and disrespectful. "I fought the war for your sort," he says at one point. "I bet you're sorry you won," replies Ringo.

I didn't analyze the scene at the time. I just felt instinctively that I was on the side of the Beatles in this battle against pomposity ("And we'll have that thing off as well, thank you"), monotony ("I take this train twice a week"), and rigidity ("An elementary knowledge of the Railway Act will tell you that I'm perfectly within my rights"). When the Beatles leave the carriage Paul says, "Let's go and have some coffee and leave the kennel to Lassie." I'd never heard someone of Paul's age being so rude to someone of my parents' generation. It was as though a war had been declared.

Another scene that affected me was the one in which the Beatles find the exit door to the theater, burst out, and run down the iron staircase to the explosive sound of "Can't Buy Me Love." Up until this point in the film they've been confined to carriages, cars, hotel rooms, and a stage—hemmed in, chased, organized, directed. Now they can do whatever they want, and they careen up and down what looks like a large playing field expressing their liberty by reverting to playful, infantile behavior. Alun Owen later told me that here in the script he wrote the direction: "The boys come out and down the fire escape. It is the first time they have been free. They run about and play silly buggers."

It was a visual metaphor for what the Beatles were about—escaping from the humdrum and leaping into the unknown. Once in the wide open space that lay beyond the world of timetables and restrictions, the film is speeded up for comic effect and the Beatles revert to absurdity and childishness—dancing, racing, falling over, playing hide-and-seek, staging mock battles. As the music stops, the voice of officialdom breaks the reverie as the owner of the field appears on the scene. "I suppose you realize that this is private property?" Again, the world of rules and regulations, ownership and rights, intrudes on their freedom. "Sorry that we hurt your field, Mister," retorts John.

The words of Beatles songs began to register with me with *Rubber Soul* in December 1965. That year lyrics had become a talking point in the British music press with Donovan ("Colours," "Catch the Wind"), Dylan ("Like a Rolling Stone," "Positively 4th Street"), and protest songs such as "Eve of Destruction," by Barry McGuire, and "Good News Week," by Hedgehoppers Anonymous all entering the charts. The Who's "I Can't Explain," "Anyway, Anyhow, Anywhere," and "My Generation" were other examples of songs with words you couldn't fail to notice. When Roger Daltrey sang Pete Townshend's lines "People try to put us down / Just because we get around" in "My Generation," I totally identified with them. The loud, thrashing music embodied the sense of frustration in the lyric.

I had never wondered what made the Beatles feel fine, how they thought they could work it out, and where day trippers went. I hadn't seen "Help!" as a cry from the heart. The only thing that mattered was that the words felt right. They fit snugly into the music. But "Nowhere Man" made me think. I might even have heard a BBC radio program dissecting the lyric just as I'd once heard "Blowing in the Wind" teased apart for its references to racism and imprisonment. "Nowhere Man" was great fodder for preachers and sociologists.

I'd started writing poetry in 1965 and on November 5 had attended my first reading, where an American read from William Blake's *Songs of Innocence* and the writings of the eleventh-century Tibetan Buddhist Milarepa in a room over a pub near London's Liverpool Street station. John's publication of his humorous stories, poetry, and sketches made writing seem cool. Newspapers were referring to him as the "literary Beatle."

An interview Paul gave to the teenage magazine *Rave* in April 1966 opened new vistas for me. I hadn't exerted much effort at school. Study and homework didn't seem compatible with having a good time. In this view I'd been encouraged by the Beatles, who'd promoted the attitude that you should follow your dreams rather than the instructions of your parents and teachers. Degrees were irrelevant. "Be a bum," was George's advice. "Do anything." Because the Beatles had been so successful at their chosen profession, it seemed advice worth taking. In fact, it was often implied that there was a direct connection between their originality and their rudimentary education. They hadn't been spoiled. They were noble savages. If they'd learned orchestration and composition, it would have doused their spark.

I took this quite seriously at sixteen. I wanted my creative spirit to be unsullied by academia. I hadn't read the theories of the Romantics, but they had obviously filtered down to me. Yet, now they were in their mid-twenties, and the Beatles were perhaps regretting their truncated education. They were all hungry for information. In the *Rave* interview Paul spoke about the sitar, Karlheinz Stockhausen, painting, reading plays, and writing music for films. "I've got thousands, millions, of new ideas myself," he said. "I want to read a lot more than I do. It annoys me that so many million books came out last year and I only read twenty of them. It's a drag."

Paul's enthusiasm to learn more—"to listen to everything and then make your mind up"—was infectious. I underlined several quotes in the story—probably the first time I'd ever highlighted something a Beatle had said—and started out on my own adventure. I was still interested in getting boots and shirts like theirs, but for the first time I could see that learning the right things could be as hip as having the right haircut. You could be interesting to listen to as well as to look at. "Sooner or later it hits you that the average life span of the British male is seventy-five years, and you've had more than twenty of them," said Paul. "So you better make the most of what's left. Then the brain starts working, and John and I rush out and buy loads of books."

The fruit of this learning, for the Beatles, was *Revolver*. This was intelligent pop, influenced not just by other pop but by religious tracts, classical music, television theme tunes, street rhymes, and drugs. With this album I felt for the first time that the Beatles were in another dimension—as though they knew so much more than any of us did. There was an assurance about what they did, and I longed to be that confident and that cool. I had just started visiting London one day a week and spending most of that time in the King's Road, and *Revolver* perfectly captured the essence of hip London in late 1966: boutiques like Granny Takes a Trip and Hung on You; pot smoke and joss sticks; languid aristocratic dropouts and stem-legged girls; cool, stoned detachment and long-collared shirts.

The Beatles stirred interest in drugs not through open advocacy but by producing such great music while apparently under their influence. They may not have actually recorded while stoned, but they certainly wrote while in that condition. They gave the impression that pot, and LSD in particular, literally enlarged the consciousness, and that anyone not stoned or tripping was having to make do with a narrow mind. They were miles above us because they had the secret knowledge that drugs provided.

In January 1967 I bought a copy of *IT* (*International Times*) from Granny Takes a Trip, one of the few places in London that sold the radical underground newspaper. In it was an extensive interview with Paul conducted by his old friend Barry Miles, the first question-and-answer session with a lone Beatle. The conversation was unlike any other I had ever read with a pop star, not just for the range of the cultural reference points (from rockabilly guitarist Carl Perkins to nineteenth-century French playwright Alfred Jarry), but for its speculative rambling. "The most important thing to say to people is, 'It isn't necessarily so, what you believe. You must see that whatever you believe in isn't necessarily the truth.' No matter how truthful it gets, it's not necessarily ever the truth because the fact that it could be right or wrong is also infinite, and that's the point. The whole being is fluid and changing all the time and evolving. For it to be as cut and dried as we've got it now it's got to be cut and dried in an unreal way. It's a fantastically abstract way of living that people have got into without realising it. None of it's real. . . ."

I envied the way he spoke. It was as though he'd encountered deep mysteries and was trying to pass them on. I was too scared to take LSD, despite the assurances of various rock stars that it would provide access to a previously unused 90 percent of my brain. I was too worried that I might end up somewhere that I couldn't return from or that the 10 percent of my brain that I'd been using might get accidentally erased. I read books about LSD, hoping that I could acquire the same insights, without having to do anything illegal or dangerous.

I tried pot out of curiosity but didn't feel any wiser. Once I sat on a Welsh mountain overlooking a river trying to write poetry that would be the equal of anything Dylan or the Beatles had written but ended up with a page of doggerel. I'd imagined a puff on a joint could give me insights that had eluded Wordsworth, but I was wrong. Drugs couldn't stimulate an imagination that hadn't already been developed through observation, practice, and study.

In May *IT* ran an interview by Miles with George Harrison that was even weirder than the one with Paul. Appropriately, it was headlined "The Way Out Is In," and in it George extolled the virtues of chanting Krishna, saying that it was "such a buzz, it buzzes you out of everywhere. It's nothing to do with pills or anything like that. It's just in your own head, the realisation. It's such a buzz, it buzzes you right into the astral plane." He spoke of having met yogis in India the previous year who were "like Christ." He claimed that they "can walk on the water and materialise bodies."

This was astonishing to me because I'd never seen a fit between the Beatles and religion. My church background was in a small, nondenominational setting where clothing, music, and cultural references were almost all pre-1950. The future was never viewed as an exciting prospect, and the "secular world" of arts, entertainment, and media was in theory guarded against and in practice ignored. It was like entering a parallel universe. I couldn't imagine that the concerns of the church would ever cross the minds of the Beatles and, ridiculous as it may seem, this affected my willingness to entertain these concerns. If the Beatles were more popular than Jesus, a lot of it was because the Beatles were cooler and more exciting and more in touch with contemporary needs than Jesus. As Devin McKinney observes in *Magic Circles: The Beatles in Dream and History*: "That their [the Beatles'] faith spoke more urgently to the times than did Christ's . . . was another reason the Beatles were so loved, and why they were so hated."

Yet here in 1967, after all the fame and the drugs, a Beatle was spending two large pages talking not about rock 'n' roll but about God and prayer and hymns. He even quoted the Bible. In support of his theory that chanting the name of Krishna united you with God, he referred to John 1:1, "In the beginning was the word." Evidence of the law of karma was found in "Whatsoever a man soweth, that shall he reap" (Gal. 6:7). Proof that divinity was to be found in actions of humility was illustrated by Christ's washing of the feet of his disciples.

George didn't confess to drug taking in this interview, but his comment that it was better to get high without chemicals implied some personal knowledge. "Nobody can be a drug addict if they're hip," he declared "It's obvious if you're hip that you've got to make it. The buzz of all buzzes, which is the thing called God, you've got to be straight to get. . . . The thing is, if you really want to get it permanently, you have got to do it, you know. . . . Be healthy, don't eat meat, keep away from those night clubs and meditate."

I bought *Sgt. Pepper's Lonely Hearts Club Band* in Rugby, a town ten miles from my home, on June 5, 1967. There had been more anticipation of this album than any other made by the Beatles. From November 1966 on, there had been photos of them coming in and out of Abbey Road in an array of different costumes, headwear, moustaches, and shades. "We are working every night on the album from seven o'clock until two in the morning," George Martin told *Disc*. "It's even more way out than *Revolver*."

I understood that the people pictured on the album cover came as a recommendation for further cultural exploration. It was the Beatles' way of telling us how to get hip. Considerately, the *Daily Express* had run a key to some of the people on the Beatles "zaniest" sleeve, revealing that if we looked hard enough we would find people like comedian Lenny Bruce, artist Aubrey Beardsley, poet Stephen Crane, playwright George Bernard Shaw, psychologist Carl Jung, children's author Lewis Carroll, novelist William Burroughs, and actor Marlon Brando. The inclusion of the Beatles' earlier selves as Tussaud's waxworks I assumed was an indication that they were no longer the four mop tops. They'd grown and matured. They'd become wise beyond their years.

It was Paul who was the first Beatle to spell it out about drug taking and also to make the connection between that and the new interest in God. "Beatle Paul's Amazing Confession: 'Yes—I took LSD'" was run in a Sunday newspaper on June 18, 1967. This followed an earlier interview with *Life* that had been published in America. Not only did he show no regret but he claimed that it had made him "a better, more honest, more tolerant member of society—brought closer to God."

All this God talk gave a new dignity to churchgoing. So, OK, John, Paul, George, and Ringo weren't reciting the Lord's Prayer, taking communion, and singing hearty choruses, but at least they were putting the big questions on the agenda for a generation that had been characterized as living only for "kicks." On June 27 I went to a Billy Graham rally that was being transmitted on closed-circuit TV at a local cinema. At this rally, Cliff Richard, the Beatles' top competitor in Britain throughout their early career, announced himself as a new Christian for the first time in public.

It was the day in August that I returned home from a holiday that I first heard of Maharishi Mahesh Yogi. The Beatles had traveled to be with him in Wales, and it was reported on the BBC radio news. I had never seen a photo of a living "guru" before, and I was slightly apprehensive about what my parents would think. Although I knew that the Beatles weren't Christians and had never claimed to be, I had always defended them from accusations of being intrinsically hostile to Christianity or of promoting attitudes damaging to the faith of Christians.

I wrote to the Spiritual Regeneration Movement for a brochure and bought a copy of Maharishi's book *The Science of Being and Art of Living*. I found Maharishi's prose almost impenetrable and probably read only to page 50. He said that "the life of the individual without the realisation of Being is baseless, meaningless and fruitless," and I underlined this because it sounded similar to the evangelistic presupposition "Life without God is meaningless." He then said (on page 30) that it wasn't the nature of Being "to be exposed to the senses . . . and it is not obviously exposed to the perception of the mind." In the margin I wrote "God?" On the next page he said, "It enjoys the status which knows no change, the status of eternal life." Against that I wrote, "God the same yesterday, today and forever," a slight misquote of Hebrews 13:8.

I wasn't really trying to find enlightenment but instead a validation of the religious ideas I was most familiar with. I would love to have found that the Beatles, after their tortuous pilgrimage, had ended with what was sitting in front of me the whole time. But it wasn't. Pure Being wasn't God, and God doesn't ignore the mind and the senses. Although Maharishi claimed to be promoting a science rather than a religion, everything he said expressed a Hindu view of the world.

On my weekly jaunts to London I would visit the Chelsea Antiques Market, which contained one of the hippest clothing stores in London. I would spend hours talking to the owners, Adrian Emerton and Vernon Lambert, envious of their hip connections. Once Keith Richards came in and stood next to me, and another time the actor Terry Stamp. In July 1967 I met a young unknown songwriter, Billy Nicholls, who impressed me by telling me that he knew the Beatles and had visited George at home. He gave me his phone number and suggested that I keep in touch.

Billy was in a unique position. Andrew Loog Oldham, former publicist for the Beatles and manager of the Rolling Stones, had hired him as a salaried songwriter for his new record label, Immediate, which had offices on New Oxford Street. Billy had his own demo studio there and was recording his debut album. I visited him there on October 12, 1967, and my diary entry for the day says: "He played me 'Magical Mystery Tour' and 'I'm a Walrus' [sic], the Beatles' next release. A group was also in the studio."

"Hello Goodbye" would actually be the next release with "I Am the Walrus" as its B side. Billy had a "white label" of the tracks and what I remember, besides the impact of being privileged to hear a Beatles track in its rough stages, was the silence between "goo goo g'joob" and "sitting in an English garden." This space was later filled in with backward guitar and sound effects. The group that was "also in the studio" listening to the preview was the Nice (Keith Emerson, David O'List, Brian Davison, and Lee Jackson). Billy's album, *Would You Believe*, suffered numerous problems in getting released but today is regarded as a cult classic.

In 1968 I began taking part in poetry readings and looked at the Beatles as fellow artists. Although I didn't think the lyrics of their songs counted as poetry (nor were they intended to), I believed that poetry could benefit if it could reach as many people as Beatles songs did and address contemporary issues in a similarly approachable fashion. Around the world there would be other nonmusicians aiming to be the Beatles of filmmaking or the Beatles of photography. Thousands if not millions of us were inspired in this way.

Role models were already available for writers looking to put pop in their poetry. The Liverpool Poets—Adrian Henri, Roger McGough, and Brian Patten—used the same reference points as Beatles lyrics and had been inspired by similar things such as rock 'n' roll, jazz, pop art, girls, and the streets of Liverpool. Henri was a painter who lectured at the Liverpool Art College, McGough was in the group Scaffold with Paul McCartney's brother, Mike, and Patten's lyrical verse was reckoned by pop culture observer George Melly to have been an influence on songs such as "Eleanor Rigby." All three were publishing in magazines and giving readings in Liverpool during the period when the Beatles were regulars at the Cavern. *Sphinx*, the Liverpool University literary magazine, featured them all as far back as 1961. When art critic and poet Edward Lucie-Smith produced an anthology of their work it was titled *The Liverpool Scene*. It featured pictures of Adrian Henri, a schoolgirl, the Beatles, and Batman on the front cover, and it had a quote from Allen Ginsberg on the back: "Liverpool is at the present moment the centre of the consciousness of the human universe."

It was something that George said that propelled me into the final stretch of my pilgrimage to Christian faith. He spoke about the importance of truth and seeking for the truth. This, to him, was the most important task. He quoted Christ's saying, "The truth will set you free." If he had given the full quote, he would have said, "If you hold to my teaching, you are really my disciples. Then you will know the truth, and the truth will set you free" (John 8:31–32 NIV).

"Truth" and "freedom" were two of the great buzzwords of the era. Everyone, apparently, wanted to be free and to know the truth. But we'd inverted the order laid down by the gospel. Instead of believing that the truth would set us free, we believed that the freedom would make us true. In other words, we thought that by following our appetites and instincts we would eventually be led to the truth about ourselves, that the road of excess, as William Blake had said, would end up at the palace of wisdom.

But Jesus insisted on truth as the prerequisite for real freedom and said that truth could only be found if we "hold to my teaching." If we didn't put truth first, we wouldn't be able to distinguish freedom from license. I hadn't made truth my benchmark. I had made fashion, feeling, convenience, comfort, intellectual respectability, or originality my benchmarks. George's statements pulled me back to what should have been my central concern. Of course, freedom could only come from truly being what I was created to be, and that could only come from knowing the truth about my creator, my spiritual condition, and the requirements for reconciliation.

I submitted my poems to Apple. I'd heard that Peter Asher, Jane's brother, had a country house near my home, and I sent them to him. I never heard back. I wrote to Paul at EMI Studios, Abbey Road, asking whether it would be possible for me to drop in on one of their sessions. *The Beatles* (The White Album) was then being recorded. I explained that although I was a fan I wasn't *just* a fan. I wrote poetry. I wanted him to know that I was interested in his work as a fellow artist. He didn't write back.

In 1969 I was introduced to the work of two men who helped me in the task of evaluating art and culture as a Christian. The tendency of the church was to totally ignore popular culture, either from fear or lack of interest, or to analyze it entirely on the basis of its adherence to the gospel. Using the latter method, the Beatles were rejected out of hand. It wasn't even necessary to prove that they were unbelievers. They had unashamedly labeled themselves as such. Additionally, they had misguided a generation by presenting drugs as a means of liberation and steered it away from monotheism and toward pantheism.

Hans Rookmaaker in *Modern Art and the Death of a Culture* and Francis Schaeffer in *The God Who Is There* took a different approach. While not denying the gravity of spiritual delusion, they encouraged Christians to remember that all art and culture existed because people were made in the image of a creator God. The instinct to make art was good and was a reflection of the original creative act, "In the beginning . . ." Consequently, however ungodly an artist might claim to be, or actually be, the work was worthy of respect and consideration. Schaeffer was more deeply moved by honest and well-executed art of existentialist angst than he was by bad and manipulative art that praised God.

Rookmaaker argued that we should look at art and ask, does it have integrity? does it show technical excellence? and is it true? Work that was true, like many hymns, could lack integrity and be technically poor. Work that was untrue, on the other hand, could have integrity and be technically excellent. In one of Jesus' parables the wheat and tares grow alongside each other, and his followers are warned against pulling up the tares because, in doing so, they may destroy the wheat. Christians frequently wanted a guaranteed wheat-only harvest when it came to culture. They couldn't cope with a mix.

The Beatles weren't mentioned much in these two books but where they were, the comments were instructive. Christians had thought "Eleanor Rigby" was an attack on the church by atheists, but Rookmaaker drew attention to the similarities the song shared with some of the judgments made by Old Testament prophets. Artists who didn't have the church's interests at heart could nevertheless offer useful criticisms of its performance. Outsiders often spotted hypocrisy before the insiders: "We must realise that in the Bible the people of God are often depicted in quite dark tones," said Rookmaaker. He viewed "She's Leaving Home" as a valid attack on the bourgeois mentality that confused respectability with righteousness. Of the parents depicted in the song, who thought they had done everything for their daughter by buying her everything she had ever wanted, Rookmaaker said, "Is that really real life? Is that what Man was created for? Is that the life Christ died for? Is that Christianity? Heaven forbid."

I read my poetry twice in Liverpool during 1969. In early August Beatles biographer Hunter Davies accepted two of my poems for publication in the

Sunday Times. For the first time I felt like a real writer. Two weeks after this acceptance, alone in the house because the rest of the family were away on holiday, I decided to write an essay on the Beatles for *The Beatles Monthly*, the group's official fan magazine. There was a piece in the current issue by a freelance journalist, and even though I'd never written an article, I thought I could do better.

I mailed the story, which was my subjective view of the Beatles and didn't think about it again. At the end of October I had a letter from the publisher, Sean O'Mahoney, thanking me for the story and enclosing payment of five pounds. I hadn't been notified that it had been accepted. I had to buy a copy from my local newsagent. On page 10, in bold writing, it said: "Guest writer Steve Turner looks at the Beatles and concludes: 'The parents who said "Ooh, you'll grow out of it" in 1963 are wondering about growing into it themselves in 1969.'" Two months later *The Beatles Monthly* ceased publication. I felt privileged to have been featured in its pages before its closure.

Sean O'Mahoney invited me to submit stories on a freelance basis to *Beat Instrumental*, another of his magazines, and eighteen months later he offered me a job. Suddenly I was a part of the world I'd looked at from afar, visiting the recording studios I'd read about and mixing with stars I'd previously only listened to on records. Although the Beatles had now disbanded, their presence pervaded the industry. There was a feeling that we were guests at a party where the hosts had gone home early. I wanted to meet them and felt myself edging closer.

On May 13, 1971, Tony Barrow, formerly the Beatles' press officer, invited me to his office for a preview of *Ram*, Paul's second solo album. Three weeks later I visited the Rhada Krishna Temple on Bury Place where I met Prabhupada, the guru who'd had such an influence on George. I asked him how ISKCON compared to other religions on offer. "Some only go up fifty steps," he told me. "Some go up two hundred steps. But you need to go up a thousand." Was his the religion to scale the thousand steps? He nodded a vigorous yes.

Then, four months into the job, I secured an interview with John and Yoko. It was set for the afternoon of July 19 at the Apple office in Savile Row. I arrived in good time and sat in the entrance hall waiting for a previous interviewer to finish. I heard the door to the front office open. Then John poked his head out and called my name. That impressed me. The voice that had first sung "She Loves You" and "Strawberry Fields Forever" was saying "Steve Turner."

The interview took place over a large office desk cluttered with phones, cups, ashtrays, staple guns, pens, and cigarette packets. John and Yoko sat on the other side. Yoko was wearing hot pants and a beret. John had on a crisp-looking dog-tooth check shirt, open at the neck. What I didn't know then was that he had recently finished recording *Imagine*, and the next month he and Yoko would leave England to live in New York. The occasion for the interview was the republication of Yoko's poetry book, *Grapefruit*.

I asked John if he'd been influenced by Yoko's poetry, which consisted mainly of brief surrealistic instructions, some of which could feasibly be followed but most of which couldn't. One, for example, told the reader to hammer a nail into a mirror and then send the shards of glass to arbitrarily chosen addresses. "The last album was pretty haiku-ish," he said, referring to *The Plastic Ono Band*. "There weren't many words to it. Pretty simple. We work well together. In films we write together and in music, too, except when I'm doing completely straight rock. It's amazing we think so alike coming from different ends of the earth. . . . It just shows that whether you're black or green doesn't come in the way of communication. You don't even have to speak the same language. . . . She was much further out than me. I was pretty far out, but she really opened up me head with all her work."

I asked whether Yoko had influenced the more personal approach of his last album. I was thinking of songs like "Mother" and "Isolation." " 'Help' was personal," he said. " 'In My Life' was personal. 'I'm a Loser' was personal. I was always on that kick, you know?" I said that I hadn't seen these songs in that way at the time because they were Beatles songs. "Yeh," said John. "That's why I stopped." Why? "Because it was all just Beatles."

Halfway through my allotted time something extraordinary happened. John stepped away from the desk to another corner of the room where Neil Aspinall and some assistants were sitting, leaving me to carry on talking with Yoko. After a few minutes he returned brandishing what looked like a newspaper. "You wanna see this!" he said, opening up the center pages of what turned out to be *Truth*, a free paper produced by a community of Christian hippies based in Spokane, Washington. There was a huge photo of John and an open letter addressed to him printed beneath it.

John read it out loud. "This is a note from the Jesus People," he said. "This is the Jesus Freaks in America. It says, 'Dear John, I've been through a lot of trips with you. When I was down I put your records on and you'd bring me back to life. I've been up mountains together with you and I know you know where it's at. But the main reason I'm writing to you is to tell you of a friend I met last June. He said He is 'The way, the Truth and the Life.' I believed him and gave my life to him. I can see now how he can boast such a claim. Since then I've heard that you don't believe in him, but I can see by your eyes that you need him. Come on home Johnny! Love, A Friend.' "

What I didn't know then but learned during my research for this book was that the letter wasn't the work of an individual but of several people, most of whom were members of a Spokane band, Wilson-McKinley, who'd become Christians after hearing local preacher Carl Parks speaking. The band became one of the better-known "Jesus Rock" bands, and Parks would preach at their concerts. He can recall the band standing around the layout table putting the letter together. "It was a composite of what each one felt at the time," says Parks. "It was about how the Beatles had affected their lives and what they would have liked to have told John Lennon if they could have sat down and talked to him. I can remember one of them saying, 'Wouldn't it be something if John read this!'"

John clearly thought I would be as amused as he was by the letter. Instead, I asked him what he thought. "I think they've got a damn cheek," he said. Earlier, after he'd told me that he thought he and Yoko were misunderstood and reviled, we'd discussed the origins of prejudice. He said it came from fear of the unknown. I asked whether his feeling toward Jesus Freaks wasn't just such an example. "I think this is insanity, not just a prejudice," he said. "The insanity and hypocrisy of these so-called Jesus Freaks and Christians who go round ramming this Lord of theirs down other people's throats at the cost of millions of lives throughout the world. . . . These Jesus Freaks are the most uptight people in the world. I mean, they're madmen. They need looking after."

I pointed out that those who were prejudiced against him and Yoko used the same argument. "That's my opinion, you know. You asked me what I thought of them and I think they're crackpots. . . . Deep down I don't like being abused or being insulted or being hurt, just like any other person. But this just makes me laugh, really. I might write to them just for a laugh and to give my point of view." Had he ever looked into what they say? "I know what the Christian jazz is," he said. "I've had it all my life. This is the Christ bit, you know—'Give yourself to Christ.' A: He's dead. B: Prove it to me."

The rest of the interview was taken up with a discussion about faith. John's view was that there was no evidence for God, miracles, or the resurrection of Christ. "You are here. Live for today, minute by minute. That's the essential way"—that was his philosophy, he explained. So why had he spent so much of his adult life investigating religion? "Looking for gurus," he said without hesitation.

You're looking for the answer that everyone is supposedly looking for. You're looking for some kind of Super Daddy. I'll tell you why we're looking for it. We were never given enough love and touch et cetera when we were children. It's as simple as that.

I think Jesus was probably a very hip guy. I think a lot of the stuff about magic and miracles is probably a lot of bullshit that was written about years later. I think he was just a very hip guy and you can read his messages. What he really says is, "You are here. Be true to yourselves. Try to love people. Love your neighbor. Help someone if they're down." They are quite practical statements. It's very aligned to communism, what he says.

Now, you can imagine if it wasn't the twentieth century [with the] kind of mysticism and guru-ism [that] has been said and put out about the Beatles. Imagine what they would put out if we were in a primitive society, if we were "four young men with long hair and strange apparel" who "appeared and drew thousands" and all that! You can imagine how this bullshit came about.

But, I said, what if people's lives were being radically changed through believing in the Beatles in two thousand years' time? "Er . . . good luck! But don't harass me with it. Don't send pamphlets through the door. I don't really mind but . . . these people are very uptight, you see, and especially these Jesus Freaks. Why should I follow Jesus? I'll follow Yoko. I'll follow myself. What the hell!"

Trying to prove the existence of God or produce evidence for the resurrection was never going to happen within an hour. Rather than defending what I believed, I decided to let him defend what he believed. In "God" he'd listed a number of belief systems and people he no longer had faith in. What *did* he believe in? "Santa Claus, love, reality," he said. Then he grinned. "I'm being childish. A friend in New York said, 'Everybody you picked on was right, but I'm so glad that you didn't say, "I don't believe in Santa Claus."' You see, I believe that Santa Claus is more real to me than Jesus Christ." And precisely what did he now believe in? "I believe in reality," he answered. I wanted to know what he considered "reality" to be. "Reality is living, breathing, eating, and dying."

I asked him if he believed in God, and he said he didn't. Not in any shape or form? "God is a concept by which we measure our pain," he said, repeating the opening line from his recently written song "God." "The more pain we're in, the more we need God. That's what God is. I believe in reincarnation. . . . I believe all that jazz about coming back started from the fact that we're all one in that sense. We're all joined together. You know—dust to flesh to dust again. So when I die my body crumbles to dust, and it might come back as a bit of cabbage that is digested by some woman as she's having a baby, so it becomes a bit of another human being. In that way, we go on and come back."

If we were no more than the ingredients of our own bodies, I questioned, what value was there to human life? "I value it highly." Why? "Because it's mine. It's the only one I've got and the only one I'll ever have." Yet, I pointed out, as raw material the human body was estimated at the time to be worth little more than thirteen shillings. "It's my life, and I think it's worth everything you can give me for it." I argued that the reason we put such a high premium on human life was the instinctive belief that we were made in God's image, unlike any other part of creation. We were worth more than a tree or a rat because of our special origin. "You don't have to have a reason," he said. "It's because it's your own. It's the only one you've got. You don't have to have an intellectual reason for loving your own body."

Looking back I feel embarrassed at some of the things I said. He'd been an argumentative nonbeliever for probably fifteen years. I'd been a believer for less than three years. We were unequally matched. I told him that in my view an existence without God would have no ultimate meaning. "What's pointless about it?" he wanted to know. I said it would seem meaningless if we came from nothing and went to nothing and life was just the pause in between. "There is no end product to life," he said. "It just is." Is it a game? "It's not a game. It just *is*. It's just life. It's very serious, but it's just life. Communication is communication. It isn't to have an end or a beginning. It just is."

For John in particular this sort of existentialism had been a consistent message. In 1963 he had said, "I don't suppose I think much about the future. I don't really give a damn." In July 1968 he and Yoko mounted an exhibition at Robert Fraser's London gallery that consisted of random charity collection boxes, a visitor's book for comments, and a white painting with the legend "You are here" at the center. Three years later John told Mick Watts of *Melody Maker* that all the great thinkers and religious leaders agreed that the minute you were living in was the only one that counted. "That's the whole game. There's no other time but the present. Anything else is a waste." Just before his death he said, "The whole Beatles' message was Be Here Now." It was both a shrug of the shoulders—being here is all we can ever objectively know—and a command: you are here, so do something about it.

Each new worldview he encountered communicated the same message to him. Jean Paul Sartre said, "There is no human nature, because there is no God to have a conception of it. Man simply is." Aldous Huxley wrote in *The Doors of Perception* that under mescaline, "interest in time falls almost to zero." The yoga expert Swami Vishnu-devananda argued that "Real knowledge is possible only when there is no past or future, and where there is no time and space." Maharishi promised that his form of meditation enabled people to reach a state of pure being which is "transcendence, the state of existence, pure consciousness, is-ness, am-ness." Zen disciple Alan Watts said that "everything, just as it is now, is IT—is the whole point of there being life and a universe."

Believing that we came from nowhere, are headed nowhere, and that our lives and actions have no ultimate meaning can be a recipe for despair. What the Beatles did was to suggest ways of self-transcendence to imbue each moment with an intensity that would make life worth living. The trick was not to expect to find a God in heaven capable of offering forgiveness, guidance, and significance but to look for the God and the heaven within our own brains. "Try to realize it's all within yourself," as George put it in "Within You without You." This is why there was so much emphasis on freeing your mind, expanding your consciousness, and opening your head. "Jesus never came down in disguise as God any more than any of us did," said John in 1968. "We're all Jesus and we're all God and he's inside all of us. That's what it's all about. As soon as you start realizing that potential in everyone you can change it, and the person themselves can change it."

In "Across the Universe," John's most purely poetic song, he asserts that nothing is going to change his world. The reason he can claim this is that his world—the world that he has control over—lies within. The images of slithering words, waves of joy, pools of sorrow, and shining suns are all placed within "my open mind." In an interview with a university magazine a few months after recording it John said, "I believe the universe is in your head— literally in your head."

These beliefs were similar to those held by the gnostics who taught that salvation came through self-exploration and challenged the early church over its interpretation of Christ's sayings, and even had additional Gospels that weren't included in the accepted canon. Some scholars suggest that Gnosticism evolved from a Christianity affected by Buddhism and Hinduism. Monoimus, a second-century gnostic, said, "Abandon the search for God and the creation and other matters of a similar sort. Look for him by taking yourself as the starting point. Learn who it is within you who makes everything his own and says, 'My God, my mind, my thought, my soul, my body.' Learn the sources of sorrow, joy, love, hate. . . . If you carefully investigate these matters you will find him in yourself."

This approach was like that which the Beatles had undertaken on drugs, in meditation, and through divination. John was aware of the gnostic tradition and spoke of it enthusiastically in his 1980 interview with *Playboy* (although the magazine erroneously transcribed it as "agnostic"). "The [Gnostics], meaning self knowledge, were the true essence of Christianity but they were stamped out or chased to the hills," said John. "The [Gnostic] tradition is similar to the Zen Buddhists, which is not quite Buddhism."

In saying "You are here," John was urging people to focus on the moment and not to be dominated by the past or intimidated by the future. At the time of his art exhibit at Robert Fraser's gallery he told the *Sunday Times*, "What I'm saying is 'You are here. What are you going to do about it?' I want it to replace 'Kilroy was here' on toilet walls. It makes more sense."

The starting place for the Beatles' gospel was the belief that most people were blind to the truth of their situation. They weren't able to live for the moment because their spiritual vision was impaired. In "Nowhere Man" this condition is referred to as blindness, in "The Word" and "Strawberry Fields Forever" as misunderstanding, in "Within You without You" as delusion, in "The Fool on the Hill" as foolishness. The Nowhere Man just sees what he wants to see, implying that his mind is preset to interpret the world in a particular way. If he wants to become "Someone" or "Somewhere," he has to reset it. He has to open his head. This was the message behind "Rain": the unenlightened person is affected by the change of weather but the enlightened person realizes that the externals don't count. Everything is merely a "state of mind."

Although there are great differences between smoking pot and chanting "Hare Krishna," all the practices the Beatles pursued during the second half of their career were attempts to become self-realized. They wanted to be equipped to take full advantage of every single moment, to see things clearly without the encumbrances handed down by convention. There were at one with William Blake when he said in *The Marriage of Heaven and Hell* (1793): "If the doors of perception were cleansed every thing would appear to man as it is, infinite. For man has closed himself up, till he sees all things thro' narrow chinks of his cavern."

Each technique they tried promised to open up those chinks: to show them things as they really are. Peter Brown, who was a director of the Beatles' management company NEMS Enterprises, said that Paul's immediate reaction to smoking pot was, "I'm thinking for the first time, really *thinking*." Paul was similarly enthusiastic about LSD almost three years later, telling Thomas Thompson of *Life* magazine, "After I took it, it opened up my eyes. We only use one tenth of our brain. Just think what we could all accomplish if we could only tap that hidden part! It would mean a whole new world."

Practitioners of some Hindu forms of meditation tried to cleanse the doors of perception by allowing their consciousnesses to transcend the "gross" level of existence, where we are deluded by relativity. "Christ said, 'Seek the kingdom of heaven that lies within,'" George told Art Unger. "Well, [meditation] takes you to that state, that state which is the kingdom of heaven within. It's within everybody. It takes you to a level of consciousness that is absolute, that is not subject to the relative state of consciousness like good and bad, black and white, and all those things that are equal and opposite to each other."

So the central advice of the Beatles is always to expand the consciousness—to open up your eyes ("Dear Prudence"), to free your mind and change your head ("Revolution"), to learn to see ("Blackbird"), to see another kind of mind ("Got to Get You into My Life"), to listen to the color of your dreams ("Tomorrow Never Knows"), to see beyond yourself ("Within You without You"), or simply to dig everything ("Dig It"). As Colin Campbell and Allan Murphy note in their excellent introductory essay "From Romance to Romanticism: Analysing the Beatles' Lyrics" in *Things We Said Today*: "Repeatedly the Beatles urge us to simply relax and let our senses work, unhindered, to 'let it out and let it in' (*Hey Jude*) or simply *Let It Be*, so that we might see, hear and feel the world directly."

The result of opening the eyes, of freeing your mind, is that the total experience of life is enhanced. Emotions are felt more deeply, colors are seen more vividly, details are observed more sharply. Where John and George specialized in the more evangelistic finger wagging that instructed people on the folly of walking through life with eyes closed and the wisdom of seeking out the truth, Paul came into his own when describing the childlike wonder of seeing the world as if for the first time. It was he, for example, who added the upbeat chorus to "Baby You're a Rich Man" with its assertion that we already have the wealth that we're searching for if we could only realize it. This offset John's rather hectoring verses that asked the "beautiful people" what they were going to do with their newly attained insights.

Paul introduced the carnivalesque aspects to *Sgt. Pepper's Lonely Hearts Club Band*. It was his idea to dress the band in costumes based on old military uniforms and to have a psychedelic inner bag composed of shades of red. *Magical Mystery Tour* was of course conceived by him. He had a way of transforming the mundane into something magical. This was best exemplified in "Penny Lane," where an ordinary street in Liverpool that few would find attractive is made to sound enchanted. He never actually says so, but the attention to detail, the celebratory tone of the brass instruments, and the central image of the "blue suburban skies" communicate that impression. This isn't the Penny Lane half-seen during the daily grind. This is Penny Lane when it's allowed to fill your ears and your eyes. The measure of its success is that the listener pictures Penny Lane as bathed in light even though the song twice reminds us that the action described takes place during a downpour.

As with John's "Strawberry Fields Forever," "Penny Lane" drew on childhood perceptions. The clarity of vision they were pursuing, the intensity of experience they desired, was something that they believed was a natural possession when they were young. They wanted to recapture the innocence of their early years, before familiarity dulled their senses. John had told me during our interview, "You're born fully aware. From then on your mind closes down. From about eighteen or twenty, or whenever it is, the brain stops even growing or moving at all. That's it." After 1965 they began writing their most childlike songs: "Yellow Submarine," "Lucy in the Sky with Diamonds," "All Together Now," "The Continuing Story of Bunglow Bill," "Cry Baby Cry," "Mean Mr. Mustard," "Her Majesty," "Maxwell's Silver Hammer."

To the obvious question—how is it possible to achieve this clear-eyed view that was, after all, their equivalent of salvation—the answer they gave was hazy. In practice, as we've seen, they employed techniques of consciousness expansion. On record, although admitting that they'd love to turn us on ("A Day in the Life") and recommending that we'd be "new" and "better" if we took a drink from Dr. Robert's "special cup" ("Doctor Robert"), they suggested a different solution. The answer, in a nutshell, was love. Love was all we needed.

This wasn't the reciprocal affection that dominated their songs up until 1965 but the altruistic, universal love spoken of in religion and in the literature of the Romantics. This was love as the primary force behind creation. The apostle John declared "God is love." The Beatles effectively turned this around and said "love is God." There was no need for God to become incarnate and then die in order to bring salvation; they were saying that we could access the love directly. Love was a pathway to the divinity within us. We could save ourselves. As George put it in "Within you without You," "With our love we could save the world, if they only knew."

This was stated most directly in "The Word" and then two years later in "All You Need Is Love." In "The Word" love is associated with being set free and seeing the light, two of the most potent images of salvation used in religious texts. In "All You Need Is Love" it's associated with knowledge, vision, guidance, being "saved," and learning "how to be you." Just how important love was to their gospel is shown by the penultimate track on their final album. "The End" was intended as a wrap-up for the recording and became a wrap-up for their career. After six repeated shouts of "Love you" the song ends with the lines:

> And in the end the love you take
> Is equal to the love you make.
>   "The End"

It was a couplet that was either deeply profound or completely nonsensical. By the love you "make" did Paul mean having sex or spreading goodwill? By the love you "take" did he mean grabbed or received? Would the song mean anything different if the "make" and "take" were transposed? The point was, when it came to summarizing what the Beatles had been about, Paul focused on love. It was the legacy he was most proud of. "The music was positive," said Ringo thirty years later when asked to say what the Beatles had meant. "It was positive in love. They did write—we all wrote—about other things, but the basic Beatles message was Love."

Where Are They Now?

Al Aronowitz, 1928–2005
The journalist who introduced the Beatles to Bob Dylan and marijuana. Aronowitz became addicted to crack cocaine in the 1970s and cleaned up in 1985. When his work with newspapers dried up, he started publishing on the Internet, labeling himself "The Blacklisted Journalist."

David Ashton, 1941–
A Woolton friend of John's who went to Sunday school and sang in the choir with him. A resident in Denmark since the early 1960s, Ashton is now an agricultural journalist.

Julia Baird, 1947–
John Lennon's half-sister, born to his mother, Julia, and her partner John "Bobby" Dykins. A teacher of French in a Cheshire school, Baird is the author of *John Lennon My Brother* (1988) and often appears at Beatles conventions.

Tony Barrow, 1937–
Press officer for the Beatles from 1962 to 1968. After leaving NEMS Enterprises Barrow went on to be an independent publicist in the London music business. He has since returned to Lancashire and is a prolific writer, a large percentage of his writing being about the Beatles. In 2005 he published a memoir, *John, Paul, George, Ringo and Me*.

Al Benn, 1940–
The journalist who broke the story of the Birmingham boycott on Beatles records. Now retired after six years as a Marine, three years as a UPI reporter, and forty years working for newspapers, Alvin "Al" Benn lives in Selma, Alabama. He has recently written a memoir of his career, *Reporter: Covering Civil Rights and Wrongs in Dixie*.

217

Tara Browne, 1945–1966
Inspiration behind the first verse of "A Day in the Life." Browne was a particularly close friend to Paul and his brother, Mike. He was killed in the early hours of December 18, 1966, when his Lotus Elan ran into a Volkswagen van at Redcliffe Gardens, West London. His passenger, the model Suki Potier, survived the accident. Browne left a wife, Noreen, and two children, Dorian and Julian.

Pattie Boyd, 1944–
Met George Harrison in 1964 and married him in 1966. After leaving George, Boyd took up with Eric Clapton and later married him. Their relationship inspired Clapton's songs "Layla" and "Wonderful Tonight." They divorced, and she now lives with property developer Rod Weston. In 2006 she had an exhibition of her photography in San Francisco.

Cyndy Bury, 1943–
Hostess of the notorious meal where John and George were slipped their first dose of LSD. Bury married John Riley in 1966 and had two children. They divorced in 1970, and he remarried the following year. She worked in corporate PR in London before leaving Britain in 1981.

Tony Carricker, 1940–
One of John's closest friends at art school in Liverpool. Carricker went into the construction business and still works as a builder. He lives in London.

John Cavill, 1928–
Lodger at John's childhood home between September 1949 and June 1950. Following his National Service in the army, Cavill studied veterinary science at Liverpool University. After a lifetime working as a vet, he has now retired.

Mark Chapman, 1955–
Murderer of John Lennon in 1980. Sentenced to twenty years to life, Chapman is serving his sentence in the Attica Correctional Facility in New York State. He was denied parole in 2000, 2002, and 2004.

Tommy Charles, 1927–1996
The first DJ to announce he was banning Beatles records following John's comparison of the group's popularity with the popularity of Jesus. Charles started on the Birmingham, Alabama, radio station WSGN and then bought WEZB, which became the Top 40 station WAQY. Within two years of the Beatles ban, WAQY had become talk radio and Charles later presented news

on local TV for WBMG, where he became notorious for such onscreen antics as throwing the day's newspapers over his shoulder.

Maureen Cleave, 1935–
The writer whose 1966 interviews with John sparked the "more popular than Jesus" controversy. Going on to enjoy an extensive career in British journalism, Cleave is best known for her penetrating interviews for papers such as the *Evening Standard* (London) and the *Daily Telegraph* (London).

Nancy Cooke de Herrera, 1922–
The Beatles' personal guide when they studied TM in Rishikesh, India. Cooke has continued to promote the work of Maharishi Mahesh Yogi in the West. She lives in Beverly Hills and recently wrote her autobiography, *All You Need Is Love*. Her son Rik, the subject of the Beatles song "The Continuing Story of Bungalow Bill," works as a photographer and lives in Hawaii.

Rod Davis, 1941–
Early member of the Quarrymen with John. Davis graduated with a degree in Modern Languages from Cambridge University, taught for a brief period in Liverpool, and then entered the travel industry. Through it all he maintained his interest in music, performing with various folk, country, and bluegrass outfits. He was an enthusiastic participant in the revived Quarrymen in 1997.

John Dunbar, 1941–
Friend to John and Paul in the mid-sixties, husband to singer Marianne Faithfull, and part-owner of the Indica Gallery where John first met Yoko. Still living in London and working as an artist, Dunbar was a contributor to a 2006 symposium on the effects of LSD. The symposium was mounted in Basel to mark the 100th birthday of Albert Hoffman, the Swiss scientist who first detected the hallucinogenic properties of the drug in 1943. Dunbar spoke on the effects of LSD on the art and popular culture of the 1960s.

Royston Ellis, 1941–
Met the Silver Beetles in 1960 and stayed at John and Stuart's apartment in Gambier Terrace. After writing several books of poetry and two books on rock 'n' roll Ellis became a novelist. He now lives in Sri Lanka and writes mostly about travel in the region.

Michael Fishwick, 1932–
Lodger at John's childhood home between October 1951 and December 1958. After getting an honors degree in biochemistry Fishwick went on to do a PhD

in the same subject. He has now retired but spent his working life in food research.

Mukunda Goswami, 1942–
Krishna devotee who played a big part in attracting George to the movement in Britain. His real name is Michael Grant. He is the brother of jazz pianist Tom Grant and now lives in New Zealand. He was the director of communications for ISKCON, 1985–1998. He describes himself as a "writer, researcher, editor, and monk." In 2001 he published *Inside the Hare Krishna Movement.* He was one of two members of the Hare Krishna movement present with George Harrison when he died.

Louise Harrison, 1931–
George's oldest sister who moved to America in 1954. George visited her in St. Louis, Illinois, in 1963, becoming the first Beatle to step on American soil. She became influenced by the teachings of Paramahansa Yogananda after George gave her a copy of *Autobiography of a Yogi.* She now spends a lot of her time involved in projects connected either with the Beatles, peace, environmentalism, or the Self Realization Fellowship.

Bill Harry, 1940–
Art school friend of John's who introduced him to Stuart Sutcliffe. After founding and editing *Mersey Beat* Harry worked in music business PR in London. He has been a prolific author of books on the Beatles (eighteen so far) and is an authority on John's art school period, the relationship between Stuart Sutcliffe and John, and the Liverpool Beat group boom of the early 1960s.

Michael Hollingshead, 1931–19??
LSD evangelist who was responsible for introducing Timothy Leary to the drug. Born Michael Shinkfeld, he changed his name (according to Joey Mellen) as an allusion to trepanning ("hole-in-head"). After establishing the World Psychedelic Centre in London in 1965 he was arrested for unauthorized possession of cannabis and was sentenced to twenty-one months in prison. After prison he lived in Norway, America, Tonga, and Nepal before returning to England. He published a memoir, *The Man Who Turned on the World*, in 1973. Unheard of for years, it is assumed that he is dead.

Ken Horton, 1940–
School friend of Stuart Sutcliffe's who corresponded with him during the Beatles' stay in Hamburg. After leaving Liverpool School of Art he became

an art teacher. He maintained contact with Stuart Sutcliffe until Sutcliffe's death. He still lives in Liverpool.

Eric Humphriss, 1904–1996
Choirmaster at St. Peter's Parish Church, Woolton, taught John the rudiments of music. Humphriss was a chemist and microbiologist employed by various dairies in Liverpool. He maintained his involvement in music up to the end of his life.

Arthur Janov, 1924–
Introduced John and Yoko to Primal Therapy in 1970, thus inspiring the content of John's album *Plastic Ono Band*. Janov lives in Malibu, California, with his second wife, France, and is still director of the Primal Center. He has written a number of books including *The Primal Scream, The Feeling Child, When You Get Sick and How to Get Well*, and *The Biology of Love*.

Morris Pryce Jones, 1906–1968
The rector of St. Peter's Parish Church, Woolton, during John's time as Sunday school pupil and chorister. Jones died at the rectory in Acrefield Road, Woolton, while still rector at St. Peter's. He had never married and was sixty-one years old.

Astrid Kirchherr, 1938–
Photographer, "Exi," and fiancée of Stuart Stuclifee. Kirchherr still lives in Hamburg, where her career is managed by Ulf Kruger. Her photos of the early Beatles have become iconic. She and Stuart Sutcliffe were the subjects of the movie *Backbeat* in 1994. She was married briefly to Gibson Kemp of Paddy, Klaus, and Gibson.

Doug Layton, 1930–
Tommy Charles's sidekick on the WAQY (Birmingham, Alabama) radio show that triggered the "Jesus" controversy in 1966. For the past thirty years Layton has been the play-by-play announcer for the University of Alabama football team. He is resigned to the fact that wherever he goes he will be asked about the notorious Beatles record ban.

Timothy Leary, 1920–1996
The most publicized advocate of LSD and other psychedelic drugs as a means of spiritual experience and a way to transform society. Arrested in 1970 and imprisoned, Leary escaped to Algeria and from there to Switzerland and

eventually Afghanistan. He was arrested at Kabul airport by American agents in 1974 and served time in Folsom Prison before his eventual release in 1976. He remained an active campaigner for expanded consciousness and in the 1990s became a great fan of virtual reality and the Internet. He had his death (from prostate cancer) filmed, and in 1997 seven grams of his ashes were sent into space aboard the Pegasus rocket.

Cynthia Lennon, 1939–

Wife to John Lennon August 1962 to November 1968 and mother to his son Julian. Cynthia married for the fourth time in 2002 and now lives in Spain. During previous relationships she had lived in Wales, France, and on the Isle of Man and had been involved in various business enterprises. Her first biography, *A Twist of Lennon*, was published in 1978. Her second, *John*, came out in 2005.

Charles Manson, 1934–

Criminal and Beatles fan who believed the group was speaking to him through their songs. Since being found guilty of first-degree murder in 1971, Manson has been imprisoned in California. Initially he was held in Vacaville but was then moved to San Quentin. He is now in Corcoran State Prison. Such is the interest in Manson and his Family that he receives thousands of fan letters a year.

Alex Mardas, 1942–

Electrician who became part of the Beatles' inner circle and inspired them with his ideas for high-tech inventions. The son of a major in the Greek secret police service, John Alexis Mardas came to Britain in 1965 and soon after linked up with the Beatles. Hired to head up the electronics division of Apple, he was eventually sacked in 1969 by Allen Klein. He went on to be a successful dealer of electronic communications, security systems, and bullet-proof limousines to foreign governments. He has sold equipment to the Nigerian police force, Saudi Arabian customs and excise, King Hussein of Jordan, and the sultan of Oman. In 2004 he sold his Beatles memorabilia through Christie's auction house in London. A necklace that had once belonged to John Lennon, with a reserved price of between ten thousand and fifteen thousand pounds was sold for one hundred thousand pounds.

Thelma McGough, 1941–

Art school girlfriend of John's. She was Thelma Pickles until she married poet Roger McGough, who was in the group Scaffold with Paul's brother, Mike. They had two children and later divorced, the breakup chronicled in

McGough's spiky poems. Thelma went on to work in television and for many years was producer for the popular Saturday evening show *Blind Date*, presented by former Brian Epstein discovery Cilla Black. In the late 1990s McGough moved to New Zealand.

Joey Mellen, 1941–

Advocate of trepanning and frequenter of the Psychedelic Centre in London. Mellen met Bart Huges on the island of Ibiza in 1965 and was converted to the idea of trepanning. He finally bored a hole in his skull in 1970 using an electric drill and claims to have been high from the result ever since. He lives in London and until recently was running an art gallery in the King's Road.

Barry Miles, 1943–

Friend of the Beatles from 1965 onward, manager of Indica Books, and the group's conduit to the emerging "underground" movement in Europe and America. Know as simply "Miles" to all his friends, he now splits his time between his London apartment and a home in France. He has written biographies of Jack Kerouac, Charles Bukowski, William Burroughs, and Allen Ginsberg. He collaborated with Paul on *Many Years from Now*, the most informative book by an ex-Beatle. His memoir of the London underground scene, *In the Sixties*, contained a lot of material about his relationship with the Beatles.

Spike Milligan, 1918–2002

Inspirational British comic and writer whose work was a favorite of John's. Milligan's humor in *The Goon Show* heralded the new attitudes toward authority and conformity that would characterize the cultural revolution of the 1950s and 1960s in Britain. Milligan went on to write poetry for children, television scripts, and a number of wartime memoirs with titles such as *Hitler: My Part in His Downfall*. He befriended John and visited Abbey Road when the Beatles were recording.

Rod Murray, 1938–

Art school friend of John's who shared a flat with John and Stuart at Gambier Terrace. Went on to be an art lecturer—recently at the Royal College of Art in London—and an expert in holographic design.

David Noebel, 1936–

One of the earliest opponents of Beatles music. Noebel started Summit Ministries in 1962, and it was through his work with teenagers in this capacity that he became interested in the effects of rock 'n' roll. He has long since lost touch with the subject but still speaks and writes on the relationship between the Bible and culture. Recent books include *Understanding the Times*, *The Battle for Truth*, and *Think Like a Christian*.

Alun Owen, 1925–1994
Screenwriter for *A Hard Day's Night*. Born in Wales but raised in Liverpool, Owen had arrived at script writing only after having been a merchant seaman, a miner, an assistant stage manager, and an actor. He wrote many memorable plays for British television, including *No Trams to Lime Street*, and he wrote the book for Lionel Bart's musical about Liverpool life, *Maggie May*.

Srila Prabhupada, 1896–1977
Founder of the International Society for Krishna Consciousness. Prabhupada maintained his contact with George and advised him that he would be of more use to the cause of Krishna consciousness as a public figure in the music industry than as a full-time devotee. He continued to travel the world until his death in India in November 1977. On his death bed he told his devotees to pass his rings to George.

Dan Richter, 1939–
Managed the lives of John and Yoko at Tittenhurst Park from 1969 to 1972. When he arrived in Britain Richter was a mime artist, having trained at the American Academy of Dramatic Arts in New York, taught at several schools, and toured America with the American Mime Theatre as its lead performer. He worked with director Stanley Kubrick on the "Dawn of Mankind" sequence in the movie *2001* (he is the ape man who throws the bone). After leaving the Lennons he returned to work as a mime artist. He is now living in California where he climbs mountains, earns money from the entertainment industry, and is writing his memoirs.

John Riley, 1930–1986
John and George's dentist who put LSD in their coffees during a 1965 dinner at his apartment. After divorcing Cyndy he was married in 1971 to a fellow dentist, and in 1978 they moved to Ireland. It was after flying back to Ireland for his eldest daughter's eighteenth birthday that he was killed in an automobile accident.

Hugh Schonfield, 1901–1988
Authored *The Passover Plot*, a book that affected John's views about Christianity when he read it in 1965. Schonfield's *The Passover Plot* caused con-

troversy in its day and went on to sell over two million copies. *Those Incredible Christians*, published three years later, didn't stir up as much trouble. He was an expert on the Dead Sea Scrolls, about which he wrote two books, *Secrets of the Dead Sea Scrolls* and *The Bible Was Right*.

Ravi Shankar, 1920–

Classical musician from India who inspired George and encouraged his exploration into Eastern religion. Shankar continues to travel, perform, and record. He was with George when he died in Los Angeles and played an important part in the Concert for George at the Royal Albert Hall in November 2002.

Pete Shotton, 1941–

Childhood friend to John who joined the Quarrymen and was later employed by Apple. Shotton became a very successful businessman, opening a chain of American-style steak restaurants, Fatty Arbuckles, across Britain. He sold them in 1998 for an undisclosed sum. In 1997 he became part of a reconstituted version of the Quarrymen that eventually played around the world.

Pauline Sutcliffe, 1944–

Younger sister to Stuart Sutcliffe. Sutcliffe qualified as a social worker, then trained as a psychotherapist at the Tavistock Clinic in London. Later trained at the Philadelphia Child Guidance Clinic, she was for many years a clinical trainer, supervisor, and lecturer. She continues to execute the estate of her brother Stuart and to contribute to books and documentaries on his work. Her home is on Long Island.

Derek Taylor, 1932–1997

Assistant to Brian Epstein, publicist for Apple, and friend to the Beatles. Taylor left Brian Epstein's employment in 1965 to publicize the Byrds, the Beach Boys, the Mamas and Papas, and others in California. In 1968 he returned to Britain to be press officer for Apple. During the 1970s he worked as an executive for Warner Brothers Records. Starting in the 1980s he wrote his own books about the period of music he knew best and helped George Harrison (*I, Me Mine*) and the Beatles (*Anthology*) write theirs. While living in Suffolk, England, he died of cancer.

Art Unger, 1924–2004

Publisher and editor of *Datebook* who ran the "more popular than Jesus" story and also did extensive interviews with the Beatles from 1965 to 1968. After

Datebook folded Unger became the movie and television critic for the *Christian Science Monitor*, a job he held for seventeen years during which he did over a thousand interviews. He died suddenly in Paris on July 9, 2004.

Ivan Vaughan, 1940–1994

Childhood friend of Paul's who was responsible for introducing him to John in 1957. After attending the Liverpool Institute where he was in the same class as Paul, Vaughan went on to Cambridge University and then became a teacher. He kept in touch with John and Paul throughout the Beatles' career. He contracted Parkinson's disease in 1977 and was the subject of a British TV documentary directed by Jonathan Miller.

Swami Vishnu-devananda, 1927–1993

Indian guru who handed George a copy of his book on yoga during the filming of *Help!* Founder of twenty International Sivananda Yoga Vedanta Centres and seven ashrams, Vishnu-devananda created the first course for yoga teachers, which has so far trained more than eight thousand certified teachers.

Jurgen Vollmer, 1941–

One of the Hamburg "EXIs" who befriended and photographed the Beatles in 1960. He has lived in Paris, New York, and Los Angeles and has mainly focused on travel essays and portraits of movie stars. His book *The Beatles in Hamburg* was published in 2004. He now lives back in Hamburg and works on European film sets.

Klaus Voorman, 1942–

Hamburg "EXI" and boyfriend of Astrid Kirchherr in 1960. After meeting the Beatles, Voorman became a musician playing with Paddy Klaus and Gibson, Manfred Mann, and the Plastic Ono Band. Voorman designed the cover for *Revolver*. After a brief period working as a producer he returned to illustration. He did the artwork for the Beatles' *Anthology* project and contributed original drawings and paintings of John, Paul, George, and Stuart for the book *Hamburg Days*. He lives and works in Munich.

Nigel Walley, 1940–

Childhood friend of John's who was on Menlove Avenue when John's mother was killed. After leaving Bluecoat Grammar School Walley became an apprentice golf professional at Lee Park Golf Club, where he arranged for the Quarrymen to play. He was also responsible for their first booking at the Cavern. He later left Liverpool and became a golf professional at Wrotham Heath Golf Club in Kent.

Colin Wilson, 1931–

Promoter of Existentialism in Britain through his literary debut in 1956, *The Outsider*. The author of over one hundred books, many of them concerned with the paranormal, philosophy, crime, literature, and the occult, Wilson lives with his wife in Cornwall. In 2005 he published his autobiography *Dreaming to Some Purpose*.

Paramahansa Yogananda, 1893–1952

Author of George's favorite spiritual book *The Autobiography of a Yogi*. Yogananda started the Self-Realization Fellowship in 1920 and in 1924 established its headquarters in Los Angeles. He toured extensively in America giving lectures and visited the White House in 1927.

Maharishi Mahesh Yogi, 1917–

Founder of the Spiritual Regeneration Movement and developer of Transcendental Meditation. Maharishi now lives in Holland. It is estimated that over five million people have been taught TM techniques. He has spent recent years establishing Maharishi Vedic Universities and Schools around the world.

Sources

The following books were referred to frequently throughout my research and were helpful in all chapters.

Beatles, the. *Anthology*. London: Cassell & Co., 2000.

———. *The Beatles Lyrics*. London: Futura, 1975.

Campbell, Colin, and Alan Murphy. *Things We Said Today: The Complete Lyrics and a Concordance to the Beatles' Songs 1962–1970*. Ann Arbor, MI: Pierian Press, 1980.

Davies, Hunter. *The Beatles*. London: William Heinemann, 1968.

Evans, Mike, ed. *The Beatles Literary Anthology*. London: Plexus, 2004.

Gabarini, Vic, and Brian Cullman with Barbara Gravstark. *Strawberry Fields Forever: John Lennon Remembered*. New York: Bantam Books, 1980.

Giuliano, Geoffrey, and Brenda Giuliano. *The Lost Lennon Interviews*. London: Omnibus Press, 1998.

Harrison, George. *I Me Mine*. London: W. H. Allen, 1982.

Lewisohn, Mark. *The Complete Beatles' Recording Sessions*. London: Hamlyn, 1988.

———. *The Complete Beatles Chronicle*. London: Pyramid Books, 1992.

Macdonald, Ian. *Revolution in the Head*. London: Fourth Estate, 1994.

Miles, Barry. *Paul McCartney: Many Years from Now*. London: Secker & Warburg, 1997.

———. *The Beatles: A Diary*. London: Omnibus Books, 2002.

———. *John Lennon in His Own Words*. London: Omnibus Press, 1980.

Pritchard, David, and Alan Lysaght. *The Beatles: An Oral History*. New York: Hyperion, 1998.

Sheff, David. *The Playboy Interviews with John Lennon and Yoko Ono*. London: New English Library, 1981.

Terry, Carol D. *Here, There and Everywhere: The First International Beatles Bibliography, 1962–1982*. Ann Arbor, MI: Pierian Press, 1982.

Thomson, Elizabeth, ed. *The Lennon Companion*. London: Macmillan Press, 1987.

Turner, Steve. *A Hard Day's Write: The Stories behind Every Beatles Song*. London: Carlton Books, 1994.

Wenner, Jann S. *Lennon Remembers*. San Francisco: Straight Arrow Books, 1971.

1. Tell Me What You See

Books

Aronowitz, Al. *Bob Dylan and the Beatles*. Elizabeth, NJ: First Books, 2003.

Blake, William. *William Blake*. London: Penguin Books, 1958.

Bromell, Nick. *Tomorrow Never Knows*. Chicago: University of Chicago Press, 2000.

Davies, Hunter. *The Beatles*. London: Heinemann, 1968.

Ginsberg, Allen. "Beatles Essay." In *Deliberate Prose*. New York: HarperCollins, 2000.

Lewis, I. M. *Ecstatic Religion: An Anthropological Study of Spirit Possession and Shamanism*. London: Penguin Books, 1971.

Marcus, Greil. "The Beatles." In *The Rolling Stones Illustrated History of Rock and Roll*, edited by Jim Miller. New York: Random House, 1980.

Mellers, Wilfrid. *Twilight of the Gods: The Music of the Beatles* (New York: Schirmer Books, 1973).

Miller, Jim. *The Rolling Stone History of Rock and Roll*. New York: Random House, 1981.

Taylor, Rogan. *The Death and Resurrection Show: From Shaman to Superstar*. London: Anthony Blond, 1985.

Williams, Paul, ed. *The Crawdaddy Book*. Milwaukee: Hal Leonard, 2002.

Youngblood, Gene. In *Kaleidoscope* (Dec. 22, 1967). Quoted in Nick Bromell. *Tomorrow Never Knows: Rock and Psychedelics*. Chicago: University of Chicago Press, 2000.

Zaehner, R. C. *Mysticism Sacred and Profane*. Oxford: Oxford University Press, 1961.

Newspapers, Magazines and Journals

"Beatle Tells Preference for Religions of India." *New York Times*, Dec. 12, 1966.

Boltwood, Derek. "'Meditation Is My Cup of Tea'" Says Ringo . . ." *Disc*, 1968.

Mann, William. "What Songs the Beatles Sang." *Times* (London), Dec. 27, 1963.

Marsh, Dave. *Creem* 2, no. 5 (1969). Quoted in Nick Bromell, *Tomorrow Never Knows* (Chicago: University of Chicago Press, 2000).

Meltzer, Richard. "The Stones, the Beatles, and Spyder Turner's Raunch Epistemology." *Crawdaddy*, May 1967.

Miles, Barry. "Miles Interviews Paul McCartney." *International Times* (London), Jan. 16, 1967.

Napier, Bunyan Davie. "The Messengers." *Time*, Sept. 22, 1967.

Thompson, Thomas. "The New Far-Out Beatles." *Life*, June 16, 1967.

Wenner, Jann. "The Working Class Hero." *Rolling Stone*, Jan. 21, 1971.

———. "Life with the Lions." *Rolling Stone*, Feb. 4, 1971.

Wilde, Jon. "Tomorrow Never Knows." *Uncut* (London), July 2004.

Wyndham, Francis. "Close-Up: Paul McCartney as Songwriter." *London Life* (London), Dec. 4–10, 1965.

2. You Can't Do That

Books

Barrow, Tony. *John, Paul, George, Ringo and Me*. London: Carlton Books, 2005.

Benn, Al. *Reporter: Covering Civil Rights and Wrongs in Dixie*. Bloomington, IL: AuthorHouse, 2006.

Lennon, John. *Skywriting by Word of Mouth*. New York: Harper Perennial, 1987.

Martin, Linda, and Kerry Segrave. *Anti-Rock: The Opposition to Rock 'n' Roll*. New York: Da Capo Press, 1988.

Noebel, David A. *Communism, Hypnotism and the Beatles*. Tulsa, OK: Christian Crusade Publications, 1965.

———. *Rhythm, Riots and Revolution*. Tulsa, OK: Christian Crusade Publications, 1966.

———. *The Beatles: A Study in Drugs, Sex and Revolution*. Tulsa, OK: Christian Crusade Publications, 1969.

———. *The Marxist Minstrels: A Handbook on Communist Subversion of Music*. Tulsa, OK: American Christian College Press, 1974.

Schonfield, Hugh J. *The Passover Plot*. London: Hutchinson, 1965.

Taylor, Derek. *Fifty Years Adrift*. Guildford, UK: Genesis Publications, 1984.

Wiener, Jon. *Come Together: John Lennon in His Time*. London: Faber and Faber, 1984.

Newspapers, Magazines and Journals

Aarons, Leroy. "Can't Express Myself Very Well.' Beatle Apologizes for Remarks," *Washington Post*, Aug. 15, 1966 (Washington D.C.)

Albert, Dora. "Sex, Religion, Politics, Causes." *Variety*, Aug. 24, 1966.

"Beatle Hit below the Bible Belt." UPI, August 1966.

"Beatles Head for America." *Waycross Journal-Herald*, Aug. 11, 1966.

"Beatles Manager Here to Quell Storm over Remark on Jesus." *New York Times*, Aug. 6, 1966.

"Beatles Mum on Local Drive." *Birmingham News*, Aug. 3, 1966.

"Beatles Perform in Capital before 32,000 Fans." *Evening Bulletin* (Philadelphia), Aug. 16, 1966.

Benjamin, C. Baron. "Letter of the Day." *Evening Standard* (London), March 9, 1966.

"Blues for the Beatles." *Newsweek*, Aug. 22, 1966.

"Christians Need Not Worry." *Carolina Israelite*, July–August, 1966.

Cleave, Maureen. "How Does a Beatle Live?" *Evening Standard* (London), March 4, 1966.

"John in His Gorilla Suit, Seeking . . . What?" *Detroit*, May 8, 1966.

"Old Beatles—A Study in Paradox." *New York Times Magazine*, July 3, 1966.

"I Don't Know Which Will Go First—Rock 'n' Roll or Christianity." *Datebook*, Sept. 1966 (New York).

Cooper, Hal. "Are Beatles in for Real 'Hard Day's Night'?" *Pensacola News-Journal*, Aug. 14, 1966.

"Comment on Jesus Spurs a Radio Ban against the Beatles." *New York Times*, Aug. 5, 1966.

"Debris Is Hurled at Beatle Concert." *New York Times*, Aug. 20, 1966.

"Do the Beatles Beat the Church?" *Christianity Today*, Sept. 2, 1966.

"Dozens of Stations Joining Ban against Beatle Records." *Birmingham News*, Aug. 4, 1966.

Ellenberg, Albert. "Beatles to the Faithful: You Got Us All Wrong." *New York Post*, Aug. 12, 1966.

"Fans, 'Brimstone' Await the Beatles." *Cleveland Plain Dealer,* Aug. 14, 1966.

Gilmore, Eddy. "Beatle Didn't Intend to Be Irreverent, Writer Declares." AP wire story, Aug. 5, 1966.

Grigg, John. "Popularity." *Guardian* (Manchester), March 7, 1966.

Harvey, Richard. "Passing over the Plot?" *Mishkan* 37, 2002.

"Jesus Was All Right, Says Beatle John." *Liverpool Daily Post*, Sept. 30, 1967.

"Jesus Comment Endangers Beatles in America." *New Musical Express*, Aug. 12, 1966.

King, James. "Beatles Sounding Off without Music." *Birmingham News*, Aug. 6, 1966.

"Lennon of Beatles Sorry for Making Remark on Jesus." *New York Times*, Aug. 12, 1966.

Lennon, John. "Being a Short Diversion on the Dubious Origins of Beatles." *Mersey Beat* (Liverpool), July 6, 1961.

McCabe, Charles. "Do Beatles Top Christ?" *San Francisco Chronicle*, April 13, 1966.

"The Messengers." *Time*, Sept. 22, 1967.

"Priests Burn Beatles Disks." *Variety*, Aug. 31, 1966.

Pritchard, Richard. "Beatles Manager Tries to Quell Storm over Remark on Jesus." *New York Times*, Aug. 6, 1966.

Rice, Basil. "Local Disc Jockeys Join 'Beatle Ban.'" *Kingsport News-Times*, Aug. 7, 1966.

Scherf, Margaret. "Beatle John Lennon Apologizes about Remarks on Christianity." *Waycross Journal-Herald*, Aug. 12, 1966.

Schneider, Matthew. "The Beatles, the Passover Plot, and Conspiratorial Narrativity." *Anthropoetics* 8, no. 2, Fall 2002–Winter 2003.

"Some Radio Stations Forgive Beatles." *Birmingham News*, Aug. 14, 1966.

"Standard Gauge." *Newsweek*, March 21, 1966.

"A Statement from Art Unger." *Datebook* (New York), October 1966.

"WAXY Bans the Beatles, Listeners Back Action." *Waycross Journal-Herald*, Aug. 6, 1966.

Taylor, Western. "BBC Ask Lennon to Play Christ." *News of the World* (London), March 23, 1969.

Transcript of Beatles Chicago Press Conference, Beatles Ultimate Experience Database, Aug. 11, 1966. www.geocities.com/~beatleboy1/

Transcript of Beatles Chicago Press Conference, Beatles Ultimate Experience Database, Aug. 12, 1966. www.geocities.com/~beatleboy1/

"U.S. Ban on Beatles over Religion." *Times* (London), Aug. 5, 1966.

Correspondence, Press Releases

Tony Barrow to Art Unger, March 9, 1966, Arthur Unger Papers, Western Historical Manuscript Collection, University of Missouri, Columbia.

Art Unger to Maureen Cleave, March 10, 1966, Arthur Unger Papers, Western Historical Manuscript Collection, University of Missouri, Columbia.

Maureen Cleave to Art Unger, March 17, 1966, Arthur Unger Papers, Western Historical Manuscript Collection, University of Missouri, Columbia.

Art Unger to Maureen Cleave, March 22, 1966, Arthur Unger Papers, Western Historical Manuscript Collection, University of Missouri, Columbia.

Maureen Cleave to Art Unger, March 24, 1966, Arthur Unger Papers, Western Historical Manuscript Collection, University of Missouri, Columbia.

United Feature Syndicate to Art Unger, March 31, 1966, Arthur Unger Papers, Western Historical Manuscript Collection, University of Missouri, Columbia.

Art Unger to Tony Barrow, April 4, 1966, Arthur Unger Papers, Western Historical Manuscript Collection, University of Missouri, Columbia.

Tony Barrow to Art Unger, April 14, 1966, Arthur Unger Papers, Western Historical Manuscript Collection, University of Missouri, Columbia.

Nemperor Artists Limited, press release, Aug. 5, 1966, Arthur Unger Papers, Western Historical Manuscript Collection, University of Missouri, Columbia.

Capitol News, press release, Aug. 5, 1966, Arthur Unger Papers, Western Historical Manuscript Collection, University of Missouri, Columbia.

Art Unger to Paul McCartney, Oct. 7, 1966, Arthur Unger Papers, Western Historical Manuscript Collection, University of Missouri, Columbia.

Unpublished Manuscripts

Unger, Art. "My Life with the Beatles," Arthur Unger Papers, Western Historical Manuscript Collection, University of Missouri, Columbia.

———."Interview with George Harrison," 1966, Arthur Unger Papers, Western Historical Manuscript Collection, University of Missouri, Columbia.

———. "Interview with John Lennon," 1966, Arthur Unger Papers, Western Historical Manuscript Collection, University of Missouri, Columbia.

Interviews Conducted by Author

Barrow, Tony. 2005.
Benn, Al. 2005.
Cleave, Maureen. 1994, 2005.
Giardina, Frank. 2005.
Layton, Doug. 2005.
Lennon, Cynthia. 1987, 2005.
Noebel, David A. 2005.
Nunez, Raul. 2005.
Purdom, Larry. 2005.
Reingold, Carmel Berman. 2005.
Tremlett, George. 2005.
Williams, Jack III. 2005.
Willoughby, J. 2005.

Recordings

"Bigger Than Jesus." BBC Radio 2, Dec. 3, 2005.
"Beatles Tapes VI: Rock and Religion 1966." Jerden Records, JRCD 7076, 2005.

3. In My Life

Books

Baird, Julia. *John Lennon: My Brother.* London: Grafton Books, 1988.
Best, Geoffrey. *Mid-Victorian Britain 1851–70.* London: Fontana, 1979.
Bocock, Robert, and Kenneth Thompson. *Religion and Ideology.* Manchester, UK: Manchester University Press, 1985.
Braun, Michael. *Love Me Do: The Beatles' Progress.* London: Penguin Books, 1964.
Coleman, Ray. *Lennon.* New York: McGraw-Hill, 1985.
Davies, Hunter. *The Beatles.* London: Heinemann, 1968.
Goldman, Albert. *The Lives of John Lennon.* London: Bantam Press, 1988.
Harry, Bill. *The George Harrison Encyclopaedia.* London: Virgin, 2003.
Henke, James. *Lennon: Legend.* San Francisco: Chronicle Books, 2003.
Humphrey-Smith, Cecil R., and Michael G. Hennan. *Up the Beatles' Family Tree.* Canterbury, UK: Achievements Ltd, 1966.
Lally, Ernest John. *History of Much Woolton.* Liverpool: Woolton Society, 1975.
Lennon, John. *A Spaniard in the Works.* London: Jonathan Cape, 1964.
Lennon, Pauline. *Daddy, Come Home.* London: Angus & Robertson, 1990.
Marwick, Arthur. *British Society since 1945.* London: Pelican, 1982.

McCartney, Mike. *Thank U Very Much*. London: Panther, 1982.
———. *Remember*. London: Merehurst, 1992.
Partridge, Elizabeth. *John Lennon: All I Want Is the Truth*. New York: Viking, 2005.
Roberts, Ted. *The Story of a Parish 1826–1987*. Woolton, UK: St. Peter's Parish Church, 1987.
Russell, Bertrand. *Why I Am Not a Christian*. London: George Allen & Unwin, 1957.
Shotton, Pete. *John Lennon in My Life*. London: Coronet Books, 1984.
Thompson, E. P. *The Making of the English Working Class*. London: Gollancz, 1963.
Thompson, Francis. *The Collected Poems of Francis Thompson*. London: Hodder and Stoughton, 1913.

Newspapers, Magazines, and Journals

Cleave, Maureen. "Paul All Alone." *Evening Standard* (London), March 25, 1966.
———. "George Harrison: Avocado with Everything." *Evening Standard* (London), March 18, 1966.
"'Come Inside and See'—First Impressions of Strawberry Field." *Deliverer* (London), August 1936.
Davies, Christie. "The Death of Religion and the Fall of Respectable Britain." *New Criterion* (London), vol. 23, Summer 2004.
"High on the Hill-Side—'Strawberry Field'—Liverpool's Beautiful New Home for Children." *Deliverer* (London), March, 1935.
Riley, Joe. "I Turned Down Paul." *Liverpool Echo* (Liverpool), Oct. 8, 2004.
"Road Death." *Liverpool Weekly News* (Liverpool), July 17, 1958.
South Liverpoool Weekly News (Liverpool), 1952–1957.
"We Must Save the Children!" *Deliverer* (Liverpool), August, 1936.

Unpublished Manuscript

Paterson, J. L. C. "Liverpool Religion: A Bane or a Boon?" Thesis, University of Liverpool, 2001.

Interviews Conducted by Author

Ashton, David. 2003, 2005.
Baird, Julia. 2005.
Best, Roag. 2006.
Best, Rory. 2006.
Capron, Keith. 2005.
Cavill, Jon. 2005.
Davis, Rod. 2003.
Fishwick, Michael. 2005.
Harrison, Louise. 2005.
Johnson, Brian. 2005.
Roberts, Canon John. 1994, 2005.
Walley, Nigel. 2003.

4. Think for Yourself

Books

Allsop, Kenneth. *The Angry Decade*. London: Peter Owen, 1958.
Best, Peter, with Patrick Doncaster. *Beatle! The Pete Best Story*. London: Plexus, 1985.

Best, Roag. *The Beatles: The True Beginnings*. Ipswich, UK: Spine, 2002.

Clayson, Alan. *Backbeat*. London: Pan Books, 1994.

———. *Hamburg: The Cradle of British Rock*. London: Sanctuary, 1997.

Davies, Hunter. *The Quarrymen*. London: Omnibus Press, 2001.

Davies, Peter. *Liverpool Seen: Post-War Artists on Merseyside*. Bristol, UK: Redcliffe Press, 1992.

Ellis, Royston. *The Big Beat Scene*. London: Four Square, 1961.

———. *Myself for Fame*. London: Consul Books, 1964.

Feldman, Gene, and Max Gartenberg. *Protest*. London: Panther, 1960.

Furlong, June. *June: A Life Study*. London: APML, 2000.

Gottfriedsson, Hans Olof. *The Beatles—From Cavern to Star Club*. Stockholm, Sweden: Premium Publishing, 1997.

Harry, Bill. *Mersey Beat: The Beginnings of the Beatles*. London: Omnibus Press, 1977.

Kirchherr, Astrid, with Klaus Voormann. *Hamburg Days*. Guildford, UK: Genesis, 1999.

Morris, Frances. *Paris Post War: Art and Existentialism 1945–1955*. London: Tate Gallery, 1993.

O'Donnell, Jim. *The Day John Met Paul*. New York: Penguin Books, 1994.

Osborne, John. *Look Back in Anger*. London: Faber & Faber, 1956.

Pawlowski, Gareth L. *How They Became the Beatles*. New York: Dutton, 1989.

Porter, Alan J. *Before They Were Beatles*. Philadelphia: Xlibris, 2003.

Sartre, Jean Paul. *Existentialism and Humanism*. London: Methuen, 1948.

Sutcliffe, Pauline. *Stuart Sutcliffe: The Beatles' Shadow*. London: Sidgwick & Jackson, 2001.

Sutcliffe, Pauline, with Kay Williams. *Stuart: The Life and Art of Stuart Sutcliffe*. Guildford, UK: Genesis, 1996.

Tynan, Kenneth. *On Theatre*. London: Penguin, 1964.

Vollmer, Jurgen. *The Beatles in Hamburg*. Munich: Schirmer/Mosel Produktion, 2004.

Williams, Allan. *The Man Who Gave the Beatles Away*. London: Coronet, 1976.

Wilson, Colin. *The Outsider*. London: Victor Gollancz, 1956.

Newspapers, Magazines, and Journals

Adams, Len. "John Is Always with Me." *Sunday People* (London), April 14, 1985.

Barrell, Anthony. "Holy Kerouac." *Sphinx* (Liverpool), Autumn, 1960.

"Beat Poetry among the Academics." *Liverpool Daily Post*, June 25, 1960.

Brown, Ken. "The Beatle Who Lost Out." *Rave* (London), 1964.

Cotkin, George. "French Existentialism and American Popular Culture 1945–1948." *Phi Alpha Theta*, 1999.

Davies, Hunter. "With a Little Help from Their Friend." *You* (London), March 20, 1994.

Doncaster, Patrick. "I Still Don't Know Why I Was Sacked." *Daily Mirror* (London), October 6, 1980.

Ellis, Royston. "The Rock Poet Explains." *Record and Show Mirror* (London), July 16, 1960.

Forbes, Peter. "This Is the Beatnik Horror." *The People* (London), July 24, 1960.

Gerrard, Mike. "With the Beatles on the Hamburg Beat." *The Independent* (London), March 24, 1990.

Harry, Bill. "The Diaries of Johnny Guitar," (1958–1959). *Mersey Beat*. http://www.triumphpc.com/mersey-beat/a-z/johnnyguitar_diaries.shtml.

"Insipid Crowd: Poet's Criticism of Students," *Liverpool Echo and Evening Express*, June 27, 1960.

Kirchherr, Astrid. "In My Life." *Get Rhythm* (London), Aug. 2001.

———. "Mach Schau!" *Mojo* (London), 1992.

Kreeft, Peter. "The Pillars of Unbelief—Sartre." *National Catholic Register*, January–February 1988.

Ledgerwood, Mike. "Do the Beatles Owe a Debt to This Man?" *Disc and Music Echo* (London), October 31, 1970.

———. "The Beatle Who Opted Out." *Disc and Music Echo* (London), Nov. 7, 1970.

Lennon, John. "Letter re Allen Ginsberg/Royston Ellis," *International Times* (London), May 31, 1973.

"The Liverpool Poetry Scene," *Sphinx* (Liverpool), Spring 1962.

Macdonald, Marianne. "Forgotten Beatle Who Will Live Again," *Independent on Sunday* (London), Feb. 6, 1994.

Marks, Cordell. "The Beatle Who Was Drummed Out." *London Times*, March 6, 1985.

Polkow, Dennis. "Paul McCartney Returns to Liverpool." *Musician*, Sept. 1991.

"The Rock 'n' Roll Poet," *Record and Show Mirror* (London), July 9, 1960.

"An Unknown Beatle Goes on Show," *London Times*, Jan. 6, 1990.

"What's His Line?" *Daily Mirror* (London), Nov. 26, 1959.

Willsher, Kim. "Fame at Last for Astrid." *Mail on Sunday*, Jan. 23, 1994.

Wilson, Sarah. "Paris Post War: In Search of the Absolute," in *Paris Post War: Art and Existentialism 1945–55*, ed. Frances Morris. Tate Gallery, 1993.

Letters, Notebooks, Catalogs

"Books to Read," notebook by Stuart Sutcliffe.
Letter from Stuart Sutcliffe to Ken Horton, October 1960.
Letter from Stuart Sutcliffe to Ken Horton, December 1960.
Stuart Sutcliffe 1940–1962, Sotheby's, London, 1990.

Interviews Conducted by Author

Barrell, Tony. 2005.
Carricker, Tony. 2005.
Chapman, Harold. 2006.
Ellis, Royston. 1991, 1994, 2005.
Fishwick, Michael. 2005.
Harry, Bill. 2005.
Horton, Ken. 2005.
Jones, Rod. 1994, 2005.
McGough, Thelma. 1994, 2005.
Murray, Rod. 1994, 2005.
Sheridan, Tony. 2006.
Sutcliffe, Pauline. 2003.
Vollmer, Jurgen. 2005.
Walley, Nigel. 2003.
Williams, Allan. 2006.
Wilson, Colin. 2005

5. Eight Days a Week

Books

Booker, Christopher. *The Neophiliacs*. London: Collins, 1969.

Bramwell, Tony. *Magical Mystery Tours*. London: Robson Books, 2005.

Braun, Michael. *Love Me Do: The Beatles Progress*. New York, Penguin Books, 1964.

Bromell, Nick. *Tomorrow Never Knows*. Chicago: University of Chicago Press, 2000.

Cohn, Nik. *AwopBopaLooBop ALopBamBoom: Pop from the Beginning*. London: Weidenfeld & Nicholson, 1969.

Hine, Al. *The Beatles in Help!* London: Mayflower, 1965.

Kane, Larry. *Ticket To Ride*. New York, Penguin, 2004.

Martin, George. *All You Need Is Ears*. New York: St. Martin's Press, 1979.

McCabe, Peter, and Robert D. Schonfeld. *John Lennon: For the Record*. New York: Bantam Books, 1984.

McKinney, Devin. *Magic Circles: The Beatles in Dream and History*. Cambridge: Harvard University Press, 2003.

Rayl, A. J. S., and Curt Gunther. *Beatles '64*. New York: Doubleday, 1989.

Robinson, John. *Honest to God*. London: SCM Press, 1963.

Shepherd, Billy. *The True Story of the Beatles*. London: Beat Publications, 1964.

Sullivan, Henry W. *The Beatles with Lacan: Rock 'n' Roll as Requiem for the Modern Sage*. New York: Peter Lang, 1995.

Newspapers, Magazines, and Journals

Aronowitz, Al. "Music's Gold Bugs." *Saturday Evening Post*, March 21, 1964.

———. "The Return of the Beatles." *Saturday Evening Post*, Aug. 8–15, 1964.

Battelle, Phyllis. "My Three Days with the Beatles," *Datebook*, Fall 1965.

Cleave, Maureen. "The Year of the Beatles." *Evening Standard* (London), Oct. 17, 1963.

———. "This Is Where the O Level World Becomes Rock." *Evening Standard* (London), Oct. 18, 1963.

———. "It's Like Living It Up with Four Marx Brothers." *Evening Standard* (London), Oct. 19, 1963.

Coleman, Ray. "It's Like Winning the Pools." *Melody Maker* (London), Nov. 7, 1964.

———. "Pop Probe." *Melody Maker* (London), Oct. 24, 1964.

Freeman, Alan. "If One of Us Quits, It's Goodbye Beatles." *Rave* (London), September 1964.

Hennessey, Mike. "Ringo the Star." *Rave* (London), 1965.

Ingrams, Peter. "I Was Shattered—They Still Daydream." *Rave* (London), February 1964.

Lydon, Michael. "Lennon and McCartney: Songwriters." (written for *Newsweek*, 1966, unpublished).

Miles, Barry. "My Blue Period." *Mojo* (London), November 1995.

Packard, Vance. "Building the Beatle Image." *Saturday Evening Post*, March 21, 1964.

Shepherd, Jean. "The Playboy Interview." *Playboy*, February 1965.

Wilde, Jon. "Tomorrow Never Knows." *Uncut* (London), July 2004.

Catalog

Sotheby's Rock 'n' Roll Memorabilia (London), Sept. 16–17, 1997 (Lennon letters to Lindy
    Ness, items 394, 413).

Interviews Conducted by Author

Baird, Julia. 2005.
Barrow, Tony. 2005.
Boyd, Pattie. 2005, 2006.
Lennon, Cynthia. 2005.
McGough, Thelma. 1994, 2005.
Milligan, Spike. 1987.

6. Nowhere Man

Books

Andrews, George, and Simon Vinkenoog. *The Book of Grass*. New York: Grove Press, 1967.
Aronowitz, Al. *Bob Dylan and the Beatles*. Elizabeth, NJ: First Books, 2003.
Barrow, Tony. *John, Paul, George, Ringo and Me*. London: Carlton Books, 2005.
Brown, Peter. *The Love You Make: An Insider's Story of the Beatles*. London: Macmillan, 1983.
Cage, John. *Notations*. New York: Something Else, 1969.
Freeman, Robert. *The Beatles: A Private View*. London: Pyramid Books, 1990.
Giuliano, Geoffrey. *The Lost Beatles Interviews*. New York: Cooper Square Press, 2002.
Huxley, Aldous. *The Doors of Perception*. London: Chatto & Windus, 1954.
James, William. *The Varieties of Religious Experience*. London: Fontana, 1960.
Lennon, John. *In His Own Write*. London: Jonathan Cape, 1964.
McClure, Michael. *Scratching the Beat Surface*. New York: Penguin Books, 1982.
Miles, Barry. *In the Sixties*. London: Jonathan Cape, 2002.
Noebel, David A. *The Marxist Minstrels*. Tulsa, OK: American Christian College Press, 1974.
Regardie, Israel. *Roll Away the Stone*. Saint Paul, MN: Llewellyn, 1968.
Reik, Theodor. *Masochism in Modern Man*. New York: Grove Press, 1962.
Taylor, Derek. *As Time Goes By*. London: Abacus, 1974.

Newspapers, Magazines, and Journals

Coleman, Ray. "Pop Probe." *Melody Maker* (London), Oct. 24, 1964.
Freeman, Alan. "Sometimes We're Treated Like Things Not Human Beings." *Rave* (London),
    June 1964.
Maymudes, Victor. Unpublished manuscript. Copyright Aerie and Jacob Maymudes.
Newman, Fred. "The Cosiest Beatle." *Mirror Magazine* (London), Nov. 29, 1969.
Smith, Alan. "On Tour with the Beatles." *New Musical Express* (London), Dec. 10, 1965.
Wenner, Jann. "The Rolling Stone Interview: John Lennon, Part One: The Working Class
    Hero." *Rolling Stone*, Jan. 21, 1971.
Wyndham, Francis. "Close-Up: Paul McCartney as Songwriter." *London Life*, Dec. 4–10, 1965.

Interviews Conducted by Author

Aronowitz, Al. 1994, 2005.
Boyd, Pattie. 2005.

Dunbar, John. 1994, 2006.
Martin, George. 1987.
Miles, Barry. 1994, 2006.
Mintz, Elliot. 1994.

7. All You Need Is Love

Books

Black, Johnny. *Recording Sgt. Pepper's*. Chorley, UK: Tracks, 1998.
Braden, William. *The Private Sea: LSD and the Search for God*. New York: Bantam Books, 1968.
Brodax, Al. *Up Periscope Yellow*. New York: Limelight Editions, 2004.
Dobkin de Rios, Marlene, and Oscar Janiger. *LSD, Spirituality and the Creative Process*. Rochester, VT: Park Street Press, 2003.
Fonda, Peter. *Don't Tell Dad*. London: Simon & Schuster, 1998.
Hieronimus, Robert R. *Inside the Yellow Submarine*. Iola, WI: Krause Publications, 2002.
Hoffman, Albert. *LSD: My Problem Child*. Los Angeles: Jeremy P. Tarcher, 1983.
Hollingshead, Michael. *The Man Who Turned on the World*. London: Blond & Briggs, 1973.
Leary, Timothy. *The Politics of Ecstasy*. London: Paladin, 1970.
Leary, Timothy, Ralph Metzner, and Richard Alpert. *The Psychedelic Experience*. New York: University Books, 1964.
Lee, Martin A., and Bruce Shlain. *Acid Dreams*. New York: Grove Press, 1992.
Lennon, Cynthia. *A Twist of Lennon*. London: Star Books, 1978.
Lewisohn, Mark, Piet Schreuders, and Adam Smith. *The Beatles London* (London: Hamlyn, 1994).
MacDonald, Ian. *The People's Music*. London: Pimlico, 2003.
Martin, George. *With a Little Help from My Friends*. London: Little, Brown & Co., 1994.
Masters, R. E. L., and Jean Houston. *The Varieties of Psychedelic Experience*. London: Anthony Blond, 1967.
Fine, Jason, ed. *Harrison*. New York: Simon & Schuster, 2002.
Stevens, Jay. *Storming Heaven: LSD and the American Dream*. London: Paladin, 1989.
Taylor, Derek. *It Was Twenty Years Ago Today*. London: Bantam Books, 1967.
Turner, Steve. (text), *All You Need Is Love* (Chorley, UK: Tracks, 1997).
Wilk, Max. *The Beatles' Yellow Submarine*. London: New English Library, 1968.

Newspapers, Magazines, and Journals

Aldridge, Alan. "A Good Guru's Guide to the Beatles' Sinister Songbook." *Observer Magazine* (London), Nov. 26, 1968.
"Beatle Paul's Amazing Confession." *People* (London), June 18, 1967.
Bieberman, Lisa. "Phanerothyme: A Western Approach to the Religious Use of Psychochemicals." *Psychedelic Information Center* (Boston), 1968.
Coleman, Ray. "Beatles—Now!" *Disc and Music Echo* (London), May 27, 1967.
Davies, Hunter. "The Beatles in a New Dimension." *Sunday Times* (London), Dec. 24, 1967.
Evans, Allen. "Beatles New LP in Full." *New Musical Express* (London), May 20, 1967.
"Fantastic Beatles Album!" *Disc and Music Echo* (London), May 20, 1967.
Gray, Andy. "Beatles Use Three Satellites to Plug Next Single." *New Musical Express* (London), July 1, 1967.

Hennessey, Mike. "Love from the Beatles." *Melody Maker* (London), July 22, 1967.

Hutton, Jack. "Beatle Listen-In." *Melody Maker* (London), May 27, 1967.

"The Messengers." *Time*, Sept. 22, 1967.

Miles, Barry. "Miles Interviews Paul McCartney." *International Times* (London), Jan. 16, 1967.

Pules, Harry. "George in Hippyland." *Melody Maker* (London), Aug. 19, 1967.

Simons, Judith. "Working Together Again—The Beatles' Last Night." *Daily Express* (London), Nov. 25, 1966.

Simons, Judith. "Sleeve Art—The Zaniest Yet . . ." *Daily Express* (London), May 19, 1967.

Thompson, Thomas. "The New Far-Out Beatles." *Life*, June 16, 1967.

Turner, Steve. "The Story of Sgt. Pepper, Part I." *Q* (London), June 1987.

———. "Sgt. Pepper, the Inside Story, Part II." *Q* (London), July 1987.

Unger, Art. "On the Road with the Beatles." *Datebook,* Winter 1966.

Wilson, James. "LSD and Me—By Paul McCartney." *Daily Mirror* (London), June 19, 1967.

Interviews Conducted by Author

Aspler, Tony. 2005.

Boyd, Pattie. 2005.

Bury, Cyndy. 2005.

Dunbar, John. 1994, 2006.

Kemp. Gibson. 2005.

Leary, Timothy. 1994.

Lennon, Cynthia, 1987, 2005.

Lownes, Victor. 2005.

Martin, George. 1987.

Miles, Barry. 1994, 2006.

Posthuma, Simon. 2005.

Schumacher, Joel. 1994.

8. The Inner Light

Books

Cooke de Herrera, Nancy. *All You Need Is Love*. San Diego, CA: Jodere, 2003.

Giuliano, Geoffrey. *The Beatles: A Celebration*. London: Sidgwick and Jackson, 1986.

———. *Dark Horse: The Life and Art of George Harrison*. New York: Dutton, 1990.

Goswami, Mukunda. *Inside the Hare Krishna Movement*. Badger, CA: Torchlight Publishing, 2001.

Goswami, Satsvarupa Dasa. *Prabhupada*. Los Angeles: Bhaktivedanata Trust, 1983.

Harrison, George, and John Lennon. *Chant and Be Happy*. Los Angeles: Bhaktivedanta Trust, 1982.

Mascaró, Juan, ed. *Lamps of Fire*. London: Methuen, 1958.

Mason, Paul. *The Maharishi*. Shaftsbury, UK: Element Books, 1994.

Michaels, Ross. *George Harrison Yesterday and Today*. New York: Flash Books, 1977.

Saltzman, Paul. *The Beatles in Rishikesh*. New York: Viking Studio, 2000.

Shankar, Ravi. *Raga Mala*. Shaftsbury, UK: Element Books, 1999.

Sire, James W. *The Universe Next Door*. Downers Grove, IL: InterVarsity Press, 1976.

Vishnu-devananda, Swami. *The Complete Illustrated Book of Yoga*. London: Souvenir Press, 1960.

Yogananda, Paramhansa. *Autobiography of a Yogi*. London: Rider and Co., 1969.

Yogi, Maharishi Mahesh. *The Science of Being and Art of Living*. London: SRM Foundation, 1966.

Newspapers, Magazines, and Journals

"Beatle Tells Preference for Religions of India." *New York Times*, Dec. 12, 1966.

Boltwood, Derek. "Rock 'n' Ringo." *Record Mirror* (London), March 30, 1968.

Coleman, Ray. "The Beatles Are Sane." *Disc and Music Echo* (London), Dec. 9, 1967.

Dunn, Cyril. "You Don't Know You're There, but You Know You've Been." *Observer Magazine* (London), Jan. 14, 1968.

Drummond, Norrie. "Paul Is Still Seeking, but George Has Found a Great Faith." *New Musical Express* (London), Sept. 9, 1967.

"The Great Meditators Get into a Whirl." *Daily Express* (London), March 2, 1968.

Housego, Michael. "Paul McCartney." *Daily Sketch* (London), March 27, 1968.

Hutton, Jack. "Ringo on Drums, Drugs, and the Maharishi." *Melody Maker* (London), Dec. 2, 1967.

Jones, Nick. "Beatle George and Where It's At." *Melody Maker* (London), Dec. 30, 1967.

Jordan, Bernard. "Why the Beatles Went Cold on the Maharishi." *Daily Telegraph* (London), May 16, 1968.

Ledgerwood, Mike. "Now They're All Leaping on the Meditation Bandwagon." *Disc and Music Echo* (London), Nov. 11, 1967.

Lennon, John. "Tribute to Brian Epstein." *Disc and Music Echo* (London), Sept. 2, 1967.

"Let John and George Explain." *Intro* (U.K.), 1967.

"Paul, Jane and a Sitar . . . in India." *Disc and Music Echo* (London), April 13, 1968.

Simons, Judith. "Why We Split from the Guru—by the Beatles." *Daily Express* (London), May 16, 1968.

Thompson, Thomas. "The New Far-Out Beatles." *Life*, June 16, 1967.

Turner, Robin. "Four People in Search of a Beautiful Experience." *Daily Express* (London), Feb. 16, 1968.

———. "Holiday with a Happiness Guarantee." *Daily Express* (London), Feb. 17, 1968.

———. "Photonews with the Meditating Beatles." *Daily Express* (London), Feb. 20, 1968.

Walsh, Alan. "The George Harrison Interview (Part 1)." *Melody Maker* (London), Sept. 2, 1967.

———. "The George Harrison Interview (Part 2)." *Melody Maker* (London), Sept. 9, 1967.

———. "Will the Real Richard Starkey Please Stand Up?" *Melody Maker* (London), March 16, 1968.

"What Is Paul Up To?" *Disc and Music Echo* (London), April 6, 1968.

Yogi, Maharishi Mahesh. "What I Believe." *Intro* (U.K.) 1967.

Radio

George Harrison interviewed by Donald Milner in Bombay. *The Lively Arts*, BBC Radio (interview Oct. 21, 1966. Transmission Dec. 11, 1966).

Interviews Conducted by Author

Boyd, Pattie. 2005.

Bruns, Prudence Farrow. 1994, 2006.

Cooke, Rik. 1994.

das Sharma, Ajay. 2005.
de Herrera, Nancy Cooke. 1994.
Donovan. 1994.
Horn, Paul. 1994, 2006.
Lennon, Cynthia. 1987, 2005.
Prabhupada, Srila. 1971.
Shankar, Ravi. 1985.
Wynne, David. 2005.

9. Let It Be

Books

Bugliosi, Vincent, with Curt Gentry. *Helter Skelter*. New York: W. W. Norton & Co., 1974.

Chang, Lit-sen. *Zen-Existentialism: The Spiritual Decline of the West*. Nutley, NJ: Presbyterian and Reformed Publishing Co., 1969.

Cott, Jonathan, and David Dalton. *The Beatles Get Back*. London: Apple, 1969. Included in *Let It Be* album box set.

DiLello, Richard. *The Longest Cocktail Party*. London: Charisma Books, 1973.

McCabe, Peter, and Robert D. Schonfeld. *Apple to the Core*. London: Sphere, 1973.

Muni, Scott, Denny Somach, and Kathleen Somach. *Ticket to Ride*. London: Macdonald, 1989.

O'Dell, Denis. *At the Apple's Core*. London: Peter Owen, 2002.

Ohsawa, George. *Zen Macrobiotics*. New York: University Books, 1965.

Ono, Yoko. *Grapefruit*. London: Peter Owen, 1970.

Quantick, David. *Revolution: The Making of the Beatles' White Album*. London: Unanimous Ltd., 2002.

Reps, Paul. *Zen Flesh Zen Bones*. New York: Anchor, 1960.

Reeve, Andru J. *Turn Me On, Dead Man*. Bloomington, IL: AuthorHouse, 2004.

Sanders, Ed. *The Family*. London: Rupert Hart-Davis, 1972.

Sulpy, Doug, and Ray Schweighardt. *Drugs, Divorce and a Slipping Image*. Princeton Junction, NJ: The 910, 1994.

Taylor, Derek. *As Time Goes By*. London: Abacus, 1974.

Vaughan, Ivan. *Ivan*. London: Papermac, 1986.

Watts, Alan W. *This Is It*. New York: Pantheon Books, 1958.

———. *Beat Zen, Square Zen and Zen*. San Francisco: City Lights, 1959.

Zaehner, R. C. *Mysticism Sacred and Profane*. Oxford: Oxford University Press, 1961.

Newspapers, Magazines, and Journals

Coleman, Ray. "John Lennon Listen-In." *Disc and Music Echo* (London), Jan. 18, 1969.

Davies, Hunter. "Lennon Here and Now." *Sunday Times* (London), July 7, 1968.

Head, Robert. "John and Paul Should Sit This One Out." *Daily Mirror* (London), April 1, 1969.

"Jane and Beatle Paul Split Up." *Sunday Mirror* (London), July 21, 1968.

Ledgerwood, Mike. "Have the Beatles Already Split?" *Disc and Music Echo* (London), Feb. 14, 1970.

"Let's Break It Up." *Daily Express* (London), Jan. 1, 1971.

"A Little Fashion Sorcery from John and Oko." *Daily Mirror* (London), Feb. 7, 1969.

Mabbs, Val. "Adam and Eve Twentieth-Century Style." *Record Mirror* (London), Dec. 27, 1969.

Miles, Barry. "Multi-Purpose Beatle Music." *International Times* (London), Nov. 29, 1968.

Mills, Paul. "Official Report on the Whereabouts of Paul." *Fusion*, December 1969.

Newman, Fred. "The Cosiest Beatle." *Mirror Magazine* (London), Nov. 29, 1969.

Norman, Philip. "The Beatle Business." *Sunday Times Magazine* (London), Jan. 11, 1970.

Palmer, Tony. "A is for Apple." *Observer Magazine* (London), Sept. 1, 1968.

Pendennis. "Yoko Ono Speaks." *Observer* (London), July 21, 1968.

Pringle, Peter. "Beatle: Leave Me Alone." *Sunday Times* (London), April 6, 1969.

"Rooftop Beatles Upset the Neighbours." *Daily Mirror* (London), Jan. 31, 1969.

Rollin, Betty. "Lennon and Yoko." *Daily Express* (London), March 12, 1969.

———. "Beatle John's 'Bossy' Girl." *Daily Express* (London), March 13, 1969.

Smith, Alan. "Beatle George Today." *New Musical Express* (London), June 1, 1968.

———. "Beatles Are on the Brink of Splitting." *New Musical Express* (London), Dec. 13, 1969.

Somma, Robert. "Beatles Get Back to Abbey Road." *Fusion*, Oct. 31, 1969.

Walsh, Alan. "We Have a Handful of Songs and a Band Called the Beatles." *Melody Maker* (London), June 8, 1968.

Wilby, Peter. "The Logic of Charles Manson." *Observer* (London), July 22, 1973.

Zec, Donald. "They're Getting Up Today." *Daily Mirror* (London), March 31, 1969.

Interviews Conducted by Author

Clapton, Eric. 1974.

Dunbar, John. 2006.

Leary, Timothy. 1987.

McCartney, Linda. 1994.

Mellen, Joey. 2005.

Miles, Barry. 1987, 2005, 2006.

O'Dell, Denis. 1999.

Posthuma, Simon. 2005.

Richter, Dan. 2005.

Wyndham, Francis. 2005.

10. Carry That Weight

Books

Fawcett, Anthony. *John Lennon: One Day at a Time.* New York: Grove Press, 1976.

Giuliano, Geoffrey. *Lennon in America.* London: Robson Books, 2001.

Green, John. *Dakota Days.* London: Comet, 1984.

Greene, Joshua M. *Here Comes the Sun: The Spiritual and Musical Journey of George Harrison.* Hoboken, NJ: John Wiley & Sons Inc., 2006.

Janov, Arthur. *The Primal Scream.* New York: Dell, 1970.

Jones, Jack. *Let Me Take You Down.* New York: Villard Books, 1992.

"Letter from John Lennon to Oral Roberts." Oral Roberts University, Tulsa, OK.

"Letter from Oral Roberts to John Lennon." Oral Roberts University, Tulsa, OK.

Pang, May. *John Lennon: The Lost Weekend.* New York: SPI Books, 1983.

Rosen, Robert. *Nowhere Man: The Final Days of John Lennon.* New York: Soft Skull, 2000.

Salinger, J. D. *The Catcher in the Rye.* London: Hamish Hamilton, 1951.

Seaman, Frederic. *John Lennon: Living on Borrowed Time.* London: Xanadu, 1991.

Wiener, Jon. *Gimme Some Truth: The John Lennon FBI Files.* Berkeley: University of California Press, 1999.

Newspapers, Magazines, and Journals

Ashby, Jonathan. "Krishna Saved My Life." *Sun* (London), June 20, 1984.
"Beatledammerung." *Time,* Jan. 25, 1971.
"Beatles Are Angels on Earth Said Maharishi." *Times of India,* Feb. 15, 2006.
Charlesworth, Chris. "Lennon Today." *Melody Maker* (London), Nov. 3, 1973.
———. "Rock On!" *Melody Maker* (London), March 8, 1975.
Charone, Barbara. "Take These Broken Wings." *Crawdaddy,* April 1976.
Ellen, Mark. "A Big Hand for the Quiet One." *Q* (London), 1987.
Fricke, David. "One for the Road." *Rolling Stone,* Feb. 8, 1990.
Garbarini, Vic. "Paul McCartney." *Musician,* May 1980.
Grant, Steve. "McCartney." *Time Out* (London), Oct. 11, 1984.
Harlow, John. "Harrison's Last Joke." *Sunday Times* (London), Dec. 9, 2001.
Harris, John. "Now That He's Sixty-Four." *Sunday Telegraph* (London), Oct. 17, 2004.
———. "Wandering Starr." *Saga* (Folkestone), November 2004.
Haywood, Jane. "Give Peace and Quiet a Chance." *Sunday Telegraph* (London), Dec. 4, 2005.
Laurence, Charles. "Harrison's Ashes Flown Secretly to India." *Sunday Telegraph* (London), Dec. 2, 2001.
Ledgerwood, Mike, and Roy Shipston. "John Lennon: Still Searching for Peace." *Disc and Music Echo* (London), July 31, 1971.
Lennon, John, and Yoko Ono. "A Love Letter from John and Yoko." *New York Times,* May 27, 1979.
Meryman, Richard. "Paul McCartney." *Life,* April 1971.
Moir, Jan. "I Will Miss Him until My Dying Day." *Daily Telegraph* (London), Jan. 24, 2005.
Norman, Philip. "Life after Lennon." *Sunday Times* (London), Aug. 24, 2003.
Peacock, Steve. "The Lennons at Home." *Sounds* (London), July 31, 1971.
———. "The Lennons at Home Part 2." *Sounds* (London), Aug. 7, 1971.
Sandall, Robert. "Nobody's Fool in the Material World." *Sunday Times* (London), July 1, 1990.
———. "Jolly George—The Untold Story." *Sunday Times* (London), Oct. 12, 2003.
Turner, Steve. "The Ballad of John and Jesus." *Christianity Today,* June 12, 2000.
Williams, Richard. "In the Studio with Lennon and Spector." *Melody Maker* (London), Nov. 6, 1971.
———. "George Harrison 1943–2001." *Guardian* (London), Dec. 1, 2001.
Woods, Vicki. "A Solo Star." *Daily Telegraph* (London), Aug. 3, 1998.

Interviews Conducted by Author

Gregory, Dick. 2006.
Janov, Arthur. 2005, 2006.

11. What Goes On

Books

Burke, John. *A Hard Day's Night.* London: Pan Books, 1964.
Henri, Adrian, Roger McGough, and Brian Patten. *The Mersey Sound.* London: Penguin Books, 1967.

Lucie-Smith, Edward, ed. *The Liverpool Scene*. London: Donald Carroll Ltd., 1967.

Melly, George. *Revolt into Style: The Pop Arts in Britain*. London: Allen Lane, 1970.

Pagels, Elaine H. *The Gnostic Gospels*. New York: Random House, 1979.

Plowman, Edward E. *The Jesus Movement in America*. Elgin, IL: David C. Cook Publishing, 1971.

Rookmaaker, Hans. *Modern Art and the Death of a Culture*. London: Inter-Varsity Press, 1970.

Schaeffer, Francis. *The God Who Is There*. London: Hodder & Stoughton, 1968.

Yogi, Maharishi Mahesh. *Meditations of Maharishi Mahesh Yogi*. New York: Bantam, 1968.

Newspapers, Magazines, and Journals

Atticus. "Lennon Here and Now." *Sunday Times* (London), July 7, 1968.

"Beatle Paul's Amazing Confession." *People* (London), June 18, 1967.

Freeman, Alan. "Inner Beatle Secrets from Paul." *Rave* (London), April 1966.

Miles, Barry. "Miles Interviews Paul McCartney." *International Times* (London), January 1967.

———. "The Way Out Is In." *International Times* (London), May 19, 1967.

Turner, Steve. "One Pair of Eyes." *Beatles Monthly* (London), October 1969.

———. "John, Yoko, Grapefruit and Jesus." *Beat Instrumental* (London), September 1971.

Watts, Michael. "George Harrison: Is There Life after Enlightenment?" *Melody Maker* (London), March 10, 1979.

———. "Lennon." *Melody Maker* (London), Oct. 2, 1971.

Interviews Conducted by Author

Cox, Tony. 1981.

Lennon, John. 1971.

McGough, Roger. 1994.

Ono, Yoko. 1971.

Owen, Alun. 1994.

Parks, Carl. 2006.

Prabhupada, Srila. 1971.

Index